Entrepreneurial Finance

I dedicate this book to three exceptional friends and scholars:

M. Lynne Markus

David Drew

James Logan

—Gary Gibbons

I dedicate this book to my great supporters:

My wife, Tina

My daughters, Kary, Katy, and Kelly

My son-in-law, Rich

My grandchildren, Rachel, Andrew, and Sara

—Robert D. Hisrich

I dedicate this book to entrepreneurs worldwide who have dedicated their lives to build meaningful companies; and

To all future entrepreneurs who do not yet realize the potential and impact their dreams can have on the world; and

Finally, I dedicate this book to all business mentors who voluntarily give their time to help the younger generation achieve success.

—Carlos M. DaSilva

Entrepreneurial Finance

A Global Perspective

Gary Gibbons
Thunderbird School of Global Management

Robert D. Hisrich
Thunderbird School of Global Management

Carlos M. DaSilva
School of Business Administration,
Fribourg, Switzerland

Los Angeles | London | New Delhi
Singapore | Washington DC

Los Angeles | London | New Delhi
Singapore | Washington DC

FOR INFORMATION:

SAGE Publications, Inc.

2455 Teller Road

Thousand Oaks, California 91320

E-mail: order@sagepub.com

SAGE Publications Ltd.

1 Oliver's Yard

55 City Road

London EC1Y 1SP

United Kingdom

SAGE Publications India Pvt. Ltd.

B 1/I 1 Mohan Cooperative Industrial Area

Mathura Road, New Delhi 110 044

India

SAGE Publications Asia-Pacific Pte. Ltd.

3 Church Street

#10-04 Samsung Hub

Singapore 049483

Acquisitions Editor: Maggie Stanley

Associate Editor: Abbie Rickard

Editorial Assistant: Nicole Mangona

Production Editor: Melanie Birdsall

Copy Editor: Gillian Dickens

Typesetter: C&M Digitals (P) Ltd.

Proofreader: Caryne Brown

Indexer: Amy Murphy

Cover Designer: Edgar Abarca

Marketing Manager: Liz Thornton

Printed in the United States of America

Library of Congress Cataloging-in-Publication Data

Gibbons, Gary E.

Entrepreneurial finance : a global perspective / Gary Gibbons, Robert D. Hisrich, Carlos M. DaSilva.

pages cm
Includes bibliographical references and index.

ISBN 978-1-4522-7417-1 (pbk.)

1. New business enterprises—Finance. 2. International business enterprises—Finance. 3. Venture capital. 4. Entrepreneurship. I. Hisrich, Robert D. II. DaSilva, Carlos M. III. Title.

HG4027.6.G53 2015
658.15′99—dc23   2014024676

This book is printed on acid-free paper.

14 15 16 17 18 10 9 8 7 6 5 4 3 2 1

Brief Contents

Detailed Contents

Preface

This book was conceived from the entrepreneurial perspective. Finance is a subject often neglected by the entrepreneur. According to the U.S. Small Business Administration, finance or, to be accurate, ignorance of finance is the root cause of 74% of small business failures. We believe that knowledge of finance is as essential to the manager's toolkit as the ability to sell, lead, and innovate. We also believe that finance should be made accessible to the entrepreneur from a pedagogical point of view. This book provides the entrepreneur the opportunity to develop the essential skills and conveys the necessary knowledge for him or her to be functional in the discipline, at least as far as his or her own business is concerned.

At the beginning of each chapter, there is a short case. In some chapters, the information in the case is used to provide expanded explanations and examples. In other chapters, the case is meant to illustrate a common circumstance encountered by entrepreneurs that illustrates the entrepreneur's need to understand the material that follows. All of the cases are real cases, although some have had company names or the names of the principals changed. Regardless, the subject matter described in the cases is real, and in our opinion, the problems faced in the cases are common to most entrepreneurs and occur regularly in entrepreneurial settings.

The field of finance is large and rapidly evolving. We have endeavored to relate information that is immediately usable and current, although not information that is subject to great controversy or rethinking. In some areas, such as understanding financial documents, ratio analysis, and cash flow management, the state of the art is settled. In other areas, such as cost of capital, capital budgeting, and valuation, much new thinking is permeating the field. In these cases, classical perspectives are provided on the techniques that are appropriate to the subject area. By making note of both the pros and cons of different methods or points of analysis, we have attempted to draw the reader's attention to some areas where new thinking is being actively put forth and debated. Also, the book provides references to some of the best sources from which the reader may find further information on the subject at hand. Finally, in the references, we have included some of the most current and interesting sources of thought on the subjects we have addressed.

In our view, finance is one of the most interesting and useful of the social science paradigms, but it is only a tool. One cannot use it blindly and without the application of skill and judgment. The entrepreneur should use his or her knowledge of finance as he or she would any other tool. By itself, finance does not provide "the answer"; one cannot use it to calculate "the solution," but it can be used to frame the problem and suggest a proper course of action. Nothing, and certainly not the discipline of finance, can replace the entrepreneur's drive, ability to convince others of the worth of his or her vision, or ability to tolerate the uncertainty that the entrepreneur faces in the pursuit of his or her dream.

Acknowledgments

We are grateful for the support, encouragement, and feedback we received during the production of this text. Several people deserve special mention for their unwavering and tireless support of this project. Carol Pacelli assisted in the preparation of many of the chapters. Francisco J. Ayala provided substantial research support and assistance in developing some of the chapters. Jonathan Beckley provided research support. Of course, any remaining errors, either of omission or commission, remain the sole responsibility of the authors.

Thanks to the following reviewers who participated throughout all stages of the book's development:

Frank W. Anderson, *University of Texas at Dallas*

Craig E. Armstrong, *University of Alabama*

David M. Ford, *University of Alabama*

Steven Frankforter, *Winthrop University*

Mary H. Harris, *Cabrini College*

Ronald Meyers, *University of Cincinnati*

Talitha Smith, *Auburn University*

David Springate, *University of Texas at Dallas*

Mengsteab Tesfayohannes, *Susquehanna University*

Xuan Tian, *Indiana University*

About the Authors

Gary Gibbons has extensive professional experience in portfolio management, securities valuation, financial modeling, and financial planning and evaluation of entrepreneurial firms. His corporate and investment clients include the Bank of Bermuda, the Agyros Foundation, Imperial Mortgage, Kaiser Steel Resources, the New Kaiser VEBA, the Kaiser Steel Benefit Trust, and many other institutions and small firms. Additionally, he has served as an expert witness or expert consultant in numerous legal proceedings; he has provided opinions that have been used in support of specific civil, tax, or regulatory positions. He has worked on both civil and criminal litigation and in court, arbitration, or mediation proceedings. Dr. Gibbons has served on the board of directors of both public and private companies. When serving on these various boards, he has generally acted in the capacity of the chief financial officer or the chair of the finance committee. Dr. Gibbons earned his PhD in business administration—with emphasis in strategy and finance—at Claremont Graduate School, Peter F. Drucker Graduate School of Management. He is the Academic Director of the Thunderbird Private Equity Center at Thunderbird School of Global Management.

Robert D. Hisrich is the Garvin Professor of Global Entrepreneurship and Director of the Center for Global Entrepreneurship at Thunderbird School of Global Management. He is also president of H&B Associates, a marketing and management consulting firm he founded. Dr. Hisrich received his MBA and PhD degrees from the University of Cincinnati and honorary doctorate degrees from Chuvash State University (Russia) and the University of Miskolc (Hungary). He has authored and coauthored 34 books, including *Marketing for Entrepreneurs and SMEs: A Global Perspective* (with Maja Konečnik Ruzzier and Mitja Ruzzier, 2014); *Managing Innovation and Entrepreneurship* (with Claudine Kearney, 2014); *Governpreneurship: Establishing a Thriving Entrepreneurial Spirit in Government* (with Amr

Al-Dabbagh, 2013); *Entrepreneurship: Starting, Developing, and Managing a New Enterprise* (9th edition; with Michael P. Peters and Dean A. Shepherd, 2013); *International Entrepreneurship: Starting, Developing, and Managing a Global Venture* (2nd ed., 2013); *Corporate Entrepreneurship: How to Create a Thriving Entrepreneurial Spirit Throughout Your Company* (with Claudine Kearney, 2011); and *Technology Entrepreneurship: Creating, Capturing, and Protecting Value* (with Thomas N. Duening and Michael A. Lechter, 2010). He has written more than 325 articles on entrepreneurship, international business management, and venture capital. He has instituted academic and training programs in Hungary, Russia, and China.

Carlos M. DaSilva has widespread experience in entrepreneurship and the startup ecosystem. He is the Director of the Founder Institute, Portugal, the world's largest early stage startup accelerator, with over 1,000 graduate companies across six continents. Dr. DaSilva is responsible for the mentoring of dozens of technology entrepreneurs every year. He is frequently invited to lecture on topics related to entrepreneurship, as well as participate in the jury of various startup competitions. Dr. DaSilva held the positions of visiting scholar at the Thunderbird School of Global Management and at the University of Southern California in Los Angeles. He is a professor of entrepreneurship at the School of Business Administration in Fribourg, Switzerland, and lectures on topics related to entrepreneurial finance and business model innovation. Prior to obtaining his PhD in technology management at the University of Ljubljana, he worked for several years as a strategy manager at an Eastern European startup venture that was recently acquired by a large multinational group.

Chapter 1

The Entrepreneurial Challenge

A Global Perspective

Learning Objectives
• To understand the importance of entrepreneurial finance
• To introduce the different types of entrepreneurs
• To expose the challenges associated with being an entrepreneur
• To identify the traits of global entrepreneurs
• To understand what is different about entrepreneurial finance

Case: CEON Solutions Pvt. Ltd.

Abhay Panjiyar, a young engineer in his second year of engineering school, had an idea while he was creating an effective administration process for Bhopal, an India-based education nongovernmental organization (NGO). Along with three friends who "believed in creating everything out of nothing" (hence the name CEON), Abhay developed an analytical problem-solving software for use in India's schools. He started participating in business plan competitions with his revolutionary idea of educational process management (EPM) software and received an invitation from IIM Ahmedabad's Centre for Innovation Incubation and Entrepreneurship (CIIE) to be their first incubator company.

Improving the quality of education is an important issue in India and other emerging countries. Abhay saw the major obstacle being the nonsharing of information among teachers, students, and parents. He filled this gap by developing software that connects all parties and helps parents become involved effectively in their students' success.

Education is a knowledge-driven sector, and it is a growing market with schools competing to improve education. In that competition, CEON's software enables better education process management for schools.

Abhay began his startup by borrowing money from his family. He ran his business at the lowest possible cost. He paid salaries out of borrowed money and got Rs. 1 lakh (USD $2,000) from his very first client. With the help of this funding, Abhay was able to double his client base and convinced GVFL, a venture capital firm, to invest additional money up to Rs. 3 crores (USD $600,000).

Today, with this software, parents are able to see whether their children have missed classes, how many questions they asked in class, whether they are showing more interest in sports than classes, and if there is a parent-teacher meeting at school. It allows personalized tools for assessment of a student with instant feedback to parents about their child's performance in school.

CEON Solutions now has two more products available—an NGO resource planning solution and police inventory management software—and is looking to expand its client base.

Abhay thinks that of the 1.2 million schools in India, at least 10% would benefit from his software. Even though CEON is creating this new market, its growth is difficult to predict. CEON's approach to use minimum resources, dedicated manpower, a research-oriented business structure, and direct marketing to quality schools is a key factor for its success.

The entrepreneurial landscape is rapidly changing. Fast-growing companies take longer to go public, secondary venture capital markets are flourishing, and new financing options such as crowdfunding are emerging. We are facing a new era in capital strategy. Private money has never been so abundant and is creating opportunity for innovation and faster company growth. In short, entrepreneurs and investors are facing both exciting and challenging times (Savitz, 2011).

However, after listening to hundreds of entrepreneurs pitching their ideas to attract funding for their business concept, we have come to understand that a large majority of **entrepreneurs** lack an in-depth understanding of financial management. Entrepreneurs make a wide variety of mistakes when trying to apply financial concepts to their nascent businesses. They attach an unjustified certainty to the valuation numbers that they generate and, as a result, irritate potential investors; they fail to understand the uncertainty that is inherent in the **financial projections** they make for their firms and, as a result, do not capture the full range of potential outcomes with respect to future revenue and cash flow needs; they think of financial ratios as being mere statements of numeric comparison rather than insights into management's style and capability, and when they do this, they lose the opportunity to use the ratio analysis to hold management accountable for its actions; and finally, they fail to appreciate that in an environment of uncertainty (as distinguished from mere statistical risk), the application of financial principles needs to be made in concert with a hefty dose of skill and judgment.

Our belief that financial principles are not given enough attention by entrepreneurs is what motivated us to write this book. Our objective is to provide entrepreneurs from all backgrounds and industries with a practical guide on how to use a better understanding of financial principles to raise capital, manage the firm, and negotiate effectively with investors or buyers. This book is targeted at both entrepreneurs and investors seeking to improve the financial lens through which they view a venture.

Before we explore in detail the financial aspects of entrepreneurship, we will briefly introduce the entrepreneurship field through a global lens.

Chart 1.1 presents a schematic representation of the material covered in this chapter.

Need for Entrepreneurial Finance

One of the most difficult aspects of starting and growing a business as occurred for CEON is finding initial capital to start a company as well as capital to grow the business further. In obtaining initial financing, the

Chart 1.1   Schematic of Chapter 1

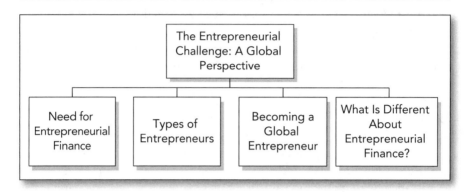

entrepreneur needs to consider the source of external funds as well as the type provided. Any external funds for the venture (those funds not personally provided by the entrepreneur) will be in the form of debt or equity. The initial source of funds almost always comes from individuals—family and friends or private individual investors often called angels. These sources provide over 80% of the funds for startups in most every country and are the key to bringing innovation to the market. Family and friends invest due to their relationship with and belief in the entrepreneur and are the most common source of financing at startup. This knowledge and familiarity help overcome part of the uncertainty and risk felt by other individual investors. Usually, this is a small amount of capital reflecting the capital needed for most new ventures. Private investors other than family and friends also provide this capital. As a part of the **informal risk capital market,** these individuals (business angels) play a very important role in the economy of every country by providing the capital needed to take innovation to the market through the creation of a new venture, which affects the gross domestic product and employment of the country.

The capital provided by family and friends and other individual investors can be in the form of debt or equity, the two general types of financing available. *Debt financing* involves an interest-bearing instrument usually in the form of a loan, which carries the obligation to pay back the total amount of funds borrowed and a fee (the interest rate) for using these funds. Often, some form of collateral or asset, such as a car, house, machine, or land, is required.

Equity financing, the more common of the two, does not require this collateral, as the family, friend, or other individual invests in the entrepreneur and new venture and obtains an ownership position in the venture.

The individual then shares on a pro rata basis in the profits and disposition of any assets, including the sale of the entire venture. The entrepreneurial financing need for the venture is often met by employing a combination of debt and equity financing.

Types of Entrepreneurs

The Global Entrepreneurship Monitor (GEM) identified three main types of entrepreneurs: (1) nascent entrepreneurs, (2) new entrepreneurs, and (3) established entrepreneurs (Acs, Arenius, Hay, & Minniti, 2005; Autio, 2007).

Nascent entrepreneurs are individuals between 18 and 64 years old who do not have a firm yet but are in the process of starting one. These individuals have been committing time and resources to founding a new venture over the past months and expect to become active owner-managers in the short term. They have assessed the opportunity and have already taken steps toward the creation of the startup company but have not yet paid salaries to anyone for more than 3 months. This means they might have already written their **business plan** or did marketing research and are serious about founding a new venture.

It is common to find nascent entrepreneurs at universities, and over the years, we have met plenty of them. They usually start developing a project or idea during their student years, with many building a successful business either before or after graduation. There are several famous examples of individuals who were nascent entrepreneurs at universities, such as Mark Zuckerberg, who launched Facebook from his dormitory room back in 2004 and today is among the 30 richest people in the world.

New entrepreneurs are individuals between 18 and 64 years old and are owner-managers currently managing a startup venture. They have paid salaries for more than 3 but less than 42 months. This period is usually the most challenging for entrepreneurs as it represents the time period where most ventures fail.

Established entrepreneurs are owner-managers of entrepreneurial firms who have been in business for more than 42 months and are currently managing a firm. They have survived the most difficult years of a startup company and may be looking to further grow their business or simply looking for an exit.

No matter the stage of entrepreneurship, this book will provide relevant information that will help the entrepreneur understand better the financial aspects of doing business in a global economy.

Becoming a Global Entrepreneur

More exciting international business opportunities are present today than any other time in the history of the world. The ability to be a global entrepreneur or to be born global is easier than ever due to the ability to communicate with and reach markets once considered impossible. What was once produced domestically is now done internationally. In fact, there is less and less distinction between foreign and domestic markets.

Global entrepreneurship creates wealth and employment benefiting individuals and countries throughout the world. International (global) entrepreneurship is "the process of an entrepreneur conducting business activities across national boundaries" (Hisrich, 2013, p. 7). It may take the form of exporting, selling goods from the Internet, opening an overseas sales office in another country, or establishing an entirely new operation. Being a global entrepreneur presents new problems but allows an individual to expand the sales/profits of a venture in ways previously not possible.

Is It the Right Time?

While an economic downturn can challenge many entrepreneurs, it doesn't mean it is not the right time to launch a new venture. In fact, history reveals that tough economic periods are appropriate for starting a new business. Out of 30 businesses from the Dow Jones Industrial Average, 16 were founded during a recession or depression: Walt Disney started in the mid-1920s and was a young startup during the Depression, Hewlett-Packard was launched in 1938 during the Great Depression, and Microsoft started to build its empire in the 1975 recession (Abrams, 2008). Instagram, a free photo-sharing application initially designed for mobile smartphones, was launched in the middle of the slowdown in 2010 (Waters & Nuttall, 2012). With only 13 employees, the company grew rapidly and acquired a large user base estimated at over 30 million in early 2012. Without ever generating any kind of revenue (their product was offered for free to users), the company was sold less than 2 years after its inception for $1 billion (Raice & Ante, 2012). At a time when companies do not even need to generate revenue in order to provide a successful exit for their founders and investors, it seems there has never been a better time than today to become an entrepreneur. Entrepreneurs look at problems as opportunities.

Is It Risky to Become an Entrepreneur?

Interestingly, there seem to be two predominant attitudes in the world toward entrepreneurs. One view is that entrepreneurs are some kind of heroes who shape the course of history and achieve tremendous success. Steve Jobs with Apple, Mark Zuckerberg with Facebook, Stelios Haji-Ioannou with easyJet, and Ratan Naval Tata with the Tata Group are inspirations who motivate others to follow their dreams and create their own ventures. Conversely, certain cultures may give merit to established entrepreneurs yet discourage nascent or new entrepreneurs to follow suit. In fact, nearly all graduates from college who visit their career centers in Europe will be offered advice on how to apply and seek a job, not advice on how to register a brand or form a company. Entrepreneurship still seems to be in most parts of the world a deviation from the norm and perceived as a risky career choice. For example, in Southern Europe, it is nearly impossible for banks to approve mortgage loans to self-employed entrepreneurs, even if their early stage venture income seems to justify a favorable decision (DaSilva, Janezic, & Hisrich, 2012). Banks prefer to give a loan to someone who has a lower salary but a "secure" job at a large corporation. This conventional position from banks and society does not seem to make sense nowadays, but still the practice prevails.

Given the mass layoffs of the past few years, is entrepreneurship riskier today than working at a big bank or law firm? A *Harvard Business Review* blog (Gibney & Howery, 2012) reveals that 215,417 jobs for attorneys will be available between 2008 and 2018, while over 430,000 new legal graduates will come out of universities during that same period. Those numbers indicate that only half will get a chance to get a job in their chosen field. There will be so many lawyers on the market for jobs that even those who get a job will probably have compensation packages that differ from the ones presently on the market. By contrast, the Kauffman Foundation did a survey of 5,000 entrepreneurial ventures started in 2004 in the United States (Robb & Reedy, 2012). Their results show that nearly 56% were still in business in the beginning of 2010 despite the world financial turmoil. Now if we consider financial rewards, entrepreneurs do have the possibility to make real money. Statistics from the venture capital industry reveal that 25% of first-time venture-backed firms are acquired for at least $50 million or file for an initial public offering (IPO) (Gompers, Kovner, Lerner, & Scharfstein, 2008).

Another positive feature of entrepreneurship is that motivated and happy people will usually perform better than individuals simply looking forward to their paycheck. In today's highly competitive market, only those who enjoy what they do and how they do it perform at a higher level.

This book will provide insights that will contribute to the success of any entrepreneur or investor seeking practical advice on how to measure performance and improve the financial state of an entrepreneurial venture in a global economy. Additionally, we will provide advice on how to reach and negotiate with investors to obtain the vital cash necessary for a venture to grow and eventually exit successfully.

Traits of a Global Entrepreneur

Several traits are common among entrepreneurs worldwide. These include cultural diversity, a strong desire to achieve, internal locus of control, clear vision, tolerance for ambiguity, integrity, and a global sense of responsibility.[1] We will cover each briefly over the next pages.

Cultural Diversity. Global entrepreneurs are individuals who are usually well traveled and who embrace cultural diversity both in and out of the workplace. They are not afraid of change or to face different sociocultural environments. They constantly seek challenges and new experiences with an "out of the box" feeling.

Desire to Achieve. Global entrepreneurs are willing to go the extra mile and face difficult and uncertain conditions to excel. Their desire to achieve allows them to go beyond cultural barriers and develop the set of skills required to succeed in an international environment.

Internal Locus of Control. Global entrepreneurs believe they and their team can intervene and influence the outcome of events and situations in a positive manner. They take responsibility for what happens and keep an open mind toward new ideas and potential solutions.

Clear Vision. Global entrepreneurs develop and maintain a clear vision as to where they are heading and make sure to share their vision with all stakeholders they interact with. They know employees must feel their work is essential for the success and prosperity of the global organization they integrate. Global entrepreneurs are positive, energetic, and confident individuals with both short- and long-term goals that express the vision of the venture.

Tolerance for Ambiguity. Global entrepreneurs face adversity with an optimistic mind-set and a willingness to learn. They have the ability to deal with contradictory or unexpected events while keeping an open mind and a focus on what their goals are.

Integrity. Integrity is critical for getting and keeping the support of employees, investors, and partners. Global entrepreneurs walk the talk by being honest, being morally upright, and meeting their commitments. Integrity is

---

[1]For a thorough discussion of these traits as well as the need for global entrepreneurs, the topic of the next section, see Hisrich (2013) and Hisrich, Peters, and Shepherd (2013).

one of the most sought-after traits by customers, vendors, and investors. Without integrity from the top, the entrepreneur, the venture will soon falter.

Global Sense of Responsibility. Global entrepreneurs care about their employees and environment where they operate. They are sensitive to their employees' and customers' needs. Their goals are to not only build a profitable global venture but also contribute toward the sustainable development of the community in which they operate.

The Need for Global Entrepreneurs

In the past, companies ventured abroad only after having established and grown a strong business at home. They would start by approaching nearby countries and progressively establish partnerships. For example, Johnson & Johnson only decided to enter a foreign market 33 years after its inception. The country they chose to enter was an easy choice, Canada, as it could be easily reached by simply driving across the border (Isenberg, 2008). Walmart went global first in Mexico, rather than Canada, despite the language difference due to its closer geographic proximity to the company's headquarters in Bentonville, Arkansas.

Nowadays, companies are born global. From outsourcing manufacturing in China, employing a team of programmers in India, seeking funding on international platforms such as Kickstarter.com, and even selling their products internationally through the Internet, entrepreneurs and investors seek the best deals worldwide with little to no boundaries.

The world has changed, and today's ventures do business in several countries before dominating their local markets. Two main explanations justify entrepreneurs crossing borders: (1) defensive and (2) offensive motivations (Isenberg, 2008). Defensive motivation leads entrepreneurs to go overseas to produce products that are competitive in the global market. When one of the authors produced his first mobile software application for the iPhone, he requested budgets from several development teams in Europe and the United States using elance.com. The average fee for a U.S.-based production was $20,000 at the time. In Western Europe, the price for the same project would fluctuate between $9,000 and $15,000. He ended up recruiting a developer from Southeast Europe who charged $3,000, which included several rounds of revisions and testing. Before he had even started the venture, he had outsourced the software development of the upcoming product at a fraction of the price it would have been to develop it in the United States.

An offensive approach occurs when entrepreneurs discover a new business opportunity that involves maintaining a presence beyond their country's boundary. This was the case of the now famous mobile game Angry Birds, created by Rovio (Kendall, 2011). While their roots are in Finland, home of Nokia Corporation, they decided to pass on the opportunity to do business locally and target their upcoming game to iPhone users predominantly present in the United States. In December 2009, Rovio launched the game Angry Birds through Apple's iPhone app store. It rapidly became a best seller, and since then, the game has been downloaded more than a billion times by smartphone owners from all over the world.

Being global is not a choice anymore for entrepreneurs. Entrepreneurial ventures need to be able to leverage the global economy and its advantages to become competitive both locally and globally.

What Is Different About Entrepreneurial Finance?

Finance for entrepreneurs is somewhat different from either corporate- or investment-oriented finance. When we consider traditional financial techniques and concepts, we see that the discipline is based on a number of key assumptions. These assumptions include readily available data, efficient markets, diversification as a way to control risk, and statistical analysis as a means to measure risk. These are the key assumptions or techniques that underlie both the theory and practice of traditional finance.

When we deal with entrepreneurs or entrepreneurial ventures, especially startups, there are two key points to consider:

1. there is usually a paucity of any historical data, and

2. entrepreneurs do not have the ability to diversify or even measure their risk in the normal way.

Thus, **entrepreneurial finance** is considerably different from main-line finance. We acknowledge that entrepreneurial finance requires an in-depth knowledge of finance theory and technique and an understanding of the strengths and weaknesses of these theories and techniques. However, the final element that needs to be equally weighted in the entrepreneurial environment is the application of skill and judgment in selecting and applying the appropriate theory or technique given the problem at hand. We do not deny that this is also important in the areas of traditional finance, but we assert that it is more acute with entrepreneurial firms. In the entrepreneurial setting, it is not just a matter of calculating the answer (which is what is usually done in the more traditional areas of finance). The entrepreneur must know:

1. What to do if historical data are not available

2. What techniques may be used when certain data are missing

3. How to compute ranges of outcomes rather than focusing on specific outcomes

4. How to use projections that are based on data that are not historical

Summary

There has never been a better time to explore international opportunities and become a global entrepreneur. Becoming an entrepreneur today is less of a trade-off than it used to be. Between corporate layoffs, foreign competition, and the decline of labor unions, the typical employee may no longer assume that his or her job will be there for the next 3 to 5 years. Entrepreneurs need to have a global mind-set to face a highly competitive global economy. Common traits identified among global entrepreneurs are cultural diversity, desire to achieve, internal locus of control, clear vision, tolerance for ambiguity, integrity, and a global sense of responsibility. Companies are born global, and internationalization is no longer a choice but a requirement for today's global competitive business environment.

Chapter 2

Business Planning for Entrepreneurs

Learning Objectives

- To understand the purpose of a business plan
- To understand the elements of a business plan
- To know the process of building a business plan
- To know how to develop the necessary financial information and statements

Case: TerraPower, Inc.

Bill Gates, Nathan Myhrvold (the former chief technology officer of Microsoft), and Lowell Wood (a renowned astrophysicist) were brainstorming about new ideas at an intellectual property incubator and licensor, Intellectual Ventures. The three knew that they needed to come up with an idea that would have significant potential by solving a large problem in the future and then developing a strategic plan and eventually a business plan to get there. While looking into the general area of energy, they focused on delivering massive amounts of emission-free energy that could occur in all kinds of weather conditions. This focus eventually led to concentrating on new designs to create and deliver nuclear energy that were technically feasible and developing the necessary plans for achieving this.

The group formed TerraPower, Inc. in Bellevue, Washington, and hired John Gilleland, founder of Archimedes Technology Group, a company that developed solutions for the disposal of nuclear waste, as CEO of the company. Since TerraPower did not require any public funding, the nuclear power startup could more easily develop an affordable endless supply of electricity through engineering an innovative traveling wave reactor (TWR) technology that would run on depleted uranium. Requiring a very small amount of enriched material to start, the wave reactor would slowly burn over decades the depleted uranium without refueling. This would provide better control of costs and reduce any opportunity for theft by terrorists.

The supply source of depleted uranium was enormous, with over 680,000 metric tons in just the United States. In addition, the coolant in the reactors would be liquid sodium, which is much softer water, just in case of an earthquake or another natural disaster such as happened in Japan in 2012.

As called for in the plan, the company had about 60 employees by March 2013 and has the objective of having a prototype ready for testing in 2022. This projected timeline is reasonable despite the technological and particularly the licensing problems associated with nuclear reactors.

The plan requires developing a brand-new supply chain for the components of the technology, a feat in itself. The distinctive fuel assemblies needed will require nontraditional materials and manufacturing techniques. Over 100 partner sources have been approached such as Massachusetts Institute of Technology, the University of Michigan, Kobe Steel, and Toshiba to develop the supply chain and conduct the necessary research.

As occurred in the development of TerraPower, Inc., a business plan is an important part of the new venture process, as it provides a road map for implementing the entrepreneurial strategy established. *Strategy* is defined in the strategic management literature as developing a plan for creating and operating a profitable new enterprise through the obtainment and development of internal and external resources in alignment with the environment (Dess & Miller, 1993; Mintzberg & Quinn, 1991; Pearce & Robinson, 1992; Thompson & Strickland, 1992). Strategy exists at various levels in a new venture, such as enterprise, corporate, business, functional, and subfunctional, so that implementation can occur throughout the firm.

A key aspect of developing a strategy at each level is establishing goals. Goals need to be difficult to achieve and represent a challenge for the new venture and yet realistic enough to be achieved with effort. Such is the case of the goal of TerraPower of having a prototype traveling wave reactor available in 2022.

To accomplish the goals established and implement the strategy, it is best to write a business plan before an entrepreneur goes very far in creating and starting a new venture. While the original plan developed will be modified and changed many times, remember, "If you do not know where you are going, any road will get you there."

Chart 2.1 presents a schematic representation of the material covered in this chapter.

Chart 2.1   Schematic of Chapter 2

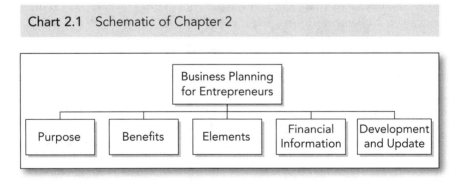

Purpose of Writing a Business Plan

Most entrepreneurs prepare a business plan for two reasons: to provide a road map for developing, managing, and operating the business and to raise outside equity or debt capital. While arguments can be made for and against writing a business plan, if financing is needed from an outside source, then a business plan needs to be written for this source to review.

Writing a business plan can be very difficult for entrepreneurs, as they are usually individuals characterized as doers, not planners. But it is not acceptable to hire someone to write the plan, as the task needs to be done personally. While outsiders (accountants, consultants, lawyers) can be used for input in terms of numbers and pieces of the plan, the final business plan needs to be developed and written by the entrepreneur and any initial top management team members when needed and appropriate. By doing this, the entrepreneur ensures that he or she is very familiar with all the details of the plan to be able to present it to outside sources of finance and make sound decisions that will affect the new venture. Every outside investor expects the entrepreneur to be knowledgeable about and totally involved in the proposed enterprise.

Developing the business plan takes energy, money, and time, with time being one of the most costly aspects. Since each business plan deals with an economy(s) and industry(s), a hidden cost of writing a business plan is a psychological one—understanding and knowing that anything can go wrong. This is particularly difficult for entrepreneurs who are overall optimistic and believe in themselves and their capabilities.

Benefits of a Business Plan

Since a business plan details the entrepreneur's vision in writing and indicates the implementation strategy and the costs involved, it has several benefits:

1. Determining the amount and timing of resources needed. The business plan indicates the existing resources of the firm, the resources needed, and some potential suppliers of these resources. This allows the entrepreneur to determine how much money is needed at various times to obtain these resources and what approach to develop and use to obtain the money as well as any other resources. The money will be obtained from outside capital providers. Other resources needed are in the areas of supply, distribution, personnel, and support services.

2. Establishing the direction of the firm. Since the business plan is a comprehensive document, it treats all the major issues faced starting and growing the venture. This enables the entrepreneur to develop strategies and contingency plans to reduce the impact of any problems.

3. Guiding and evaluating. By setting goals and milestones for the new venture, the business plan lays out the intentions of the entrepreneur as well as his or her values. Accomplishments and results can be measured and any deviations from the plan corrected in a timely manner. These results should be reported to all interested stakeholders and to outside providers of financial resources on a regular basis, usually four times a year if not more frequently, such as every month in at least the first year.

4. Avoiding conflicts. By being put together by the entrepreneur and the management team and being reviewed and revised frequently, the business plan can be used to guide decisions and help avoid conflicts among the entrepreneur, management team, employees, outside vendors, and financial providers. The amount of energy and resources needed to launch and grow something new is enormous, with the risks being high; the new firm requires reinvestment and seems to always need more time and money. This requires significant sacrifice by the entrepreneur in terms of short-term income and people and family. There are often individuals hurt by the tough personal decisions that an entrepreneur needs to make.

Elements of the Business Plan

While there are some variations on what goes into a successful business plan, they all have the same essential elements (aspects). These can be grouped into three sections:

- Section 1: Introduction
  - Title (Cover) Page
  - Table of Contents
  - Executive Summary

- Section 2: Body of the Business Plan
  - Description of Business
  - Description of Industry
  - Technology Plan
  - Marketing Plan
  - Financial Plan
  - Production (Outsourcing) Plan
  - Organizational Plan
  - Operational Plan
  - Summary

- Section 3: Support (Backup) Material
  - Exhibit A: Résumés of Principals
  - Exhibit B: Market Statistics
  - Exhibit C: Market Research Data
  - Exhibit D: Competitive Brochures
  - Exhibit E: Competitive Price Lists
  - Exhibit F: Leases and Contracts
  - Exhibit G: Supplier Price Lists

Each of these sections, as detailed in Table 2.1, will be discussed in turn.

Table 2.1 Aspects of a Business Plan

Section 1: Introduction
Title (Cover) Page
Table of Contents
Executive Summary

Section 2: Body of the Business Plan	

1.0 Description of Business
 	
  • Description of the Venture
  • Product(s) and/or Service(s)
  • Mission Statement
  • Business Model
 	
3.0 Technology Plan
 	
  • Description of Technology
  • Technology Comparison
  • Commercialization Requirements
 	
5.0 Financial Plan
 	
  • Sources and Applications of Funds Statement
  • Pro Forma Income Statements
  • Pro Forma Cash Flow Statements
  • Pro Forma Balance Sheets
 	
7.0 Organization Plan
 	
  • Form of Ownership
  • Identification of Partners and/or Principal Shareholders
	2.0 Description of Industry
	
	  • Type of Industry
	  • Future Outlook and Trends of Industry
	  • Analysis of Competitors
	  • Trends and Market Forecasts
	
	4.0 Marketing Plan
	
	  • Market Segment
	  • Pricing
	  • Distribution
	  • Promotion
	  • Product or Service
	  • Sales for First 5 Years
	
	6.0 Production (Outsourcing) Plan
	
	  • Manufacturing Process (amount subcontracted)
	  • Physical Plant
	  • Machinery and Equipment
	  • Suppliers of Raw Materials
	  • Outsourcing Aspects

7.0 Organization Plan (continued)	8.0 Operational Plan
• Management Team Background • Roles and Responsibilities of Members of Organization • Organizational Structure	• Description of Company's Operation • Flow of Orders and Goods • Exit Strategy

9.0 Summary

Section 3: Appendices (Exhibits)

- Exhibit A: Résumés of Principals
- Exhibit B: Market Statistics
- Exhibit C: Market Research Data
- Exhibit D: Competitive Brochures
- Exhibit E: Competitive Price Lists
- Exhibit F: Leases and Contracts
- Exhibit G: Supplier Price Lists

Section 1: Introduction

Section 1 contains the title (cover) page, table of contents, and executive summary. The title (cover) page is an important part of every business plan, as it has the following:

1. The company name, address, telephone, fax, e-mail address, and website.

2. Name and position of each member of the management team and the contact person.

3. The purpose of the plan, the amount of money needed, and funding increments

4. At the bottom of the title page: "This is confidential business plan number ____." A low number should be put in for each business plan given out and when, and who received this numbered plan should be tracked for a 30-day/60-day/90-day period.

The first page after the title (cover) page is the table of contents. This follows the usual format and lists at least the major subsections in each section and the corresponding page number as well as each figure, table, and exhibit. Preferably each major subsection and smaller subsections should be labeled as 1.0, 1.1, 1.2, 2.0, 2.1, 2.3, and so on. The executive summary precedes the numbering and therefore either has no number or smaller letters or Roman numerals. The tables and figures should have a separate list, as should the exhibits (appendices).

The last item in Section 1, following the table of contents, is the all-important two-page **executive summary.** This is by far the most important document in the business plan, as it is often used as the screening section by investors who often decide not to read the entire plan. Many readers, including potential providers of capital, never read beyond the executive summary. One head of a very successful venture fund, who is now managing his eighth fund of over $850 million, indicated that he receives about 1,500 business plans a year, discards 1,400 based on the cover page or executive summary, and, of the remaining 100, will discard 80 after the first 1- to 2-hour examination. Of the remaining 20, about 4 to 6 will receive investment from his fund. So the executive summary needs to be very well written to invite further reading of the business plan.

The executive summary should have the name of the company and address at the top of the first page that appeared on the title (cover) page. It should begin with defining the nature and size of the problem existing. In the case of TerraPower, the problem is a large, critical one—the need for low-cost, clean electrical energy. The larger and more critical the problem, the more interest there will be on the part of investors and others.

This needs to be followed by your proposed solution to the problem. Again, for TerraPower, this is providing low-cost, clean electricity through a new traveling wave reactor (TWR) technology that runs on depleted uranium. In this section, all competitive ways to solve the problem should be discussed showing the uniqueness or the unique selling propositions of your solution. These would include nuclear, solar, cool, and geothermal energy for TerraPower.

Following the solution is the size of the market, trends for at least 3 to 5 years, and future growth rate. The market needs to be large enough and accessible to deliver the sales needed for the profits and returns expected by investors. The need for and increasing use of electricity makes for a very exciting perspective for TerraPower.

The entrepreneur and team who will deliver these sales and profits then need to be described. The education, accomplishments, and industry experience of each known member of the top management team need to be described. The individuals involved in TerraPower are very noteworthy and include CEO John Gilleland, founder of Archimedes Technology Group, and founding members Bill Gates (Microsoft), Nathan Myhrvold (Microsoft's former CTO), and Lowell Wood (a renowned astrophysicist).

The resulting sales and profits should be summarized over a 5-year period in the following format:

	Year 1	Year 2	Year 3	Year 4	Year 5
Total Revenue					
Cost of Goods Sold					
Gross Margin					
Operating Expenses					
Profit (Loss) Before Taxes					

These numbers are taken directly from the pro forma income statement summary in the financial plan in Section 2. Note the exact calendar year is not used but rather year 1, 2, 3, 4, and 5, with 1 indicating the first year of company operations after the investment is received so that dates do not have to be changed based on the receipt of the investment.

The two-page executive summary closes with a statement of the resources needed, the increments of capital accepted, and contact information. An example two-page executive summary is indicated in Figure 2.1.

Figure 2.1   Example Executive Summary

TIDAL POINT

Phoenix, Arizona

www.tidalpoint.com

Contact: _____

Stage: Pre-launch

Industry Software Product NAICS Code: 511210

Software Consulting NAICS Code: 541512

Mission Statement

To empower our customers by providing them with better control of their IT systems through efficient, rational, and cost-effective delivery of IT products

(Continued)

Figure 2.1 (Continued)

and services. And do so by becoming our clients' most trusted advisor and partner by sharing knowledge and best practices.

Problem Being Solved

Nature of Problem: When it comes to replacement of their legacy IT systems, insurance companies struggle with cost and effort overruns, which makes the cost of transformation and cost of ownership significantly higher.

Market Segment: There are approximately 300 mid-sized to large insurance companies that need to replace their legacy IT systems. The segment growth rate is estimated to be 7% CAGR, and the total IT budget by year 2015 for COTS product and services is estimated to be USD $17.5 billion.

Importance: There is an unmet need for insurance software product providers who can combine the follow-up services required for product integration and implementation into insurance companies' operational landscape. We will offer a suite of services to the companies along with consultants and experts who can enable a smooth transition for insurance companies.

The Solution

We will provide a customized off-the-shelf product along with the services required to integrate this product into an insurance company's operational landscape. The product will be Tidal Point Policy Administration system; this system can cover all major business lines and provide an end-to-end processing capability which includes distribution, new business development, underwriting, claims, and reinsurance. The services provided will include data migration, implementation, business analysis, process consulting, and IT strategy consulting.

USP

- Provide an integrated suite of services to the clients without having them organize different activities related to legacy system transformation.
- Overall cost and time will be reduced for the clients due to:
  - Reduced time and efforts in issuing multiple RFPs and RFIs.
  - Speed to start will improve as one vendor will provide all the services.
- More effective approach as all the services would be provided by a single vendor, which will give clients better control and ease of managing the transformation.
- Lower cost of ownership for the customers.

Competition

- IBM, CSC, Guidewire, Accenture (Duck Creek), MajescoMastek, Camilion, Exigen, Insurity, AQS, CGI, Cover-All

Market

- 400 Property & Casualty (P&C), Specialty and Life Insurance companies in the U.S. market.

Market Segment

- Software (NAICS 511210): Insurance COTS product market estimated to be $17.5 billion by year 2015. Insurance software services, including consulting market, are estimated at $40.9 billion by 2015.
- Software consulting (NAICS 541512): Insurance software consulting services are estimated to be $41.0 billion by year 2015.
- Approximately 300 insurance companies (direct carriers) need to replace their legacy IT systems for at least one class of business.

Marketing Plan

- Advertisements through industry publications such as *Insurance & Technology.*
- Participating in industry conferences and sponsorship of these events.
- Personal contacts and outside sales.

Price

- COTS product: $1,250,000
- Business analysis: $650,000
- Implementation: $700,000
- Process consulting: $200,000
- Data migration: $200,000
- IT strategy: $150,000

Financial Summary

Year	2014	2015	2016	2017	2018
Revenue	1,950,000	4,641,000	5,949,762	7,603,796	11,953,167
Cost of Goods Sold	1,072,500	2,552,550	3,272,369	4,182,088	6,574,242
Gross Margin	877,500	2,088,450	2,677,393	3,421,708	5,378,925
Operating Expenses	779,500	1,738,590	2,050,380	2,392,271	2,923,929
Operating Profit	98,000	349,860	627,013	1,029,437	2,454,996

Section 2: Body of the Business Plan

Following the executive summary, which is the end of Section 1 of the business plan, Section 2 starts on a new page with its first part—1.0—Description of Business. In this section, the nature of the venture is described to provide an understanding of how the venture will operate and deliver the products/services to solve the problem identified. Information on the products/services should be in enough detail to be easily understood; this will be expanded on in two places in Section 3. If it is a technological product/service that employs a unique/new technology, it will be described with a summary copy of the patent as well as in the product section of the marketing plan (Section 4). Every product/service will be further discussed here regardless of its degree of technology. The mission statement of the company should be described as well as the business model—the entire picture of how the company does business—and if this business model significantly differs from the model of the way business is presently being done in the industry.

Section 2.0—Description of Industry—follows; this section discusses the characteristics and size of the industry, industry trends for the past 3 to 5 years, future outlook and growth rate, and a thorough analysis of competition presently filling the same need as the new idea. This is a large section with significant use of data from secondary sources. Sometimes there are so much data that only part appears in the body of the plan, with the rest appearing in an appendix at the end of Section 3. Graphs, charts, histograms, and other graphics should be used to thoroughly explain the industry, its growth projection, and the competitors. A graph showing the market growing is important based on the trends of this market to date. The market, the market segment, and target market for the first year will be further discussed in the first section of the marketing plan.

Following the description of the industry is Section 3.0—Technology Plan. Some business plans where there is not a technological advancement in the product/service being offered might not have a technology plan. For example, one author founded a rainbow decal and sticker company with no significantly new technology, so there was no technology plan in the business plan of the company. Whenever the product/service has a patent or patent pending or application, there will always be a technology plan as the patent adds value to the venture. A general rule is if you are having a hard time deciding whether to have a technology plan, then put one in, as it is better to have one than not in this circumstance. The *technology plan* describes the state of the technology presently available and how the new technology revolutionizes the way things are done. This was the case for the traveling wave reactor (TWR) technology running on depleted uranium of TerraPower, discussed in the opening of this chapter.

The *marketing plan,* the next section, begins with a discussion of the market segment and target market for the product/service. It defines, usually through using one or more segmentation techniques, the most appropriate overall market and target market and its size. Of the many available segmentation techniques (demographic, geographic, psychological, benefit, volume of use, and controllable market elements), the two most widely used ones, particularly for entrepreneurs and **small- and medium-sized enterprises (SMEs),** are demographic and geographic, as this is the way that much of the secondary data are published. SMEs are smaller enterprises defined by size category that varies by the industry the company is in; it is established by the government of the country. In the United States, the U.S. government allows SMEs in the construction industry to be larger than SMEs in consulting.

If the venture is BtoC (business to consumer), then the most important market data are the demographics of the selected geographic market. The most widely used demographic variables are age, income, and gender to determine the size of the market and a typical customer profile. For a BtoB (business to business) venture, then the business market needs to be identified using the classification (country) system of the country for the industrial (business) customer being served. The North American Industry Classification System (NAICS) code in the United States, the Standard Industrial Classification (SIC) code in Korea, and the SIC code in China each use a numbering system to classify each industry and specific products/services in that country. A sum of all the output of these numbers is the gross national product of the country. This procedure will provide the trends, size, and growth rate of the particular industry market, which can be used to develop the typical customer profile.

Following the delineation of the target market, a marketing plan needs to be developed to successfully reach and sell to that target market. The marketing plan has four major areas—product/service, price, distribution, and promotion—as indicated in Table 2.2. The product/service part describes the characteristics and quality of the offering, the assortment of items to be offered, the guarantee, any servicing provided if needed, and the packaging. The latter can be very important for entrepreneurs and SMEs in the BtoC market as it can be a major area of distinctiveness as well as a sales tool in the distribution center(s) used.

The second variable, price, is closely related to the product/service, particularly the quality level. The price, the most badly executed of the marketing areas by entrepreneurs and SMEs, needs to reflect the competitive

Table 2.2 Elements of the Marketing Plan

| Product/ Service | Price | Distribution Mix | | Promotion |
		Distribution Channels	Physical Distribution	

• Quality
• Assortment
• Guarantee
• Servicing
  (if needed)
• Package
	• Price/
	  consumer
	  reactions
	  relationships
	• Price/cost
	  relationships
	• Price/
	  competitive
	  reactions
	  relationships
		• Retailers
		• Wholesalers
		• Representatives
			• Storage
			• Inventory
			• Transportation
				• Advertising
				• Personal
				  selling
				• Publicity
				• Sales
				  promotion
				• Social
				  media

prices, the costs, and the consumer reaction to the price. If a distribution system is used, then there will be a chain of markups on the cost, as indicated in Chart 2.2.

The distribution area has two major aspects: distribution channels and physical distribution, which together is called supply chain management. The distribution channels include entities handling the product, such as retailers, wholesalers, and representatives. The physical distribution, or logistics, is becoming an increasingly important area and includes transportation, storage (warehousing), and inventory.

The final area of the marketing plan is the promotion area, which is composed of advertising, personal selling, publicity, sales promotion, and social media. The latter three are particularly important for entrepreneurs and SMEs as they can be used to produce multiple exposures cost-effectively. Social media, including the website of the new venture, are a particularly useful area. A marketing budget needs to be prepared for the first year indicating where the money will be specifically allocated to promote the company and achieve the initial sales of the first year. This first-year sales figure concludes the marketing part of the business plan and is a good start for the next section—the financial plan.

The *financial plan,* the next part of Section 2, focuses on a discussion of the created statements indicated in Table 2.3. These will be discussed later in this chapter following the discussion of the business plan.

Following the financial plan is the *production or outsourcing plan,* which indicates how the offering will be developed and produced. Some service

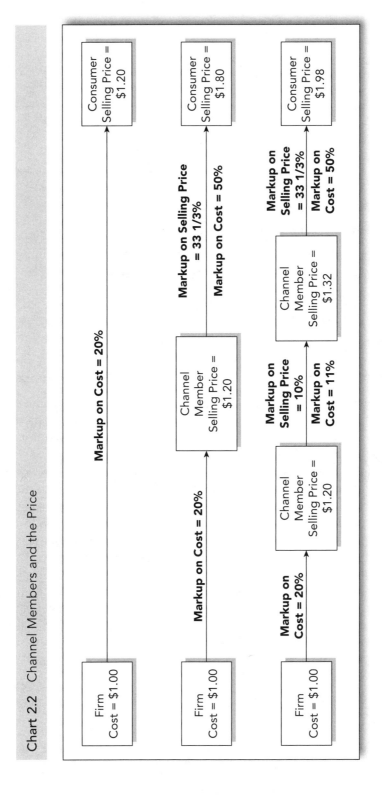

Chart 2.2 Channel Members and the Price

Firm
Cost = $1.00

Markup on Cost = 20%

Consumer
Selling Price =
$1.20

Firm
Cost = $1.00

Markup on Cost = 20%

Channel
Member
Selling Price =
$1.20

**Markup on Selling Price
= 33 1/3%**

Markup on Cost = 50%

Consumer
Selling Price =
$1.80

Firm
Cost = $1.00

**Markup on
Cost = 20%**

Channel
Member
Selling Price =
$1.20

**Markup on
Selling Price
= 10%**

**Markup on
Cost = 11%**

Channel
Member
Selling Price =
$1.32

**Markup on
Selling Price
= 33 1/3%**

**Markup on
Cost = 50%**

Consumer
Selling Price =
$1.98

Table 2.3   Financial Statements

Sources and uses of funds statement

Pro forma income statement—5-year summary

Pro forma income statement—First year by month

Pro forma income statement—Second year by quarter

Pro forma income statement—Third year by quarter

Pro forma cash flow statement—5-year summary

Pro forma cash flow statement—First year by month

Pro forma cash flow statement—Second year by quarter

Pro forma cash flow statement—Third year by quarter

Pro forma balance sheet—Year 1

Pro forma balance sheet—Year 2

Pro forma balance sheet—Year 3

ventures will not have this part in their business plan as they are not producing or outsourcing anything. Each individual cost needs to be specified so that an understanding is provided of the actual costs involved in the final offering and how much this can be reduced through economies of scale. All suppliers or outsourcing firms should be described in detail.

Following the production (outsourcing) plan is a short section—the *operational plan*. This describes in detail how the company will operate, including the flow of goods and orders. An important aspect discussed here is the exit strategy by which investors will get their equity and a return on equity, hopefully in a 5- to 7-year period of time from the initial investment. There are basically three ways to provide this exit and return desired: (1) retained earnings of the venture, (2) selling to another financial institution or firm, or (3) going public and being a publicly traded company. The most likely exit avenue is selling to another firm and, if this is mentioned, then three to four likely exit firms in the industry area need to be identified and discussed. Section 2 concludes with a brief summary that completes this section of the business plan.

Section 3: Support (Backup) Material

Section 3 contains all the backup material to support areas in Section 2. This includes secondary support data, any research data, contracts or leases, the patent document, and most notably the résumés of the entrepreneur and members of the management team. Nothing new should be introduced in this section.

Financial Information

The financial information contained in the financial plan consists primarily of the 11 **financial statements** indicated in Table 2.3. All but one of these are actual statements of any operating company. While having the same content, the difference in these statements is that they are forecasted—pro forma—statements that at the end of the time period will become actual statements. The one new statement is the first one—the sources and uses of funds statement—which describes how much money is needed (uses) and where it will come from (sources). The uses part often includes money for renovations, inventory, working capital, and/or reserve for contingencies. Each use statement will include working capital—the money needed until the venture positively cash flows, the point in time when the revenues from operations exceed the cost of operations. Sources of money will always include the entrepreneur and usually friends and family. The other sources of finance include banks, private investors, venture capitalists, and/or grants, which are described in Chapter 9.

Business Plan Development and Update

The business plan is a very important document both for providing direction for the new venture and for raising financial resources. It is important that it be well written and edited. The best way for an entrepreneur to proceed is to develop and write everything in draft format and then go back and rewrite. Keep in mind during this process the audience for your plan and arrange the material in a way, such as the one suggested in this chapter, that makes items flow smoothly from start to finish. Clear and concise writing is needed, and all numbers need to be consistent. If possible, have a friend or colleague critique the final business plan. If needed, you can always pay a professional writer at the end to make sure the plan flows smoothly.

A question frequently asked is how long (how many pages) a business plan should be. While that depends on the nature of the product or service, whether the business contains a technology plan and/or a production (out-sourcing) plan, and the extent of Section 3 (exhibits and appendices), most business plans are around 30 to 50 pages. Remember, you have 12 pages of financial statements and several pages of résumés. Most important, you want all the necessary material covered in a clear, concise manner.

Summary

Every new venture needs a business plan to set the direction for the firm and obtain financial resources. The essential elements of a business plan are contained in three sections, with the main elements being in Section 2. The most important document in the plan is the executive summary, as most potential investors do not read beyond it.

Each business plan needs to be well written and organized and address as many anticipated questions as possible. It needs to flow smoothly and consistently without errors so that the reader has a clear understanding about the details and future success of the new venture. Time will tell whether TerraPower meets its plan of having a prototype ready for demonstration in 2022.

Chapter 3

Understanding Financial Documents

Learning Objectives

- To foster an understanding of how financial documents are used in entrepreneurial ventures

- To analyze the components of the basic accounting equation

- To understand the logic of an income statement

- To understand the relevance of the statement of cash flow

Case: Hostess Brands LLC

Little did the founders of the Continental Baking Company know in the 1920s that the company would go through two bankruptcy proceedings by 2013. Through a series of mergers, the company at one time was the largest commercial bakery in the United States, with its Wonder Bread and Hostess cake products becoming Hostess Brands LLC in 1930.

Despite having multiple owners, including International Telephone and Telegraph, Interstate Bakeries Corporation, Ralston Purina, Ripplewood Holdings, Silver Point Capital, Monarch Alternative Capital, and today Apollo Global Management LLC and Metropoulos & Co., the famous Twinkies brand has not had any significant change since invented by James Alexander Dewar in the Depression era of the United States.

Over the years, even though millions of Hostess products were being sold, the company was not keeping a close watch on the numbers, and the income statement of the company was in bad shape due mostly to the company's high fixed-cost structure. The labor unions had negotiated generous pensions and health care benefits not in line with the market. When sales declined in the 1980s and 1990s with people consuming fewer carbohydrates and no successful new product introductions, Hostess Brands LLC had $450 million in debt in 2004 when it filed for its first bankruptcy in September of that year.

During the years in bankruptcy, Hostess Brands LLC attempted to restructure its debt and its unfunded pension funds and had several purchase offers, including one for $580 million in 2007 from its biggest competitor, a part of the giant Mexican bakery firm Bimbo Bakeries USA, Grupo Bimbo. The company stayed intact and emerged from bankruptcy in 2009 by (1) obtaining a $130 million equity infusion for controlling interest by Ripplewood Holdings, a private equity firm; (2) debt providers, including Silver Point Capital and Monarch Alternative Capital, two hedge funds having about 30% of the debt, keeping their loans; and (3) the labor unions agreeing to reduce the number of jobs and salaries by $110 million.

Again, the numbers were not watched carefully; the company had 12 different unions with 15,000 members, 40 different pension plans, and $2 billion in pension liability, and again it was forced to file for bankruptcy in January 2012. As a result of not being able to reach an agreement with the unions and creditors, mismanagement, and not watching the numbers, the company stopped producing its brands of Twinkies, CupCakes, Ding Dongs, and Ho Hos in November 2012. The company sold its Wonder Bread brand to Flowers Foods and Hostess Brands LLC to Apollo Global Management LLC and Metropoulos & Co. Twinkies and Hostess CupCakes were back on the shelves for purchase on July 15, 2013. It is hoped that the numbers will be carefully watched this time to avoid a third bankruptcy.

Financial statements are extremely important for any business, regardless of size or industry, as they provide information on the operating, financing, and investment activities of the venture and help keep a company from filing for bankruptcy protection as occurred twice in the case of Hostess Brands LLC. They are a fundamental tool for raising capital and assessing the financial health of the venture. They allow projections, comparisons, and the evaluation of past performance and future cash flow. In a nutshell, financial statements are a necessary tool for assessing a venture's current and future earnings and associated cash flow. In this chapter, we will cover three basic financial documents: the balance sheet, the income statement, and the statement of cash flow. Chart 3.1 presents a schematic representation of the material covered in this chapter.

Chart 3.1   Schematic of Chapter 3

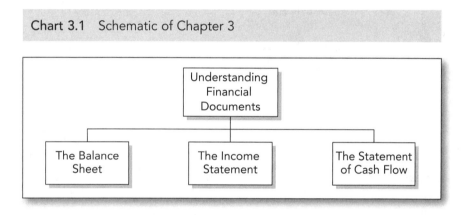

The Balance Sheet

The **balance sheet** allows venture owners to assess how healthy the business is in comparison with other past periods. It records what the company has in the form of assets, debt, and equity at the end of a month, fiscal quarter, or year. It is a "snapshot" of the firm's financial status at an instant in time. Table 3.1 provides an example of a balance sheet.

Assets are defined as the resources of the venture. Such assets were financed through liabilities or equity. **Liabilities** represent obligations the venture has to pay in the future, while equity defines the ownership interest of the venture. The relation between those three elements is the core of the balance sheet and is known as the accounting identity:

$$\text{Assets} = \text{Liabilities} + \text{Shareholders' Equity}$$

Table 3.1   Year-End Balance Sheet

Assets	
Current assets	
Cash	$200
Accounts receivable	400
Less: Allowance for bad debt	(10)
Inventory	610
Total current assets	**$1,200**
Property, plant, and equipment	
Real property	$5,000
Buildings	5,000
Less: Accumulated depreciation	(1,000)
Equipment	4,000
Less: Accumulated depreciation	(1,000)
Total property, plant, and equipment (net of depreciation)	**$12,000**
Other assets	
Automobiles	$4,500
Patents	1,000
Total other assets	**$5,500**
Total assets	**$18,700**
Liabilities and Shareholders' Equity	
Current liabilities	
Accounts payable	$500
Short-term debt	900
Current portion of long-term debt	700
Total current liabilities	**$2,100**
Long-term liabilities	
Bank loans	$4,000
Mortgages	5,000
Total long-term liabilities	**$9,000**
Shareholders' equity	
Contributed capital	$5,000
Retained earnings	2,600
Total shareholders' equity	**$7,600**
Total liabilities and shareholders' equity	**$18,700**

Assets

Assets represent the tangible and intangible property that the venture owns and has accounting value. It is important to note that assets can be both physical assets and intangible assets. Examples of **physical assets** are inventory, company cars, and real estate. Examples of **intangible assets** are patents, copyrights, trademarks, and goodwill. Assets are usually ordered in the balance sheet in order of their liquidity. The most liquid assets appear first on the balance sheet followed by the least liquid ones. Current assets represent the most liquid assets of a venture, meaning they can more easily be turned into cash. Examples of **current assets** are cash, marketable securities, and accounts receivable.

A venture's requirement for current assets is dependent on its operating cycle. The operating cycle is measured based on the time it takes to convert an investment in cash into inventory and then back into cash proceeds from its sale to customers. As a general rule, the longer the operating cycle, the larger the venture's need for liquidity (i.e., cash).

Noncurrent assets may not be readily converted into cash and are usually subject to wide swings in value. These assets are composed of buildings, land, mineral interests, and equipment (ranging from computers to furniture). Assets in this category are "depreciated" over time. **Depreciation** is the "expensing" or "writing off" of an asset over its economic life. Depreciation affects the value of such items on the firm's books. The value of the asset is and lowered by a certain amount each year. The annual amount of depreciation depends on the type of item. The depreciation amount appears on the income statement (which we will cover next) and reduces taxable income. Accumulated depreciation is the cumulative sum of depreciation for physical assets such as property and equipment.

Intangible assets are assets other than real or tangible property and have no physical existence. They may or may not be reported on the balance sheet. Intangible assets can be and usually are amortized over time.

Liabilities

Liabilities are usually presented in order of their due date and divided in two main sections: current liabilities and long-term liabilities.

Current liabilities are generally due within 1 year, with most items usually having a cycle shorter than 12 months. Several of the items in this category are associated with day-to-day operating expenses and are usually paid within 30 to 180 days depending on the country and culture. Current liabilities may consist of the following:

1. Accounts payable (payments due to other parties)

2. Wages and salaries (payments due to employees)

3. Current portion of long-term debt

4. Short-term loans (from banks or other sources)

Long-term liabilities are obligations that are due beyond 1 year. These can include the following:

1. Notes payable and bonds

2. Mortgages and capital leases

3. Deferred taxes (taxes that may have to be paid in the future)

Shareholders' Equity

Equity represents the shareholders' stake in the firm. The book value of equity known as shareholders' equity or stockholders' equity is the portion of firm capital provided by its investors. This amount is the cumulative amount shareholders have invested in the venture, plus or minus cumulative earnings or losses, minus distributions to owners. This section of the balance sheet is composed of the following:

1. Par value (nominal amount per share of stock or stated value if the stock has no par value)

2. Capital surplus (amount paid for shares of stock by investors in excess of par or stated value)

3. Retained earnings (prior and current periods' earnings and losses minus dividend payment)

4. Accumulated other comprehensive income or losses (accumulated unrealized gains and unrealized losses such as foreign currency hedges or unrealized pension costs)

Reaching a Balance

The basic accounting equation must always be maintained; total assets must equal total liabilities plus total shareholders' equity. With some effort and interpretation, assets, liabilities, and equity can be used to generate a picture of the company's health at a particular moment in time. In the real world, the venture's balance sheet will undoubtedly be composed of more items than have been described here, but the format of the balance sheet will be similar to the one presented.

All entrepreneurs need to develop a clear understanding of accounting principles. The first accounting concept should be the balance sheet. The balance sheet represents a view of the firm at a particular point in time.

In Chapter 4, we will explore the balance sheet using ratio analysis. Analysis of the balance sheet can be very helpful in generating insights into management's capabilities, trends in the firm's performance over time, and the firm's performance **vis-à-vis peer groups at a point in time.**

The Income Statement

The **income statement** describes the results of a company's operations over a specific interval of time. This interval could be a month, quarter, or year. The purpose of the income statement is to describe how much revenue was generated and what the associated level of expenses was. With these two pieces of information, we can determine whether the company is making a profit or not (see Table 3.2). The basic formula for the income (i.e., profit and loss) statement is simple:

$$\text{Revenue (for the period)} - \text{Expenses(for the period)}$$
$$= \text{Net Income or Loss (for the period)}$$

A second use of the income statement is to provide the basis for calculating various measures of profit and cash flow. Various measurements of profit and cash flow include pretax net profit, net income (NI), and earnings before interest, taxes, depreciation, and amortization.

Pretax operating income is the primary measurement of the total earnings generated by the firm without regard to taxes and net interest income (expense). This measurement is an intermediate measure of firm performance that helps describe the firm's economic results over a period of time (see Table 3.2).

Table 3.2 Year-End Income Statement

Net revenues (net of returns and allowances)	$8,000
Expenses	
Cost of goods sold (direct material/direct labor)	2,000
Gross profit	$6,000
Operating expenses	
Wages and salaries (supervision and corporate)	$1,000
Rent	300
Selling expense	400
Depreciation	500
Amortization	300
Total operating expenses	$2,500
Pretax operating income (net profit before net interest and taxes)	$3,500
Interest expense	200
Profit before taxes	3,300
Income tax expense	1,320
Net income	$1,980

Net income is the primary measurement of the after-tax total earnings of the firm. This measurement takes into account the firm's tax liability (see Table 3.2).

Earnings before interests, taxes, depreciation, and amortization (EBITDA) represent the profit generated after all expenses related to operations are paid. EBITDA is useful for comparison and valuation purposes as it paints a basic picture of the venture's operating capability as well as its ability to cover nonoperating payments such as taxes, interest payments, and principal (see Table 3.3).

Cash Versus Accrual Accounting

Two main methods used in accounting are the cash accounting method and accrual accounting method. The **cash accounting** method records revenues when received and expenses when paid. The results can be difficult to understand and get a clear picture of the company as expenses may be registered

Table 3.3   Example of EBITDA Calculation

Net income	$1,980
+ Interest expense	200
+ Taxes	1,320
+ Depreciation	500
+ Amortization	300
EBITDA	$4,300

several months before or after the associated revenue is made (see Table 3.4). Because of this poor matchup between revenue and expenses, this method is not good for larger, more complex firms with large inventories, but it is perfectly appropriate for small businesses with limited or no inventory.

Table 3.4   Cash Versus Accrual Accounting Example

	Cash Method		Accrual Method	
Revenues	Collected	$600,000	Billed	$1,000,000
Costs	Paid	$400,000	Accrued	$500,000
Profit before taxes		$200,000		$500,000
Taxes (50% rate)	Paid	$100,000	Accrued	$250,000
Profit after taxes		$100,000		$250,000

The **accrual accounting** method registers revenues billed but not necessarily when the actual cash is received; similarly, this method registers expenses as incurred (accrued) but not necessarily as they are paid. The advantage of this method is that it provides a clear picture of a venture with respect to relating costs and revenues. On the other hand, this method does not give a precise picture of how the company is doing in terms of liquidity. To be more specific, it does not show whether the venture is about to run out of cash.

Revenues

Revenues represent the money received or billed for services or products sold. Revenues may also result from sources other than sales, such as returns on investments (interest earned), franchising fees, or even rental income from a property. When revenues are recorded in the income statement will depend on the accounting method chosen, as discussed previously.

Expenses

Expenses represent a cost associated with the selling of services and products. Expenses are composed of the cost of goods sold (COGS), operating expenses, financing expenses, and tax expenses. Again, expenses are recorded in the income statement depending on the accounting method chosen.

Cost of Goods Sold (COGS). The **cost of goods sold** (COGS) includes everything directly connected with the purchasing or production of the services or products that are ultimately sold. These expenses include the wages of the direct labor involved in the production of the product or service, the materials used, parts or components purchased, and repairs made to the equipment of the facility used for production of the product or service. These are expenses directly related to the venture's production of goods or services. If we subtract these expenses from revenue, the resulting sum is gross profit. Gross profit (when gross profit is measured as a percent of sales, it's called gross margin) is defined as the difference between sales of the company's goods and services and the cost of goods sold.

Operating Expenses. The **operating expenses,** also known as OPEX, represent a category of expenditure directly connected with operating the venture and not directly connected with the production of the product or service. This category includes accounting and legal services, advertising and marketing costs, insurance coverage, office equipment and supplies, office rent (factory rent for production may or may not be included in the COGS depending on the accountant), salaries not directly tied to the production process, utility bills (could also be classified in the COGS depending on the type of business), depreciation (allocation of the cost of a tangible asset spread throughout its economic life), and amortization (allocation of an intangible asset's cost over that asset's useful life).

Other Expenses. Other expenses cover financing expenses (interest paid on loans) and tax expenses associated with the company's profit.

The Statement of Cash Flow

The **statement of cash flow** describes the venture's cash flow. It analyzes cash flow, calculating cash flow attributed to three different activities: operations, investment activities, and financing activities. Questions include how much cash the company spent or where the cash came from. A simplified cash flow statement is shown in Table 3.5.

Table 3.5   Example Statement of Cash Flow for Fiscal Year-End

Cash Flow From Operating Activities	
Net income	$2,000
Add: Depreciation	1,000
Subtract: Increase in accounts receivable	(200)
Add: Decrease in inventory	150
Add: Increase in accounts payable	50
Add: Increase in wages payable	50
Cash flow from operations	$3,050
Cash Flow From Investing Activities	
Capital expenditures	($3,000)
Cash flow from investing	($3,000)
Cash Flow From Financing Activities	
Dividends paid	($100)
Cash flow from financing	($100)
Net changes in cash	($50)

Cash flow from operations is defined as the cash generated or used by virtue of the day-to-day operations of the venture. Collected accounts receivable and cash from cash sales represent positive cash flow. Paid expenses related to generating those sales represent outflows of cash. The sum of these two flows is referred to as *cash flow from operations,* and this normally represents the bulk of the cash inflows and outflows that pass through the company.

Cash flow from investments includes cash generated or consumed by the purchase or sale of buildings, equipment, and marketable securities (stocks or bonds). It may also include loans advanced to suppliers or customers as well as payments related to acquisitions of parts of another venture.

Cash flow from financing activities includes cash generated or consumed by investments, investors, loans from banks, dividend payments, stock repurchases, and repayment of debt principal.

The firm's net cash flow is the cumulative sum of the above three subclasses of cash sources and uses. In short, the net cash flow equals cash sources minus cash uses. This computation is used to describe how the venture generates cash to fund operations, pay off liabilities, or pay dividends to investors. By analyzing the cash flow of a venture, it is possible to make conclusions about management's capabilities and the firm's overall efficiency. For example, if external financing from investors is the main source of cash for a large period of time, without significant inflows from operations, it is an alert that the firm could face upcoming financial challenges or is already experiencing difficulty in making and selling its product.

Summary

In this chapter, the three basic financial statements were presented and explained. Each of these statements provides information about the status and health of the venture. Later chapters will provide more tools for a deeper understanding of how to analyze and interpret each of the reports covered. The balance sheet is a comparison tool where the performance of the firm is assessed at a certain point in time. The income statement gives an overview of how much the company made and spent in a specific period of time. The statement of cash flow defines how much cash is generated and how it is used over a period of time.

Chapter 4

Financial Ratio Analysis

Learning Objectives

- To explain the use of financial ratios
- To learn where to source information to calculate and compare ratios
- To distinguish between the different types of ratios and their purposes
- To understand the limitations of financial ratio analysis

Case: Old Pueblo Lithographers

Old Pueblo Lithographers, the largest lithographer in New Mexico and headquartered in Santa Fe, is a family firm that dates back to the 1950s. The company specializes in high-quality, fine art, book, and commercial printing for customers in New Mexico and the southwestern United States, with some commercial customers in Mexico. The firm is managed by James Logan, a third-generation printer who is approaching retirement. The issue at the firm is what to do about choosing the next leader of the company.

James has one child, a daughter, Sydney, who works in the business. By all accounts she is very good at her job. She is excellent with clients, is well respected by her peers, and knows the production process inside and out. She had a meeting with her father and has asked him to consider appointing her the new president of the corporation. James turned her down. She took offense at what she perceived as a slight; hurt and dejected, she stalked out of her father's office, slamming the door.

Later when she had calmed down, she approached her father and asked why he had turned her down in her bid to lead the company. His answer was simple and direct: "You cannot read financial statements." He went on to say, "Without this ability, you will not be able to manage the company well enough to keep it on track with the requirements of its banks, nor will you be able to assure that the customers would pay their bills appropriately and that the company would pay its bills in the most efficient manner. You would not have any idea about how to give credit terms or take advantage of terms offered by the firm's suppliers. You would not know what the impact of production scheduling changes or capital purchases would have on the firm and would thus not know the impact of any decisions you made in these areas. In short, if you can't read the financial statements, you won't know how to manage the firm's cash flow and, ultimately, you would not be able to keep the company on an even financial keel."

Sydney wanted to know how she could learn to "read financial statements." Her father suggested two things: (1) learn about the firm's financial statements and (2) understand ratio analysis.

Chapter 3 indicated the role that financial statements play in providing relevant and timely information about the overall health of the company to entrepreneurs, investors, and other stakeholders. Financial statements provide a wealth of information that can be used to assess the risk of the firm, evaluate management's efficiency, and determine future needs of capital. However, it is sometimes difficult to interpret all this information without first putting it into context. For example, suppose a firm has total assets of $1,250,000 on the balance sheet. Is this good, bad, or neither? Is the firm going in the right or wrong direction? Based on this number alone, it's hard to tell. By looking at the financial statement in isolation, it can be difficult to get a clear picture of how the firm's performance is progressing over time and how the firm compares to its peers. **Financial ratio analysis** helps make sense of this problem by providing a method for making better use of the information in the financial statement. It is an extremely useful management tool that improves the understanding of financial results and trends over time and provides key indicators of organizational perfor-mance. In this chapter, we will look at how we can use *financial ratios* to perform a complete and efficient analysis of the firm. Chart 4.1 presents a schematic representation of the material covered in this chapter.

Chart 4.1   Schematic of Chapter 4

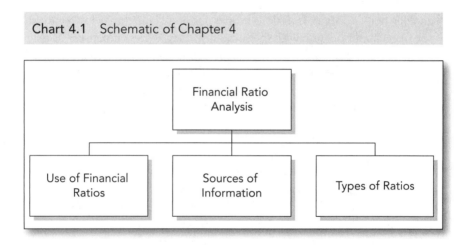

Uses of Financial Ratios

Before delving into the ratios themselves, we must first understand how we can use ratios in the business environment. Like financial statements, financial ratios are not very useful on a stand-alone basis; they must be benchmarked against something. The two benchmarks useful for financial ratios are comparing the firm to its own past performance (time-series) or against other companies (cross-sectional). While the computation and ratios don't change in either form of use, each context of use provides a different perspective and benefit.

Time-Series

The **time-series benchmark** of the financial ratios is used to assess the trends at the company over a specific time frame. This allows the entrepreneur to see how his or her firm's operations are progressing throughout the time period being analyzed. An examination of the ratios at different points in time can help identify if the firm is headed in the right direction; if the ratios are improving, then management is doing a good job in running the firm. Conversely, deterioration in the ratios from period to period can help identify areas in the management of the firm that are causes for concern.

Cross-Sectional

While the time-series approach compares the firm to itself at different points in time, the **cross-sectional benchmark** approach compares the firm to two or more companies at a specific point in time. Unless it's a monopoly, a firm does not operate in isolation; it operates in a competitive environment. If the firm cannot operate with the same efficiency as its competitors, it risks having financial difficulties and eventually being insolvent. By comparing the financial ratios of the firm against other firms or the industry, investors and management can get a better idea of what management's and the firm's strengths and weaknesses are in relation to its peers.

Sources of Information

In time-series ratio analysis, the most important source of information is the firm's historical financial statements, as these are the ones that will reveal the trends within the firm's operations. While the firm's balance sheet, income statement, and statement of cash flows are the major sources of information, it's also important to look elsewhere in the financial statements for other pieces of data needed to calculate the ratios. For example, lease payment amounts, needed to calculate the fixed charges coverage ratio (discussed later in the chapter), are usually lumped into the sales, general, and administration (SG&A) expenses in the income statement. Often small details like this will have to be researched by the analyst to perform a complete analysis.

In a cross-sectional ratio analysis, not only are the firm's financial statements needed, but information from the industry and other competitors is also required. Many publications provide financial ratios for various industries and individual companies. Financial ratios for industries are published each census period by the U.S. Department of Commerce at www.commerce.

gov. The *Almanac of Business and Industrial Financial Ratios* provides an annual publication of industry ratios by the North American Industry Classification System (NAICS). Individual company ratios can be found on the web by companies such as Fintel, Standard & Poor's, Bloomberg, and Hoover's.

For demonstration purposes, we will be calculating each of the 2013 financial ratios discussed (except for market ratios) for Old Pueblo Lithographers (OPL) based on the information provided by its financial statements included in the Appendix (Balance Sheet, Income Statement, and Statement of Cash Flows) at the end of this chapter. A summary of all financial ratios for 2012 and 2013, as well as industry averages for 2013, is included in Table 4.1 in the summary section of this chapter.

Types of Ratios

Ratios can be classified in terms of the information they provide to the reader. This means that analysis of the different types of ratios helps identify certain aspects of performance for the firm. Chart 4.2 provides a graphic view of the five types of ratios.

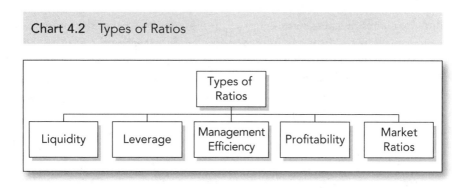

Chart 4.2   Types of Ratios

Liquidity

These types of ratios may be used to analyze the firm's financial ability to meet short-term liabilities. This form of liquidity analysis focuses on the relationship between current assets and current liabilities, as well as the speed with which receivables and inventory can be converted into cash during normal business operations. This class of ratios is particularly important to bankers. **Liquidity ratios** in general are used extensively to qualify loan applicants for loans. Bankers view both the trend and the point-in-time peer group comparative measurements to be important.

The two most common measurements are the current ratio and the quick ratio. The **current ratio** is the ratio of current assets to current liabilities:

$$\text{Current Ratio} = \frac{\text{Current Assets}}{\text{Current Liabilities}}$$

$$\text{Old Pueblo Lithographers' Current Ratio} = \frac{\$2,229,176}{\$949,007} = 2.349$$

The **quick ratio** is the ratio of the quick assets to current liabilities. Quick assets are those assets that can be most readily converted to cash. In most situations, the least liquid of the current assets is inventory; hence, inventory is typically excluded when calculating the quick ratio:

$$\text{Quick Ratio} = \frac{\text{Current Assets} - \text{Inventory}}{\text{Current Liabilites}}$$

$$\text{Old Pueblo Lithographers' Quick Ratio} = \frac{\$2,229,176 - \$668,407}{\$949,007} = 1.645$$

The greater the current ratio and the quick ratio, the higher the company's liquidity and the greater the firm's ability to pay its current liabilities when due. By comparing these ratios using a time-series approach, the entrepreneur can see if the firm has improved its liquidity from one period to the next; increasing ratios demonstrate a positive trend, and lowering ratios indicate declining liquidity. A cross-sectional view of the numbers can indicate if the company is more or less liquid than its peers or how the company ranks against the peer group average.

Leverage

A company's **leverage ratio** measures how much debt the firm has on its balance sheet. Leverage ratios represent another measure of financial health. Generally, the more debt a company has, the riskier its stock is. This escalating risk comes from two primary impacts that accompany higher debt: (1) the firm's breakeven point goes up because of the higher fixed costs associated with the debt, and (2) the volatility of return on equity becomes less predictable and more volatile when debt increases.

The **debt to equity ratio** measures how much of the company is financed by its debt holders compared with the equity contribution of its owners (shareholders). A company with a lot of debt will have a high debt to equity ratio, while one with little debt will have a low debt to equity ratio. Assuming everything else is identical, companies with lower debt to equity ratios are less risky than those with higher such ratios. The debt to equity ratio is calculated as follows:

$$\text{Debt to Equity} = \frac{\text{Short-Term Debt} + \text{Long-Term Debt}}{\text{Total Shareholders' Equity}}$$

$$\text{Old Pueblo Lithographers' Debt to Equity} = \frac{\$120,104 + \$1,143,796}{\$2,140,600} = .590$$

Also known as the debt ratio, the **debt to total assets ratio** can be interpreted as the portion of a company's assets that is financed by debt. The higher this ratio, the more leveraged the company and the greater its financial risk. (We discuss financial risk in greater detail in Chapter 11.) Debt ratios vary widely across industries, with capital-intensive businesses such as utilities and pipelines having much higher debt ratios than other industries like technology. A debt ratio of greater than 1 indicates that a company has more debt than assets. The debt to total assets ratio is

$$\text{Debt to Total Assets} = \frac{\text{Short-Term Debt} + \text{Long-Term Debt}}{\text{Total Assets}}$$

Old Pueblo Lithographers' Debt to Total Assets

$$= \frac{\$120,104 + \$1,143,796}{\$4,589,403} = .275$$

The **interest coverage ratio** (also known as the times interest earned ratio) compares the firm's operating earnings to its interest expense; the more the firm can produce in **operating profit** to cover its interest expense, the lower the risk of defaulting on its debt. It is calculated as follows:

$$\text{Interest Coverage} = \frac{\text{Operating Profit (EBIT)}}{\text{Interest Expense}}$$

$$\text{Old Pueblo Lithographers' Interest Coverage} = \frac{\$125,855}{\$58,905} = 2.137$$

A stricter version of the interest coverage ratio is the **fixed charges coverage ratio,** which is calculated as

$$\text{Fixed Charge Coverage} = \frac{\text{Operating Profit } (\text{EBIT}) + \text{Fixed Charges}}{\text{Interest Expense} + \text{Fixed Charges}}$$

Old Pueblo Lithographers' Fixed Charge Coverage

$$= \frac{\$125,855 + \$91,028}{\$58,905 + \$91,028} = 1.447$$

The fixed charges coverage ratio relates the interest and fixed charge payment that the firm is required to pay to the funds that the firm has available to pay them with. Fixed charges are expenses that are incurred and must be paid regardless of sales, profits, or production.

Management Efficiency

Regardless of what kind of industry a company is in, it must invest in assets to perform its operations. **Management efficiency ratios** measure how effectively the company uses these assets, as well as how well it manages its liabilities.

The **accounts receivable turnover ratio** measures how effective the company's credit policies are. It is calculated as

$$\text{Accounts Receivable Turnover} = \frac{\text{Sales}}{\text{Accounts Receivable}}$$

Old Pueblo Lithographers' Accounts Receivable Turnover

$$= \frac{\$7,893,755}{\$1,317,566} = 5.991$$

This ratio essentially measures how many times a company "turns over" its accounts receivable during the course of the year. If accounts receivable turnover is too low, it indicates the company is being too generous granting credit or is having difficulty collecting from its customers. All else equal, higher receivables turnover is better. A similar measure of efficiency is the **days sales outstanding (DSO) ratio,** calculated as

$$\text{Days Sales Outstanding} = \frac{365}{\text{Accounts Receivable Turnover}}$$

$$\text{Old Pueblo Lithographers' Days Sales Outstanding} = \frac{365}{5.991} = 60.923$$

This ratio measures the number of days' worth of sales that are tied up in accounts receivable. You can think of it as the average lag between the date of sale and the date the payment is received on the average account receivable. Entrepreneurs want to keep this number low, as having money tied up in accounts receivable affects the firm's working capital.

Working capital is also affected by the amount of inventory that a firm holds on its balance sheet. A measure of how well managers manage the firm's inventory is the **inventory turnover ratio,** calculated as

$$\text{Inventory Turnover} = \frac{\text{Cost of Goods Sold}}{\text{Inventory}}$$

$$\text{Old Pueblo Lithographers' Inventory Turnover} = \frac{\$6,300,807}{\$668,407} = 9.427$$

Notice that the numerator has cost of goods sold and not sales. This is because inventory is valued at cost, and therefore the cost of goods sold measure gives a better representation of the inventory's value. Like the accounts receivable turnover ratio, the more times a firm can "turn over" its inventory, the more efficiently it handles its assets. The **days of inventory ratio** is

$$\text{Days of Inventory} = \frac{365}{\text{Inventory Turnover}}$$

$$\text{Old Pueblo Lithographers' Days of Inventory} = \frac{365}{9.427} = 38.720$$

It measures the number of days that a firm sits on its inventory before it is sold. The firm would want to hold onto its inventory the least amount of days possible to avoid inventory obsolescence and to increase working capital.

On the liabilities side, the **accounts payable turnover ratio** measures how a company manages paying its own bills. High accounts payable turnover is a signal that a firm isn't receiving very favorable payment terms from its own suppliers or isn't paying its accounts payable in a timely manner. All else being equal, average to slightly lower payable turnover is better. It is calculated as

$$\text{Accounts Payable Turnover} = \frac{\text{Cost of Goods Sold}}{\text{Accounts Payable}}$$

Old Pueblo Lithographers' Accounts Payable Turnover

$$= \frac{\$6,300,807}{\$502,303} = 12.544$$

While the above ratios focus on current assets and liabilities, a firm must also understand how efficiently management uses the long-term assets they have been entrusted with. The **total asset turnover ratio** is a catch-all efficiency ratio that highlights how effective management is at using both short-term and long-term assets and measures a company's ability to generate sales given its investment in total assets. It is calculated as

$$\text{Total Asset Turnover} = \frac{\text{Sales}}{\text{Total Assets}}$$

$$\text{Old Pueblo Lithographers' Total Asset Turnover} = \frac{\$7,893,755}{\$4,589,403} = 1.720$$

Generally speaking, the higher the ratio, the better it is since it indicates the company is generating more revenues per dollar of assets.

One can also analyze the efficiency of the firm's organizational structure (a topic not reported on the balance sheet). The **sales to employee ratio** describes how well employees are generating sales for the firm. This measurement can be interpreted as being derivative of the firm's organizational success. The calculation is straightforward:

$$\text{Sales to Employee} = \frac{\text{Sales}}{\text{Total Employees}}$$

Old Pueblo Lithographers' Sales to Employee

$$= \frac{\$7,893,755}{45} = \$175,416 \, / \, \text{employee}$$

The ratio can be especially insightful for firms in the "people business," such as retailers, consultants, and software companies.

It is important to note that, if annualized data are being used, ratios that involve balance sheet items (accounts receivable, inventory, and total assets) are usually calculated as the average of the beginning and ending balances. This is done to account for changes in these items throughout the year. If shorter periodicity is in the play, then the values for the end of each period are used.

Profitability

Some of the management efficiency ratios are measurements of the firm's ability to generate sales given its asset size. These ratios don't address how much of the sales turn into profit. A firm that can generate substantial sales but cannot turn those sales into profits is not generating any returns for its owners. **Profitability ratios** focus on a firm's ability to generate earnings as compared to its direct expenses and other relevant costs. These types of ratios are usually calculated at different "levels" of the income statement to evaluate the firm's efficiency at different stages of the process.

The first level of profitability is **gross margin.** You will recall from the discussion of the income statement in Chapter 3 that gross profit is simply the difference between a company's sales and the cost to produce those goods (cost of goods sold). The gross margin ratio is calculated as

$$\text{Gross Margin} = \frac{\text{Sales} - \text{COGS}}{\text{Sales}}$$

Old Pueblo Lithographers' Gross Margin

$$= \frac{\$7,893,755 - \$6,300,807}{\$7,893,755} = .202 = 20.2\%$$

This ratio shows how efficiently a business is at using its materials and labor in the production process, and the ratio gives an indication of the pricing, cost structure, and production efficiency of the business. The higher the gross margin ratio, the better.

One step down in the profitability analysis is the **operating margin.** Operating margin captures how much a company makes or loses from its core operations. It is a much more complete and accurate indicator of a company's performance than gross margin, since it accounts for not only the direct cost of goods sold but also the other important components of operating income, such as marketing and other overhead expenses. Operating margin is calculated as

$$\text{Operating Margin} = \frac{\text{Operating Income (EBIT)}}{\text{Sales}}$$

Old Pueblo Lithographers' Operating Margin $= \dfrac{\$125,855}{\$7,893,755} = .016 = 1.6\%$

Analyzing the operating margin is important because the income statement can sometimes be significantly affected by nonrecurring transactions that are not part of a company's core business, such as gains or losses on sales of equipment or tax penalties. The operating margin is a way to measure only the core operations of the firm that are expected to be sustainable into the future.

The final profitability measure is the **net profit margin,** which is calculated as

$$\text{Net Profit Margin} = \frac{\text{Net Income}}{\text{Sales}}$$

$$\text{Old Pueblo Lithographers' Net Profit Margin} = \frac{\$47,342}{\$7,893,755} = .006 = .6\%$$

Net profit margin considers how much of the firm's revenue it keeps when
all expenses or other forms of income have been considered, regardless of
their nature. A firm that manages to deliver a greater percentage of its sales
as income is doing a good job at keeping costs and other expenses low. The
net profit margin indicates what percent of sales is available to shareholders
and for reinvestment into the firm.

While net profit margin is important to take note of, net income often
contains quite a bit of "noise," both good and bad, which does not really
have much to do with a company's core business, such as gains or losses on
property or machinery. Such events can distort both the company's bottom
line and the profitability analysis.

The profitability ratios we have considered so far involve only items in
the income statement. Another form of profitability analysis is to measure
earnings versus a balance sheet item. The two most widely used are **return
on assets** (ROA) and **return on equity** (ROE). ROA measures a company's
ability to turn assets into *profit.* This is similar to the total asset turnover
ratio discussed earlier, but total assets turnover measures how effectively a
company's assets generate *revenue* rather than profit. ROA is calculated as

$$\text{Return on Assets} = \frac{\text{Net Income} + \left[\text{Interest Expense}^*(1-T)\right]}{\text{Total Assets}}$$

where T = firm's tax rate.

$$\text{Old Pueblo Lithographers' Return on Assets}$$

$$= \frac{\$47,342 + [\$58,905^*(1-.3889)]}{\$4,589,403} = .018 = 1.8\%$$

Notice that the company's after-tax interest expense is added to net income
in the calculation. This reflects that return on assets measures the profitability
a company achieves on all of its assets, regardless of whether they are
financed by equity holders or debt holders; this being the case, we add back

what debt holders are charging the company to borrow money. The higher the ROA ratio, the more profit the firm is able to generate from its assets.

The ROE ratio measures a company's return on its investment by shareholders; it tells common shareholders how effectively their money is being employed. ROE is calculated as

$$\text{Return on Equity} = \frac{\text{Net Income}}{\text{Total Shareholders' Equity}}$$

$$\text{Old Pueblo Lithographers' Return on Equity} = \frac{\$47,342}{\$2,140,600} = .022 = 2.2\%$$

Analyzing ROE is important because a company can create shareholder value only if the ROE is greater than its cost of equity capital (the expected return shareholders require for investing in the company given the particular risk of the company). If a firm cannot deliver ROE that is greater than its cost of equity capital, then the firm is actually destroying shareholder wealth. (We examine cost of equity in Chapter 7.)

Because ROA and ROE involve balance sheet items in their calculation, common practice is to use the average of the beginning and ending balances to calculate the ratio for the same reasons discussed above. However, when shorter periods of time are involved with the calculation, then only ending balances can be used.

Quality of Earnings

The ROE ratio can be decomposed to provide a more specific source of a firm's superior or inferior performance. Remember that ROE equals Net Income divided by Shareholders' Equity. We can rewrite the formula as

$$\text{ROE} = \frac{\text{Net Income}_{\text{Pretax}}}{\text{Sales}} * \frac{\text{Sales}}{\text{Total Assets}} * \frac{\text{Total Assets}}{\text{Shareholders' Equity}} * (1 - T)$$

where T = firm's tax rate.

$$\text{ROE} = \frac{\$77,474}{\$7,893,755} * \frac{\$7,893,755}{\$4,589,403} * \frac{\$4,589,403}{\$2,140,600} * (1 - .3889) = .022 = 2.2\%$$

By doing the math, this formula condenses to the ROE formula above. You may also notice that we have already seen some of these ratios (profit margin, total asset turnover). The purpose of the formula is to see what is actually driving ROE based on other performance measurements. While some of these drivers are desirable as sources of ROE, others are a source of risk, being unsustainable sources of shareholder value creation.

The first term on the right-hand side of the equation is the profit margin ratio discussed previously, although here we use pretax income. A higher profit margin ratio means that the firm is converting more of its sales to net income available to equity shareholders. Ideally, a firm would like to increase this ratio to improve ROE. The second term is the total asset turnover ratio discussed in the management efficiency section. We previously indicated that a higher ratio indicates that management is efficiently using its assets to generate sales. A firm that is able to generate a higher ROE than its competitors because of its asset turnover has a competitive advantage in efficiency.

The third term in the equation is another way of expressing financial leverage. While financial leverage is discussed more in depth in Chapter 11, it is necessary to point out here that a higher ratio is not necessarily better and can in fact introduce more risk into the firm. Recall from Chapter 3 the basic accounting equation: Assets = Debt + Equity. If assets are financed by either debt or equity, then a higher financial leverage ratio means that the firm is using more debt to finance its assets (a larger numerator and a smaller denominator). While having some debt in the firm's capital structure is encouraged due to the tax deductibility of interest, at least in the United States, having too much debt can put the firm in a financial bind and can lead to insolvency. An ROE that is driven largely by financial leverage, therefore, is not sustainable and can indicate that managers provide a return to equity holders only by introducing more financial risk into the firm.

The last component of the formula above, $1 - T$, specifies how much of the firm's ROE is due to its tax rate. A lower tax rate will increase the value of this multiplier and hence increase ROE. While it is in the best interest of the firm to have the lowest tax expense possible, increases in ROE due solely to a lower tax rate are not sustainable and could indicate that management is trying to manipulate ROE. All else being equal, a firm that is able to generate a higher ROE due to increased profit margin and/or increased total assets turnover is preferable to one that relies on financial leverage and an abnormally low tax rate.

Market Ratios

If the firm has equity that is publicly traded, one can use **market ratios** to get an indication of how the market values the firm versus peers (cross-sectional) or relative to its own historical performance (time-series). Because the price of equity is determined by market supply and demand forces, management can be evaluated on how the market views their performance; market value ratios give management an idea of what the firm's investors think of the firm's performance and future prospects. The most common market ratio is the **price to earnings** (P/E) ratio, calculated as

$$\frac{P}{E} = \frac{\text{Price per Share}}{\text{Earnings per Share (EPS)}}$$

Note: Old Pueblo Lithographers does not trade in the public market; therefore, no examples of market ratios are available to use as examples.

The ratio specifies how much the market is willing to pay for $1 of the company's earnings. Earnings are a chief driver of investment value, and a higher P/E ratio versus its peers indicates that the market is confident in the firm's ability to generate future earnings. The P/E ratio can be calculated based on the firm's last 12 months' EPS (trailing P/E) or on the next 12 months' expected EPS (forward P/E).

The P/E ratio has some drawbacks that derive from the characteristics of EPS. First, EPS can be negative, and the P/E ratio does not make economic sense in that case. Second, the EPS calculation may have large transient components that do not adequately reflect the ongoing operations of the firm. Finally, managers have flexibility in the application of accounting standards used in calculating earnings. In making such choices, managers may distort EPS as an accurate reflection of economic performance. All these factors may affect the comparability of P/Es among companies.

Certain types of privately held companies, including companies organized in partnership form, have long been valued by a multiple of annual sales. The **price to sales** (P/S) ratio is calculated as

$$\frac{P}{S} = \frac{\text{Price per Share}}{\text{Sales per Share}}$$

where Sales per Share = Annual Sales/Shares outstanding.

The P/S market valuation alleviates some of the concerns that are present in the P/E ratio. For example, sales are generally less subject to distortion or manipulation than are EPS. Also, as long as the company has begun selling its products or services, the sales figure will always be positive even though EPS can be negative. This point, however, is also a drawback of the P/S ratio, as companies can have sales but consistently post negative earnings. A final reason is that sales are generally more stable than EPS, which reflects operating and financial leverage, and is therefore more meaningful for the firm's economic performance.

The **price to book value** ratio (P/BV) is also a popular measure of market value. The book value represents the investment that common shareholders have made in the company. The P/BV ratio is

$$\frac{P}{BV} = \frac{\text{Price per Share}}{\text{Book Value per Share}}$$

where Book Value per Share (BVPS) = Shareholders' Equity/Common stock shares outstanding.

Because the purpose of this ratio is to value common stock, any value attributable to preferred stock must be subtracted from **shareholders' equity.** Like the P/S ratio, the P/BV can be used even if EPS are negative. Book value is also more stable and can be used if EPS are abnormally high or low.

Numerous other market valuation measures can be calculated, including price to cash flow (P/CF) and enterprise value to EBITDA (EV/EBITDA). The purpose here is not to list them all but rather give an overview and demonstrate how market ratios can be used to gauge how the market values the company. By comparing these ratios against peer companies or historical firm measures, management can get a sense of whether the market agrees on the firm's trajectory.

Limitations of Financial Ratios

There are some important limitations to using financial ratios. First, some firms operate in very unusual, different industries. For these companies, it is difficult to find a meaningful set of industry-average ratios when performing cross-sectional analysis. Second, macroeconomic events such as inflation or recessions can distort a company's financial statements during these disruptive periods. A time-series ratio analysis that covers a disruptive period of time must be interpreted carefully using both skill and judgment. Similarly, seasonal factors can distort ratio analysis. Understanding seasonal factors that affect a business can reduce the chance of misinterpretation. For example, a retailer's inventory may be high in the summer in preparation for the back-to-school season. As a result, the company's days of inventory will be high and its ROA low in summer before the back-to-school sales period. In general, ratio analysis conducted in a mechanical, unthinking manner does not provide good, useful information. On the other hand, if used intelligently, ratio analysis can provide insightful information.

Summary

Using financial ratios is part art and part science. The technique is referred to as "quantitative" because the ratios themselves are calculated mathematically. However, the methodological technique actually provides both a quantitative measurement and a lens through which to view the organization. On one hand, the lens is a quantitative lens because it allows us to view trends and make comparisons using numeric calculations. On the other hand, it is a fundamental qualitative lens because the interpretation of the ratios provides information about the capabilities of management and the quality of the choices and decisions made.

Recall the discussion of "quality of earnings." For any firm, the desired quantitative outcome is high ROE (when measured as a trend and when benchmarked against a peer group); however, it is always preferred that the firm's ROE be generated via a qualitatively superior process, and ratio analysis is helpful in identifying the quality of that process. By being proficient in using ratio analysis, the ROE of the firm can be quantified and the qualitative manner in which management has achieved the results understood. Virtually all ratios do not just tell us what the quantitative measurement is; rather, each measurement implies a management choice or capability (or failure) with respect to the choices that generated the numbers that are measured by the ratio.

The summary of a ratio analysis for Old Pueblo Lithographers is shown in Table 4.1.

Old Pueblo Lithographers has generated results as follows:

1. With respect to liquidity, the company has been able to improve its position in both ratios year over year, and it also is above the industry average for 2013. The firm seems to be in a good position for meeting its short-term obligations.

2. The leverage ratios indicate a mostly positive story. Old Pueblo Lithographers has been able to lower its debt to equity and debt to total assets ratios, indicating less financial leverage. It also has improved on its times interest earned and fixed coverage charge ratios in the past year. Compared to industry averages, the firm has a lower debt structure, but it is below average in both coverage ratios.

3. The profitability ratios, however, tell a different story and indicate an area that the firm must focus on improving. Gross profit margin, net profit margin, and ROE improved year over year, while operating margin and ROA had slight deteriorations. The compelling

Table 4.1   Financial Ratio Analysis

	2013	2012	2013 Industry Average[a]
Liquity			
Current ratio	2.349	2.127	2.01
Quick ratio	1.645	1.391	1.52
Leverage			
Debt/equity	0.590	0.693	0.81
Debt/total assets	0.275	0.320	0.47
Times interest earned	2.137	1.406	3.29
Fixed coverage charge	1.447	1.208	2.52
Profit			
Gross margin	0.202	0.178	0.262
Operating margin	0.016	0.017	0.083
Net profit margin	0.006	0.004	0.061
ROA	0.018	0.025	0.054
ROE	0.022	0.013	0.034
Management efficiency			
Receivables turnover	5.991	8.450	12.850
Days sale outstanding	60.923	43.197	28.405
Inventory turnover	9.427	8.173	19.910
Days of inventory	38.720	44.658	18.332
Accounts payable turnover	12.544	16.025	15.470
Total asset turnover	1.720	1.564	2.940
Sales/employee[b]	$175,416.78	$166,547.60	$164,953.00

Note: ROA = return on assets; ROE = return on equity.

a. Source: *Almanac of Business and Industrial Financial Ratios, 2013.*

b. Based on 45 employees.

issue is that for 2013, the firm was below industry standards for all profitability ratios. Operating margin and net profit margin were 5.2 times and 10.2 times, respectively, higher for the industry than for Old Pueblo Lithographers. Since gross profit margin was only slightly below industry averages, a close examination of expenses below the gross profit line is warranted, including SG&A and interest expense.

4. The management efficiency ratios paint a mixed picture and high-light areas for improvement. Receivables turnover and, in turn, days sales outstanding deteriorated in the past year, pushing days sales outstanding to over twice the industry average. The same is true for inventory turnover and days of inventory, although there was a slight improvement in the firm's year-over-year performance. This indicates that the firm must do a better job of handling its current assets. The accounts payable turnover is slightly below industry average and therefore in an ideal position. Total asset turnover improved slightly in the past year but still trails the industry substantially. Finally, the sales to employee ratio showed improvement year over year and is now even higher than the industry, a positive sign for the firm's use of human capital.

Appendix

Old Pueblo Lithographers

Balance Sheets

As of May 31, 2013 and 2012

Assets		
	2013	**2012**
Current assets		
Cash and cash equivalents	$189,861.00	$354,043.00
Accounts receivable, net	$1,317,566.00	$886,978.00
Note receivable	$–	$23,056.00
Note receivable, shareholder	$–	$84,595.00
Inventories	$668,407.00	$754,070.00
Prepaid expenses	$19,342.00	$12,519.00
Deferred income taxes	$34,000.00	$64,000.00
Total current assets	$2,229,176.00	$2,179,261.00
Property and equipment, net	$2,025,122.00	$2,295,149.00
Other assets	$322,156.00	$317,156.00
Note receivable	$12,949.00	$–
Total assets	$4,589,403.00	$4,791,566.00
Liabilities and Shareholders' Equity		
Current liabilities		
Notes payable, bank	$–	$30,000.00
Current portion of long-term debt	$120,104.00	$392,553.00
Accounts payable	$502,303.00	$384,591.00
Accrued expenses	$303,600.00	$185,717.00
Income taxes payable	$23,000.00	$31,600.00
Total current liabilities	$949,007.00	$1,024,461.00
Long-term debt, net of current portion	$1,143,796.00	$1,111,847.00
Deferred income taxes	$356,000.00	$442,000.00
Total liabilities	$2,448,803.00	$2,578,308.00

Shareholders' equity		
Common stock, no par value; 1,000,000 shares authorized		
800 shares issued	$80,000.00	$80,000.00
Retained earnings	$2,660,600.00	$2,733,258.00
Treasury stock, 300 shares at cost	$(600,000.00)	$(600,000.00)
Total shareholders' equity	$2,140,600.00	$2,213,258.00
Total liabilities and shareholders' equity	$4,589,403.00	$4,791,566.00

Old Pueblo Lithographers

Statements of Income

Years Ended May 31, 2013 and 2012

	2013	2012
Sales	$7,893,755.00	$7,494,642.00
Cost of sales	$6,300,807.00	$6,163,155.00
Gross profit	$1,592,948.00	$1,331,487.00
Depreciation and amortization	$464,273.00	$482,675.00
SG&A[a]	$1,002,820.00	$723,903.00
Income from operations (EBIT)	$125,855.00	$124,909.00
Other income (expense)		
Interest expense	$(58,905.00)	$(88,867.00)
Interest income	$1,465.00	$3,418.00
Gain of sale of assets	$9,059.00	$2,300.00
Income before taxes (EBT)	$77,474.00	$41,760.00
Income tax expense[b]	$(30,132.00)	$(11,987.00)
Net income	$47,342.00	$29,773.00

a. Includes lease payments of $91,028 and $84,595 for 2013 and 2012, respectively.

b. The firm's tax rate is $30,132/$77,474 = 38.89%.

Old Pueblo Lithographers

Statement of Cash Flows

Years Ended May 31, 2013 and 2012

	2013	2012
Cash flows from operating activities		
Net income	$47,342.00	$29,773.00
Adjustment to net income		
Depreciation and amortization	$464,273.00	$482,675.00
Gain on disposal of assets	$(9,059.00)	$(2,300.00)
Deferred income taxes	$(56,000.00)	$(35,585.00)
Provision for bad debts	$(57,837.00)	$–
Changes in operating assets and liabilities		
Accounts receivable	$(372,751.00)	$180,356.00
Inventories	$85,663.00	$(28,336.00)
Deposits and prepaid expenses	$(6,823.00)	$11,424.00
Other assets	$(5,000.00)	$(22,921.00)
Accounts payable	$117,712.00	$(47,821.00)
Accrued expenses	$117,883.00	$(27,197.00)
Income taxes payable	$(8,600.00)	$23,344.00
Total adjustments	$269,461.00	$533,639.00
Net cash provided by operating activities	$316,803.00	$563,412.00
Cash flows from investing activities		
Purchases of property and equipment	$(195,155.00)	$(226,334.00)
Proceeds from disposal of assets	$9,968.00	$2,300.00
Advance on note receivable	$–	$(33,000.00)
Collections on note receivable	$10,107.00	$122,937.00
Collections on note receivable, related party	$84,595.00	$86,376.00
Net cash used in investing activities	$(90,485.00)	$(47,721.00)

Cash flows from financing activities		
Dividends paid to shareholder	$(120,000.00)	$(180,000.00)
Net borrowings on note payable	$(30,000.00)	$30,000.00
Net repayments on long-term debt	$(391,955.00)	$(412,250.00)
Proceeds from long-term debt	$151,455.00	$–
Net cash used in financing activities	$(390,500.00)	$(562,250.00)
Net increase/(decrease) in cash	$(164,182.00)	$(46,559.00)
Cash beginning	$354,043.00	$400,635.00
Cash ending	$189,861.00	$354,076.00

Chapter 5

Cash Flow Management

Learning Objectives

- To understand the meaning of working capital
- To understand the different types of cash flow
- To understand the cash flow cycle
- To learn strategies for improving cash flow management

Case: De Werks, S.A.

It was Friday afternoon, and the staff were about to leave early for the weekend. Carlos was sitting in the same office as Roberto, CEO and founder of De Werks, S.A. De Werks is a company founded in 2004 and headquartered in northern Italy. The company had become the largest advertising portal for jobs in the country and had expanded its operations to Serbia, Bosnia, and Herzegovina. The numbers posted on the wall of its office looked good. The company had exceeded its sales projection by a large amount, and there was a feeling of well-earned success among its sales team. For the company's staff, it felt almost as if the stress associated with its startup phase was finally over. Now everyone believed the company was heading toward better times.

As Carlos and Roberto were discussing their plans for the weekend, the venture's accountant entered the office with a confused look and a pile of papers in her hands. The topic of her report involved cash, and the essence of her report was decidedly bad news. After 20 minutes of lively conversation, she left the room with a concerned expression on her face. Roberto kept looking at the papers, confused and shocked at the same time. Finally, Carlos and Roberto looked at each other and exclaimed, "We are out of cash." All of this despite the fact that for the last 2 months, the sales figures were terrific, at least on paper. "We have no cash to pay salaries next week," Roberto said. "How will we do it?" asked Carlos. The company indeed was doing well in terms of revenues, but clients were not paying on time, and their delays were affecting the company's cash flow. By focusing its efforts on increasing revenues, management had forgotten that cash flow is the blood that runs through a company's veins. When Roberto sent out a companywide e-mail message explaining what was going on and asking for a delay in paying salaries, employees were far from understanding. Employees could not understand why their wages were postponed to an undefined future date when the company seemed to be doing so well.

I f "cash is king," cash flow is the blood that keeps the heart of a king beating. The proper management of cash flow is one of the most critical components of success for entrepreneurial ventures. Without cash, an entrepreneur will not be able to pay suppliers, bills, salaries, or even taxes. In fact, a profitable business on paper can end up in bankruptcy if the cash coming in does not exceed the cash going out of the venture. In this chapter, we will explain the importance of *cash flow management* and how managers and entrepreneurs can prevent cash flow issues as well as creative ways to collect accounts receivable and delay account payables. Chart 5.1 presents a schematic representation of the material covered in this chapter.

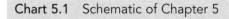

Chart 5.1   Schematic of Chapter 5

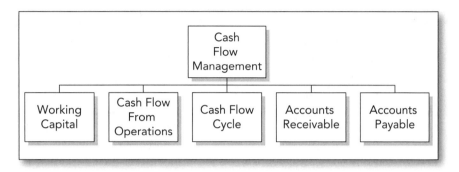

Working Capital

How does a venture generate income? If the venture manufactures a product, it uses funds to purchase inventory, transform the inventory into products, and then convert those goods through sales into cash or accounts receivable. Each component mentioned is a current asset (i.e., cash, accounts receivable, inventory, or marketable securities) if it can be converted into cash within 1 year through the normal operation of the venture. Conversely, current liabilities (i.e., accounts payable, salaries, utilities) are obligations due during the same relative period of time.

Working capital is the difference between current assets and current liabilities. It defines a venture's solvency as well as its capacity to make large purchases and take advantage of bulk discounts, as well as its ability to attract customers by offering credit terms. The working capital can be either positive or negative. Having a positive working capital balance means that the assets of the venture are more than enough to cover liabilities that are due soon. Having a negative working capital means the venture runs the risk of being unable to pay its upcoming bills with the cash, collectible receivables, or other liquid assets that can be turned into cash within a short period of time. Without these current assets, the firm will be forced to borrow cash or solicit new equity investments.

The difference between working capital and cash flow is that working capital is a balance concept explained by the relationship between current assets and current liabilities, while cash flow measures the venture's ability to generate cash over a certain period of time via its operations, investing, and financing activities. We will now explore certain aspects essential to the proper management of a venture's cash flow management.

Cash Flow From Operations

Cash flow from operations, in its most basic form, is a movement of funds in and out of a venture that originates with the firm's creation of its goods or services. There are also two types of cash flows: positive and negative cash flow.

Positive operating cash flow occurs when the cash entering the venture (e.g., sales, accounts receivable) exceeds the amount of the cash leaving the venture (e.g., cost of goods sold, salaries, accounts payable, etc.).

Negative operating cash flow is the opposite and occurs when the outflow of cash exceeds incoming cash. Negative cash flow should be closely monitored, and solutions must be found to keep the company running. For every dollar of negative operating cash flow, the company must find a dollar of debt or a dollar of equity.

In accounting literature, operational cash flow is often referred to in a shorthanded manner as earnings before interest, taxes, depreciation, and amortization (EBITDA). EBITDA represents the money available to face the venture's expenses ranging from buying inventory to paying taxes, as calculated in Method 1.

Method 1

EBITDA = Operating Profit (Income) or
EBIT + Depreciation Expenses + Amortization Expenses

Adding noncash expenses (i.e., depreciation and amortization) back to operating profit allows entrepreneurs and investors to generate an *approximate* picture of the cash flow of the venture. While both depreciation and amortization are considered costs for tax purposes, they are noncash expenses, and thus no money is flowing out of the venture.

To estimate precisely free cash flow (cash flow available in excess of the venture's and equity owners' immediate needs), we can extend Method 1 by subtracting the net result of the firm's capital expenditures (i.e., the purchase of new capital equipment minus the sale of old capital equipment) and subtracting any dividends to shareholders and adding or subtracting the changes in working capital (see Method 2).

Method 2

Estimated Free Cash Flow = Operating Profit (Income) or
EBIT + Depreciation Expenses + Amortization Expenses ± Capital
Investments – Dividends ± Change in Working Capital

As useful as these two estimates of cash flow are, we should remember that cash available is time sensitive. Cash available at any point in time will vary based on when accounts receivable are collected and when expenses are paid. When we project cash flow for valuation purposes, we do not need to adjust for timing because it averages out over the longer time frame of the valuation model. Thus, we can use Model 1 (EBITDA) or Model 2 (Estimated Free Cash Flow) as a proxy in this context. However, when we are interested in forecasting available cash to estimate future short-term or cumulative long-term capital needs, we should make an attempt to adjust for the timing of both accounts receivable collection and expense payments. Only after accounting for the lag in collecting accounts receivable and the lag in paying accounts payable is the system as accurate as possible.

Some entrepreneurs still mistake profits for cash flow. Knowing if a venture made a profit or a loss is not the same as knowing what is happening to its cash. While profit is a result of our accounting practices (revenues minus expenses), invoicing a customer for a product or service creates revenues but not necessarily cash inflow. The money inflow happens only once the money is collected from the customer. There are countless stories of entrepreneurs who reach a high level of sales and consequent revenues but do not have the cash to finance daily activities of the venture, which is exactly what was happening in De Werks. Maintaining optimal and necessary available cash is one of the key jobs of management. To succeed, entrepreneurs must establish control systems capable of monitoring and managing cash receipts and payables in a predictable and useful manner.

For a practical example of the difference between profitability and cash flows, consider the former New York Stock Exchange–traded company Lehman Brothers Holdings, Inc. At the end of 2007, Lehman Brothers Holdings was the fourth-largest investment bank in the United States with more than 25,000 employees worldwide (Humer, 2012). In March 2008, Lehman Brothers announced quarterly profits of $489 million. In September 2008, only 6 months later, the firm was filing for bankruptcy. Despite 4 repeated years of record-breaking profits, the firm ran out of cash to support its operations and to fulfill its obligations to creditors. It had no choice but to file for bankruptcy. This case clearly demonstrates how a blind focus on revenue and profits may lead a venture to fail. Entrepreneurs must understand their cash flow needs. They must be able to predict how much cash the venture will have each month and where the cash will come from, where it will go, and what internal or external factors could affect cash flow. Cash flow forecasts allow entrepreneurs to define their financing needs and create contingency plans. Understanding cash flow projections will also help entrepreneurs make better decisions when opportunities arise. It could be an unexpected opportunity to acquire a competitor, purchase new equipment, or face an unexpected large order from a new customer. If the management team understands various input variables affecting their cash flow, the chances of making a wrong decision are significantly reduced.

Cash Flow Cycle

The **cash flow cycle** describes the various activities undertaken by a venture to produce cash inflow. It reveals how a venture transforms cash today into cash in the future. The ultimate goal is converting as little cash today into the largest cash payoff possible in the future. The cash flow cycle in Figure 5.1 gives a simplified overview of the process.

It starts as cash that comes from either equity investment (from entrepreneurs themselves or from other sources) or debt (from investors, banks, and other debt sources). As the venture undertakes its activities to produce goods or services, it has to acquire various key resources (ranging from raw materials to a qualified labor force). Resources are then transformed into finished products, which are sold on a cash and/or credit basis. The distinction between payments in cash or in credit is very important. Just because accountants recognize income once an invoice is generated does not mean that the invoice was paid and cash was received. Sales made on credit generate accounts receivable, not cash. Entrepreneurs need to be aware of the difference between accounting for income and accounting for cash flow. Once the cash is effectively received, it is used to pay creditors, taxes, dividends (or other forms of reward to investors), or simply reinvested within the company.

The goal of good cash management is evident: have cash when the venture needs it. While conceptually easy to understand, it is a challenging task even for experienced financial managers. The magic behind cash flow management is timing. On one side, venture owners will want to receive payments from their customers as soon as possible. On the other, they will want to pay their suppliers and vendors as late as they can. The following sections expand on this process and provide more detailed information on how to improve cash flow management.

Accounts Receivable

Whenever we go to a grocery store to buy bread, we get the bread and then go to the cashier to pay for it. It is a simple transaction where money is

Figure 5.1 Cash Flow or Working Capital Cycle of a Company

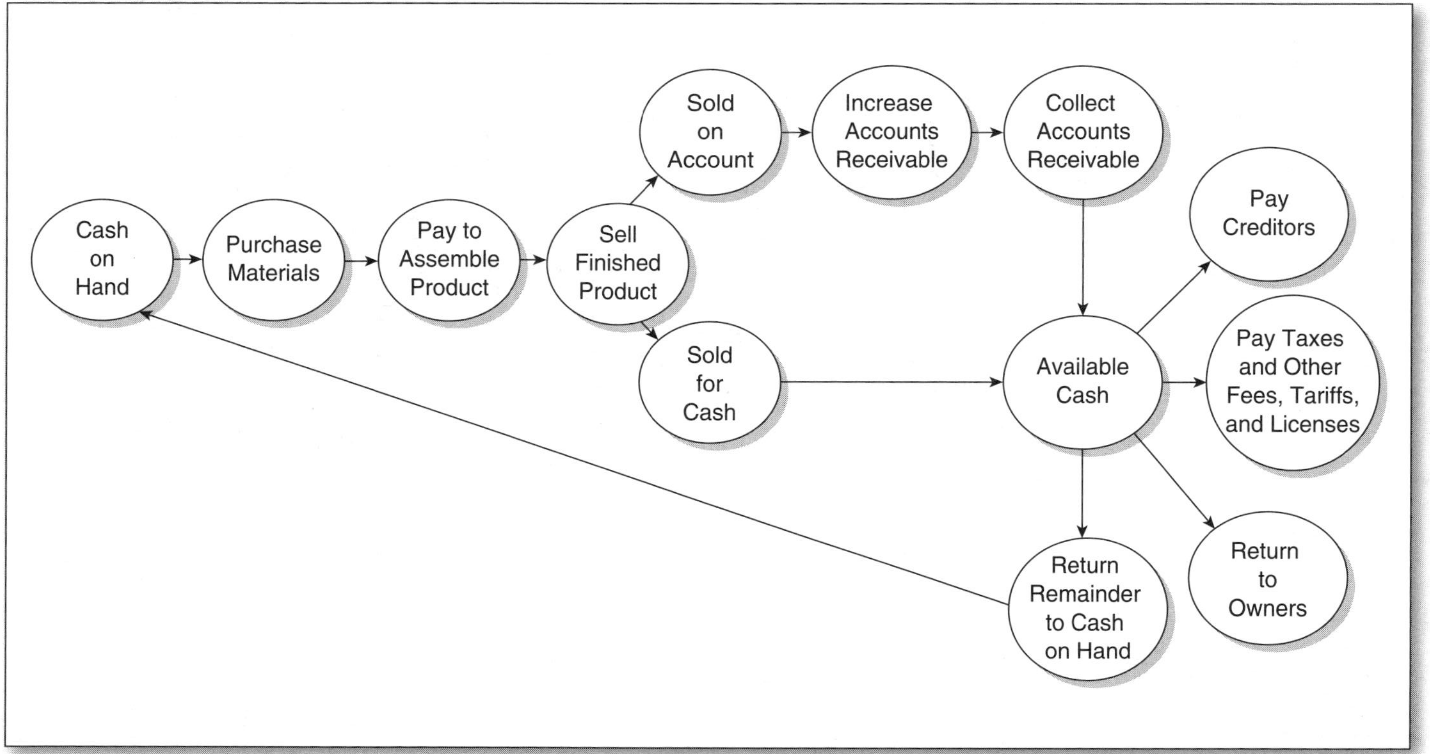

exchanged for a product. However, in the business world, ventures are usually willing to sell their products on credit. By allowing customers to pay on credit, ventures are able on one side to boost their revenues and on the other open themselves to the possibility of not receiving the cash when the invoice amount becomes due. Two distinct things occur:

1. There is an increase in credit sales.

2. This leads to an increase in accounts receivable from customers.

If the customer does not pay the amount he or she owes, a credit loss expense will be registered in the income statement, and the accounts receivable on the balance sheet will be adjusted downward.

The asset accounts receivable represents the cash owed to the venture by customers for goods and/or services that have been sold to them but not yet paid for. As entrepreneurs usually focus most of their efforts on generating sales, they end up giving little attention to customers who have not paid. Progressively, accumulation of accounts receivable from credit customers can ultimately lead to a serious cash shortage. We recommend entrepreneurs pay special attention to accounts receivable and not be afraid to confront their clients when payment is due. If the entrepreneur is not comfortable taking care of the issue, someone else needs to take care of this task. Under *no* circumstance should an entrepreneur ignore cases of outstanding accounts receivable.

Below is a series of strategies that will help entrepreneurs maximize their chances of receiving their payments on time and minimize losses:

1. Research the Potential Customer. When a venture grants credit to a customer, it is essentially loaning its own money without any guarantee that money will be repaid. Therefore, entrepreneurs should research their customers' creditworthiness before extending credit. The process can be as simple as making a phone call to the client's bank, or it can involve a more thorough investigation. One option is to have the customer fill out a basic application for credit. Standard forms are available on the Internet and require information such as the names of the principals of the business, the business address, contact information, and so on. If a customer hesitates to give you this information, it usually means he or she has bad credit (Dahl, 2010). You should also ask how long the company has been in business, who its major clients and suppliers are, and what its payment terms are. Calling suppliers is also a good option. In addition, searching online for clues that may indicate a company has or is facing financial issues or is involved in lawsuits is also recommended.

Traditional credit analysis involves three basic elements of assessment: capacity, collateral, and character.

a. *Capacity* refers to the ability of the venture to pay on a timely basis.

b. *Collateral* refers to the assets that can be pledged to guarantee payment.

c. *Character* refers to the basic character traits of the entrepreneur(s).

The extent of research on the credit-seeking customer needs to be adequate to resolve these key issues. Many professional firms specialize in doing credit and background checks on both individuals and firms, or you can use a company like Dun & Bradstreet yourself to check the credit rating and payment history of potential customers (Dahl, 2010).

If after the research the conclusion is that the client is worth the risk, the entrepreneur should discuss and establish the payment schedule with the client. If the customer does not meet your criteria, we recommend you either request 100% payment before or at the time of delivery or an upfront payment that covers the order's costs of goods sold (COGS) with the balance of the invoice due upon delivery.

2. Invoice Promptly. Send invoices to customers as soon as the goods or services are shipped or delivered. Do not wait or postpone this important task. Making sure customers receive the invoice quickly will hopefully lead to faster payment.

3. Take Action With Respect to Customers That Have Outstanding Balances on Their Accounts. In the event a customer does not pay within the time frame established, entrepreneurs should not delay taking action. There should be a regular procedure the venture follows to deal with slow-paying customers. The important thing is to take immediate action. If no action is taken, it gives a message to customers that they are allowed to delay their payments past the due date without consequences.

4. Credit Limits. Establish an appropriate credit limit for each customer. If a customer exceeds his or her credit limit, management may request partial or full payment up front in cash or ask for some form of collateral.

5. Offer Discounts. Entrepreneurs may offer customers a discount on the amount of the order if it is paid within a certain time frame.

Collection of Past Due Accounts Receivable

Collecting outstanding balances from customers can be an intimidating experience for entrepreneurs. As a result, third-party companies offer "trade credit insurance," where the insurance company assumes the responsibility for collection.

In severe cases, entrepreneurs may have to hire a lawyer. While this action may be effective in the United States, it may not work as well in other parts of the world. As a result, ventures may have to use collection agencies, as they may be faster than courts in resolving these types of issues. One of the most original collection agencies is the Madrid-based company El Cobrador del Frac (EL COFRAC) (www.elcobradordelfrac.com) (Abend, 2009). This enterprise specializes in debt collection by having its employees, dressed in old-fashioned, black frock coats and top hats carrying a suitcase saying in big letters "DEBT COLLECTOR," follow debtors everywhere they go, including restaurants, stores, and clients' premises. What happened to a couple who decided to not pay their $83,000 wedding bill to a wedding company indicates the effectiveness of this company (Harman, 2010). EL COFRAC asked the unsatisfied wedding company for the list of people who attended the wedding and started phoning the attendees one at a time. Upon confirmation of their presence at the wedding, EL COFRAC asked them if they had the lobster or the chicken as the main course, following with a request for their address where they could mail the bill. The money eventually was collected, and the collection agency is in high demand, given its outstanding success rate and has expanded its services to the neighboring countries of Portugal and France.

Days Sales Outstanding (DSO) Ratio

The days sales outstanding (DSO) ratio is used to assess the average number of days a venture takes to collect its receivables after they have been invoiced. This ratio provides information about how efficient the venture is at collecting payments from its customers:

$$DSO = \frac{\text{Accounts Receivable}}{\text{Invoiced Sales in Period}} \times \text{Days in Period}$$

In a strictly cash business, the DSO will be zero. However, most ventures do give customers credit terms, which generate accounts receivable. A low DSO ratio means the venture takes a relatively short time to collect accounts receivable. Too low a ratio may indicate that the venture's credit policy is too rigorous, which may be limiting its revenue potential. A high DSO reveals whether the venture's customer base has credit issues and/or the venture has a deficient debt collection system. The average DSO will vary from one industry to another and will vary based on whether the venture has only domestic customers or also sells internationally.

Let us consider the following scenario: a venture that started in January 2012 with $50,000 in accounts receivable (represents unpaid invoices from the last year or even earlier) and had invoiced sales of $900,000 by the end of the year 2012 on 30-day payment terms. This leaves the company with "credit sales" for 2012 of $900,000. Throughout 2012, the venture got payments on invoiced bills of $800,000. Thus, the accounts receivable at the end of 2012 amounted to $50,000 that were initially in the account, plus $900,000 of new invoiced sales, minus $800,000 that were paid during the period. It does not matter if the payments were made for invoices sent out during 2012 or before; all that matters is the final balance of accounts receivable at the end of the period. The accounts receivable at the end of 2012 was $150,000. The DSO for the period considered (365 days) is $150,000/$900,000 × 365 = 60.83.

This means that on average, it takes this venture approximately 61 days to convert *accounts receivable* into cash. Customers are paying an average 30 days later than they should since the venture's payment terms are 30 days. The venture is wasting capital that could be reinvested within the company or used to reduce debt or return to shareholders. Collection inefficiencies are often overlooked by entrepreneurs who do not understand how to measure the cost of delayed payments from customers. Below is a formula that quantifies the benefit of faster collection in terms of dollars saved (Fraser, 2000). Faster collection means the venture will rely less on its own credit line or its shareholder equity while waiting for customers to pay their invoices.

$$\frac{\text{Gross Annual Invoiced Sales} \times \text{Annual Interest Rate}}{365} \times \text{Days Saved} = \text{Dollar Savings}$$

To find "Days Saved" in the equation above, simply subtract the venture's improved DSO from its original DSO.

For example, a venture with gross annual invoiced sales of $10 million, borrowing at a rate of 6%, which improves its DSO by 7 days, will save more than $11,000 a year.

$$\frac{\$10,000,000 \times 0.06}{365} \times 7 = \$11,507$$

Accounts Payable

The best scenario in cash flow management is to collect receivables as fast as possible and pay outstanding bills as late as possible while keeping a good relationship with your customers and suppliers. There often are advantages associated with paying outstanding bills early. If a supplier is willing to provide a discount if the invoice is paid within 10 days instead of the regular 30 days, it might be worth doing this.

As an example, suppose a supplier offers a 2% discount if paid within 10 days (otherwise the payment should be made within 30 days). Here is the formula to use:

$$[(\% \text{ Discount}) / (100 - \% \text{ Discount})] \times (365 / \text{Number of Days Paid Early}) = \text{Annual Interest Rate}$$

In this case, a 2% discount for paying within 10 days (20 days earlier) would represent the following annual interest rate saving:

$$2\% / 98\% \times (365 \div 20) = 37.24\%$$

In this case, it is probably even worthwhile borrowing money to take advantage of the discount offered by the supplier.

The average number of days a venture takes to pay its bills, known as the days payable outstanding (DPO), can be measured with a procedure similar to the accounts receivable.

$$\text{DPO} = \text{Accounts Payable} / (\text{Annual Cumulative Accounts Payable Incurred} / 365 \text{ Days})$$

Some traditional accounting and finance books calculate this ratio differently by replacing the "annual cumulative accounts payable incurred" by annual total cost of goods sold (COGS). We agree with this procedure as long as all costs (both those paid in cash and on account) are included. A small entrepreneur, especially in less developed parts of the world, may incur some COGS that are not invoiced as they are required to be paid in cash. Again, this ratio can be high or low depending on the type of industry and whether a firm is dealing with international suppliers.

For entrepreneurs seeking to improve their accounts payable, there are several recommendations:

1. Negotiate longer payment terms with your suppliers, justified by the volume purchased and/or the trust built over time.

2. Request that your suppliers invoice you only upon your receipt of the product (especially with international suppliers).

3. Set priorities. Pay the bills that incur an obligatory interest charge or that extend a discount first.

4. Invest in a good accounting system to organize bills, payments, and warning alerts.

5. Test suppliers by delaying payments. They may have set a 30-day payment simply as a standard but may not mind if they receive payments within 50 days.

6. Study the local culture and offer payment terms that are in line with the local conditions.

Summary

Working capital is the difference between current assets and current liabilities. Positive working capital implies that the venture can pay upcoming liabilities without increasing debt or adding to shareholder equity, while negative working capital signals upcoming difficulties for the venture.

The main differences between working capital and cash flow were also discussed. Working capital has to do with the way management controls the magnitude of its current assets and current liabilities. Cash flow has to do with the amount of cash the firm has after it collects its revenues and pays its bills. When measuring cash flow, the manager must control for the existence of non-cash items like depreciation, as well as cash outlays that are not part of the firm's cost structure, dividends, capital expenditures, and principal payments of loan balances or amortization of intellectual property.

In this chapter, we described working capital is a financial metric to measure the operating liquidity of a venture; as such, it is most germane to the credit worthiness of the venture and represents an indication regarding the ability of management to control the relationship between current assets and current liabilities. Also in this chapter, we described cash flow as the ability of a venture to generate spendable cash from its operations. Again management's ability is measured; the ability to generate cash flow is a measurement with respect to (1) how well management collects the firm's revenues, (2) how well management controls the firm's expenses payments, and (3) how well management plans out the firm's capital budget and dividend payment policy.

An important point that was emphasized in this chapter is the difference between profits and cash flow. Profits are revenues minus expenses computed under an appropriate accounting convention, while cash inflow only occurs once the cash is collected from the customer and appropriate expenses are deducted and paid.

The cash flow cycle is the process through which the firm transforms initial revenues into cash that can be used in operations. How well management manages the cash flow cycle represents a key metric with respect to management's job performance.

Chapter 6

Financial Projections for the Firm

Learning Objectives

- To understand the basic typology of projections
- To learn to deal with information (or lack of information)
- To understand revenue and cost relationships
- To understand seasonality

Case: Desert Divers

Larry Gibbons and his friend Alex Huhn were having dinner and discussing their favorite hobby, scuba diving. Both were local businessmen in Tucson, Arizona. Their discussion centered on the need for a dive shop in Tucson. The Sea of Cortez was only a 6-hour drive from Tucson, and there was a steady supply of enthusiasts who were either already active in the Tucson dive community or interested in receiving the training to become divers. The men were not happy that the dive shop that had historically served the community was closing down, not because of lack of demand for diver training, equipment sales, and dive trips to the Sea of Cortez but because of mismanagement. The existing firm had gone bankrupt and discontinued its business. Both knew that historically there had always been a good market for a dive shop in the desert. Out of this discussion, the concept of Desert Divers was born.

Within a short time the name was secured, the lease on the old dive shop location became available, inventory was identified, instructors were found, and it became time to put in the money. The two friends had the money, but they did not want to put it into the company until they knew what to expect with respect to its financial performance. How much would the cash flow be? What would the profitability look like? How much initial inventory should there be? They didn't have the answers to these and many other questions. They wanted to be responsible and invest enough money to cover the worst case that they might expect during their startup phase. To find the answers they needed, they decided to make a projection for the first 2 years of the new Desert Divers Company.

Making financial projections is as much art as science. It is an activity that has both ideal and practical aspects. The "idealized" aspects of the process include two main factors:

1. The identification and a conceptualization of what the underlying inputs to the projection should be

2. How the underlying assumptions regarding these inputs should be assembled together to produce projected outcomes that will react to varying inputs in the same way as the firm would react to those same inputs in practice

Basically, the firm's financial projection should "work" the way the firm "works." In financial projections, the practical problems aren't ones of conceptualization and model building but rather problems of a best practice and implementation nature. Key problems are

1. Determining the proper time horizon for the projection

2. Overcoming the paucity of historical information

3. Creating shorthand explanations of what may otherwise be complicated relationships

This chapter addresses these questions and others. Remember, *always* do financial projections with a projection of units sold and their price. This cannot be emphasized enough. The most common mistake made in making or conceptualizing projections is to initially project sales in currency (dollars) instead of units sold and their selling price. This is true for both manufacturing and service companies. Every firm sells a unit of something, whether a unit of manufactured product, a unit of time to use something (like an office or a piece of equipment), or a unit of time in which a service is provided (like an hour with an attorney or an accountant). Often firms sell a hierarchy of products—for example, an hour of a senior partner's time, an hour of an associate's time, an hour of paralegal's time, and an hour of a typist's time. However, it must be emphasized that projections that are done in dollar units instead of product unit are next to worthless. Only with product units does the analyst have the flexibility to vary both units sold and price per unit to produce projections that are flexible and robust.

Finally, as with many business problems, the actual execution is difficult, time-consuming, and problematic. Financial projection as a subject matter has been given color and texture by a very large body of research, a wide range of analytical techniques, and many diversities of opinion. All of these factors make implementation difficult. While it is impossible for one chapter to fully explain all or even a majority of the rich variety of technique and practice embraced by this subject matter, Chart 6.1 presents a schematic

Chart 6.1   Schematic of Chapter 6

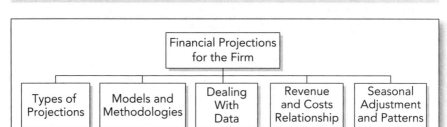

representation of the material covered in this chapter. This information is a good starting point for understanding the overall subject.

Making projections is a process that involves several basic steps:

1. Obtaining data (where and how it is obtained is discussed later)

2. Using a model to represent the data so that it can be understood and manipulated

3. Applying an analytical method to the manipulated data to make a projection beyond the data range

Types (i.e., Forms) of Projections

In the discussion of different types of projections, confusion can occur. One may suppose that the "type of projection" may be defined by the technique being used to make it (for example, linear regression), or one may presume that the type of projection may refer to the thing being projected (for example, sales projection). When discussing types, we are referring to neither technique nor subject but to form. The form of the output defines the projection just as clearly as does the technique and the subject matter. To understand projections, it is best to start with form. While many techniques can be brought to bear on many diverse subject matters, there are only four forms of output: flat projections, untrended projections, trended projections, or patterned projections.

Our discussion must start with the introduction of data that explain the construction of various forms of projection. Table 6.1 is a table of historical unit sales data for years 20xx through 20zz. As can be seen in the table, annual unit sales have been increasing over the 3-year period. The rise from 20xx to 20yy was small, a .28% increase, and then from 20yy to 20zz, sales increased by a larger amount, 10%. Chart 6.2 shows these unit sales data graphically.

Flat projections are projections where no new information is used and no new assumptions are made. In essence, the projection for the coming year is exactly what happened for the past year. This type of projection can take two forms: Monthly unit sales will be exactly the same as they were in the past, or total sales can be used to calculate a monthly average and then forecast the next year's monthly sales based on the average monthly sales from last year. Either way, the projection of total sales will equal what it was last year. The only difference between the two methods employed is using an average monthly amount or last year's actual

Table 6.1 Three Years of Historical Unit Sales Data

	January	February	March	April	May	June	July	August	September	October	November	December	Total
Historical unit sales													
20xx	12,505	12,908	13,207	11,906	14,250	14,700	16,780	15,640	15,500	15,780	22,305	17,009	182,490
20yy	13,200	13,027	13,140	10,907	13,798	14,020	16,203	16,240	17,090	16,729	21,910	16,750	183,014
20zz	14,163	14,290	14,517	12,570	15,454	15,825	18,174	17,566	17,957	17,912	24,362	18,601	201,393
Total units sold by month	39,868	40,225	40,864	35,383	43,502	44,545	51,157	49,446	50,547	50,421	68,577	52,360	566,897

Note: Totals may vary slightly due to rounding.

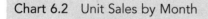

Chart 6.2   Unit Sales by Month

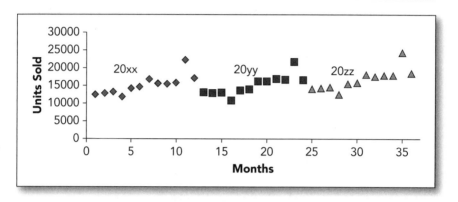

monthly amount as the projected amounts. Flat projections are limited in nature, but they do have two redeeming features:

1. This type of projection is easy to make.

2. This type of projection can be used to test the impact of single variables (for example, unit sales or unit price or cost of direct material) on the bottom line given the assumption that the firm is performing exactly as it did in the immediate historical past.

In Table 6.2 and Chart 6.3, we see a flat projection that uses the average monthly amount of unit sales in 20zz (16,783 units) to forecast next year's total unit sales of 201,393 (totals may vary slightly due to rounding). This 201,393 of annual unit sales is the same as in both the historical period and the projection period.

An *untrended projection* works in a way that is similar to a flat projection; however, it does not assume that total unit sales are the same in the projected period as they are in the prior period. When making this type of projection, sales are assumed to increase (or decrease) by some amount, for example, 10% (see Table 6.3 and Chart 6.4). In the untrended projection shown in Table 6.3 and Chart 6.4, unit sales are 10% higher than in the historical year 20zz.

The easiest way to make an untrended projection is to apply an annual growth rate to either the average monthly unit sales of the prior period or to the monthly unit sales amounts. Either way, the total unit sales for the projection period will end up being higher than the unit sales in the prior period. This type of projection is called untrended to distinguish it from a flat projection. A flat projection assumes no growth, indeed no change from the

Table 6.2 Flat Projection of Monthly Unit Sales (Based on Last Year's Historical Data)

Projection start point through projection end point	January	February	March	April	May	June	July	August	September	October	November	December	Total
	13	14	15	16	17	18	19	20	21	22	23	24	Total
Average monthly units sold	16,783	16,783	16,783	16,783	16,783	16,783	16,783	16,783	16,783	16,783	16,783	16,783	201,393

Note: A flat projection is the one that is the average periodic amount that will sum to the total of the prior year.

Table 6.3 Untrended Projection of Higher Monthly Average Unit Sales (Assumes a 10% Increase Over Last 20zz's Data)

Projection start point through projection end point	January	February	March	April	May	June	July	August	September	October	November	December	Total
	13	14	15	16	17	18	19	20	21	22	23	24	Total
Average monthly units sold with 10% growth	18,461	18,461	18,461	18,461	18,461	18,461	18,461	18,461	18,461	18,461	18,461	18,461	221,532

Chart 6.3   Actual Sales Versus Flat Projection Sales

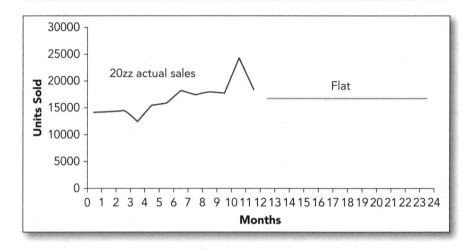

Chart 6.4   Actual Sales Versus and Untrended Projection With 10% Increase

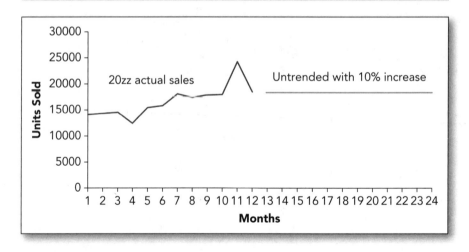

prior period. An untrended projection may have a flat look, but it does assume a change from the prior period, if only an annual increase or decrease.

Untrended projections are useful starting points.

1. They are easier to use and make than trended projections.

2. They can be turned into trended projections without much effort.

In projections, more information is captured than a simple repeat of the prior year or a fixed upward revision in prior year sales. Most of the time, one wants to closely reproduce whatever patterns are inherent in the business, and linear trends provide more information than either a flat or an untrended projection. Analysts have identified three basic types of trend patterns:

1. Linear

2. Nonlinear

3. Seasonally adjusted

In the remainder of this section, we will deal with *linear trended projections* and then seasonal adjustments and patterns dealing with nonlinear and seasonally adjusted trends. Linear trends are most useful. These types of projections produce a sense of direction in unit sales as well as an expression of the gross impact of year-to-year or period-to-period changes. There are basically two ways to produce a linear projection:

1. Applying an appropriate periodic growth rate equally through a 12-month period, thus producing a trended projection resulting in a desired annual unit sales projection (after which the trend may continue should the analyst desire)

2. Using a linear regression methodology to produce a trended projection of unit sales for the desired period

Table 6.4 and Chart 6.5 indicate what turning an untrended projection that has increased by 10% over the prior year (20zz) into a trend looks like. If each of the monthly unit sales amounts in the projection are added together, their total will be equal to the projected sales in total unit sales in Table 6.3 (the untrended example). There is a small difference due to rounding.

To make a *trended projection using an annual growth rate,* one needs only make a choice regarding the starting point and the annual growth rate. To further develop an example, let's assume that we wish to start our projection at 201,393 units per year (this is the level of unit sales indicated in Table 6.2 for year 20zz; totals may vary slightly due to rounding). Using a desired annual increase of 10% would mean in the projection period, 221,532 units would be sold. This is the annual unit sales that were indicated in Table 6.3. However, unit sales in Table 6.3 are untrended. To work

Table 6.4 Trended Projection of Higher Monthly Unit Sales (Assumes a 10% Increase Over Last 20zz's Data)

Projection start point through projection end point	January	February	March	April	May	June	July	August	September	October	November	December	Total
	13	14	15	16	17	18	19	20	21	22	23	24	Total
Trended monthly units	17,630	17,777	17,925	18,075	18,225	18,377	18,530	18,685	18,840	18,997	19,156	19,315	221,532
January initial value (without monthly growth)	17,484												

Notes: Calculate monthly growth rate (slope of projection) as follows:

For 10% annual growth, the monthly amount is .10/12 or 0.008333.

Calculate monthly projected unit sales as follows:

For the first period, use the average monthly amount, in this case 18,461. Then multiply this amount by 1 plus the periodic growth rate (.008333), in this case (1 + .008333).

For each of the other periods, multiply the prior month's unit sales times 1 plus the periodic growth rate. For February, we would multiply January's unit sales by (1 + .00833), and so on.

Center the trend. This means that the trended projection should cross the untrended projection in late June.

We can ensure this by adjusting the initial average monthly amount downward to 17,485 from 18,461. The amount is arrived at via trial and error. Excel's Goal Seek function can be used to determine January's initial value (before adding monthly growth) that is necessary to make the annual unit sales total 221,532.

We have done this in this case to arrive at January's initial value of 17,484.

Chart 6.5 Actual Sales Versus Trended Projection Sales With 10% Increase

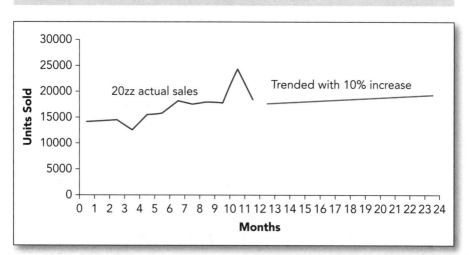

out a trended forecast, the following steps are used to calculate a monthly projection of units sold for the next 12 months:

1. Determine the periodic trend rate. Mathematically, it is the annual trend rate divided by the desired number of projection periods in the year; in our example, it is (10% / 12) = .08333.

2. Except for the first monthly projection, each projected monthly value is going to be a function of the prior period. Mathematically, the values for projection period 2 through period N will be determined as follows: Unit projection for each period n = Unit projection period $n - 1 * (1 + .08333)$.

3. For the first projection period, a little more work needs to be done. We know the projection needs to total 221,532 annual units. We know that the average monthly units for annual unit sales of 221,532 are 18,461 units. However, if we compute the first period's projection by using the 18,461 number, we will end up with too many annual units (231,973 versus the expected 221,532). To end up at the correct point, we need to reduce the 18,461 unit number to a lower number that then results in the annual sum of the trended projection being very close to 221,532 units. Through trial and error, we can identify 17,630 units as the starting point for period 1. That starting point will produce an annual total of 221,531, which is very close to the desired 221,532.

The disadvantage of trended projections is that they do not anticipate new information. The trends continue unless new information is incorporated into the historical data being used to calculate them.

Another type of linear trended projection is a *linear regression*. This type of projection has two basic characteristics:

1. The projection is a purely mathematical construct. There is no input in the growth rate, the boundaries, or the limits of the projection.

2. The projection is entirely dependent on the amount of historical data used in the process. Relatively more or less data will have a large impact on the regression projection.

Linear regressions are built around the idea that a straight line can be drawn through a plot of historical unit sales (or other data) and that that line can be drawn in such manner so as to describe the data very well. The line can then be used, via extension, to project the data in a meaningful way into a future projection period. The formula for such a line is $^\wedge Y = a + bX$, where $^\wedge Y$ = the value for the output value on the Y axis given a constant of a (the line's intercept on the Y axis) given a line slope of b at point X on the X axis. The placement of the line within historical data is somewhat involved and beyond the scope of this chapter. Basically, the line passes through the data set in such a way that the sum of the perpendicular distance from each data point on the top of the line to the line equals the sum of the perpendicular distances of each data point on the bottom of the line to the line.

In Table 6.5 and in Chart 6.6, the regression projection for unit sales for the next 12 months (periods 13 through 24), given the data of the past

Chart 6.6   Actual Sales Versus Regression Projection Sales

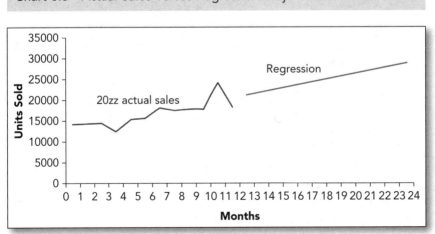

Table 6.5 Regression

Historical Data for Regression Input

	January	February	March	April	May	June	July	August	September	October	November	December	Total
Data starting point through data end point	1	2	3	4	5	6	7	8	9	10	11	12	Total
Actual unit sales 20zz	14,163	14,290	14,517	12,570	15,454	15,825	18,174	17,566	17,957	17,912	24,362	18,601	201,393

Regression

	January	February	March	April	May	June	July	August	September	October	November	December	Total
Projection start point through projection end point	13	14	15	16	17	18	19	20	21	22	23	24	Total
Predicted units (^Y)	21,302	21,997	22,693	23,388	24,083	24,779	25,474	26,169	26,864	27,560	28,255	28,950	301,514

Notes: Totals may vary slightly due to rounding. The regression formula is $^\wedge Y = K + bX$, where

The period to project (X) = the value of the period on a sequentially numbered time line,

Constant (K) = 12,500,

Coefficient (b) = 678.38.

12 months (periods 1 through 12), is provided. Projections done using the linear regression technique are worthwhile if the projection period is kept short, such as no more than 2 or perhaps 3 years.

Types of models and methodologies that produce outputs that exhibit various *patterns* include various types of curvilinear analysis and higher-order polynomial math functions, and while we do mention these techniques, we will not spend much time trying to master them. We do deal with these types of techniques in the section "Seasonality and Patterns."

Models and Methodologies

To date in this discussion, the models or methods have not been addressed that can be used to

1. Process data

2. Duplicate within the planning model the firm's day-to-day activities

3. Make projections or test hypotheses

4. Assess the performance or effectiveness of management or existing firm processes

By reviewing the types of projections, we were in fact reviewing generic types or forms of projection. The common types of projections encountered in business fall into the categories that were previously discussed. Following is a discussion of the types of models and methodologies that can be used to handle data and make projections.

Models are analytical means used to summarize or describe data. Methodologies are analytical means used to make projections from the raw data or models of data available (Armstrong, 2001). It is possible and often the case that a particular model may also be a methodology; for example, a linear regression may be used to describe historical data and to project the linear trend of that historical data into the future. Table 6.6 lists a number of models and methodologies that are commonly used.

Four classes of mathematical techniques can be used as models or methodologies (and sometimes both):

1. Average based

2. Trend following

3. Statistical systems

4. Miscellaneous

Table 6.6   Models and Methodologies

	Mathematical Technique	Model—Summarizes or Describes Data	Methodology—Used for Projection
Distribution averages	Arithmetic average	✓	✓
	Moving average	✓	
	Weighted average	✓	
Trends	Simple trend	✓	✓
	Linear regression	✓	✓
	Multivariable regression	✓	✓
	Curvilinear	✓	✓
Statistical distribution	Monte Carlo simulation		✓
Miscellaneous	J-curve	✓	✓
	Econometric		✓
	Seasonal adjustment	✓	✓

With respect to the techniques classified as *average-based* systems, there are three primary types:

1. Arithmetic average, the simplest form of average calculation, is employed in the normal way by adding the various sample numbers together and dividing by the sample size. The formula is

$$\text{Arirthmetic average} = \frac{\Sigma_{t=1}^{N}X_i}{N}$$

2. Moving average is another type of computation involving averages. When calculating this type of average, a predetermined number of sequential data points are used to compute their average. This average becomes the model output for the last day of the input sequence. The second step is to then drop off the first data point in the series, add the next data point, and recompute the average. This average becomes the model output for the next period. This process can continue as long as there are data. Inputs may be in series lengths that are chosen by the analyst (for example, 3 days, 9 days,

20 days, or any other relevant period). Moving averages serve to smooth data, eliminating extremes in either direction. The formula is

$$\text{Moving average} = \frac{X_t + X_{t-1} + \ldots + X_{t-(N-1)}}{N}$$

where N = number of observations.

3. Arithmetically weighted moving averages are similar to moving averages except the data are weighted in proportion to their proximity to the most recent date of the series. For example, if we are computing a 3-day arithmetic moving average, we would weigh the data from the third day more than the data from the second day, and we would weigh the data from the second day more than the data from the first day. It would look like the following:

$$\text{3-day weighted moving average} = \frac{3X_t + 2X_{t-1} + 1X_{t-2}}{6}$$

where 6 = sum of the weights applied to the data points.

The strength of all the analytical techniques that involve averages is that they are easy to compute. They also yield results that are close to recent historical results so they are not usually prone to spectacular error. Their weakness is that they contain very little information about trends or patterns in the data.

Trend-following models are data models where the data are expressed as a linear but sloped line. There are two basic forms of these models: (1) the trended linear model and (2) a linear regression model. The trended linear model is used when a linear trend is desired to increase or decrease a variable in a straight-line manner. An example of a linear trended projection is presented in Table 6.4 and in Chart 6.5. Those examples are relevant to this discussion. Linear trends are most often characterized as

$$V_t = V_{t-1}(1 + g)$$

where

V_t = value at point t,

V_{t-1} = value at point $t - 1$,

g = growth rate from one period to the next.

One important issue regarding these types of trend computations is that the growth rate is usually based on some estimate provided. The motivation behind the estimate is usually either subjective in nature or loosely based on recent historical trends. In either case, the linear trended projection is not good at identifying patterns within the seasonal cycle of the firm, nor is it good at closely fitting the slope of the trend line to the historical data that are available.

Linear trends may also be calculated via linear regression. Linear regression was discussed earlier, with examples given in Table 6.5 and Chart 6.6. As a data analysis technique, it is one of the most common. The big advantage of linear regression is that the resulting trend line is closely fitted to the historical data used. This represents a clear advantage if historical data are important to the projection. However, just as with the models we have discussed to this point, linear regression is not useful in capturing the impacts of business cycles or seasonal data. The linear equation is the equation for a straight line: $^\wedge Y = a + bX$, where $^\wedge Y$ = the value for the output value on the Y axis given a constant of a (the line's intercept on the Y axis) given a line slope of b at point X on the X axis. The important feature of this technique is that the "line" is placed in the historical data in the most optimal spot in terms of generating explanatory power, as previously discussed.

Other trend-following models can be used when we want to summarize existing data and project future performance based on trends exhibited within the data. *Multiple regression analysis* assumes that the relationship of more than one independent variable X is related to the status of the dependent variable Y. If various independent variables $X_1 \ldots X_n$ are examined, then the movement of Y is projected on the basis of its relationship to each of the Xs examined in turn. Multiple regression analysis adds value in making a projection in that the increased number of independent variables will likely allow for more finely tuned explanatory power; the regression output will still be inadequate in capturing seasonality and business cycle impacts because the relationships are still linear in nature. The results are completely captive to a historical relationship between variables.

If linear explanations of existing data and trends are not desired or if they will not be adequate in their explanatory power, then *curvilinear regressions* may be used. In this type of model, the projection is a function not only of the linear equation but of higher order contributing polynomial relationships. In this technique, trends may be described that are nonlinear, a clear advantage. The explanatory power of these models will likely be higher than with linear models. The disadvantage is that this technique is no longer as amenable to informal problem formulation and computation.

With curvilinear regression, rigorous problem setup and computer process-ing time need to be used. Basically, users of this method must be knowledge-able and skilled in more math and more computer science than those who use other techniques. Curvilinear output does capture data in a unique way. Chart 6.7 shows an example of a curvilinear regression.

The classic technique used to summarize the *statistical distribution* of outcomes is the *Monte Carlo simulation*. This method is often used to proj-ect the most likely outcome given the statistically determined movements of input variables. A model is built to describe the relationship among firm inputs of unit sales, prices, direct costs, general and administrative costs, and taxes. The designed methodology projects net income (or some other output such as EBITDA or cash flow) given a specified level of unit sales. The values of the variables in this analysis are described on the basis of their historical behavior (or expected behavior). This means that each variable (for example, the cost of raw material) will have a unique statistical profile. It will have an average, a standard deviation, and a distribution profile (normal, discrete uniform, etc.).

When operating a simulation program, the average, standard deviation, and distribution profile for each variable will be input into the model. The computer will then step through the model one variable at a time and select a value for each variable; that value is calculated based on the variable's

Chart 6.7 Curvilinear Regression Example

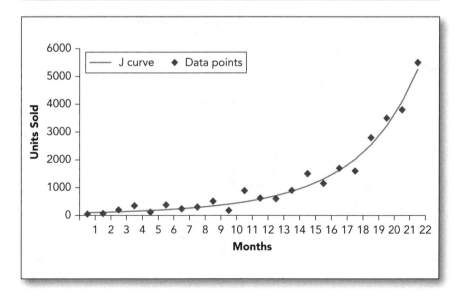

entered statistical characteristics. Once all variables have been assigned values, the program will then calculate the value for the desired output (i.e., dependent variable). This calculated output will be a result of statistics, not scenario or history.

The final step in the program is to perform the calculation thousands of times and summarize the results statistically. The final projection of the desired output is an average of thousands of calculations based on statistical estimates of the behaviors of input variables. Monte Carlo simulation offers an interesting perspective on the expected value and range of behavior of an identified output variable. However, the methodology is not useful for observing how the day-to-day work of the firm proceeds.

There are a couple of other models of data treatment. These techniques are not easily placed in the previous classifications. The first is called *econometric*. This modeling technique is often used to view problems in a "top-down manner" in light of the many linear relationships between the desired projected variable and a number of other independent variables. In one sense, the econometric model is the same as multiple regression analysis. However, as a matter of scope, it is usually a much broader formulation of the environment. Banks and trust companies use an econometric approach to project next year's investment climate. In their models, input variables range from gross domestic product (GDP) growth to interest rates to energy prices to money growth and industrial productivity. Many hundreds of variables can be brought into the analysis as independent variables. Historical relationships dominate the process, and specific relationships between variables are hard to assess since those relationships make relatively small contributions to the overall outcome of the projection. This is a method involving large databases and many hours of computer time.

Finally, all data can be "seasonally" adjusted. *Seasonal adjustment* should not be thought of as a means of projecting magnitude or trend but a means of analyzing the inherent seasonal patterns of the firm and adjusting output data so that these seasonal patterns stay intact. Seasonal adjustment will be discussed later in this chapter.

Dealing With Data (or Lack of Data)

Bringing all of the various views regarding type of projection, model, and methodology together is difficult. Not just because there is a plethora of information and concepts to learn but because the concepts overlap and duplicate both form and function. For example, a model used to describe data such as a simple average can also be used to project results. In fact, most models can also be methodologies that can be used to make projections. A type of a projection, such as a trended projection, may also seem to be a method of projection, and indeed it is once the starting point and growth rate for the trend have been determined. Once the decision is made about the assumptions and how to describe projected results, then types of projections and methods of data summary become full-fledged projections. Put another way, once historical data have been identified and key assumptions have been made, then constituent parts of the process lead to a coherent useful projection. Chart 6.8 summarizes the discussion in this section.

Chart 6.8   Dealing With Data

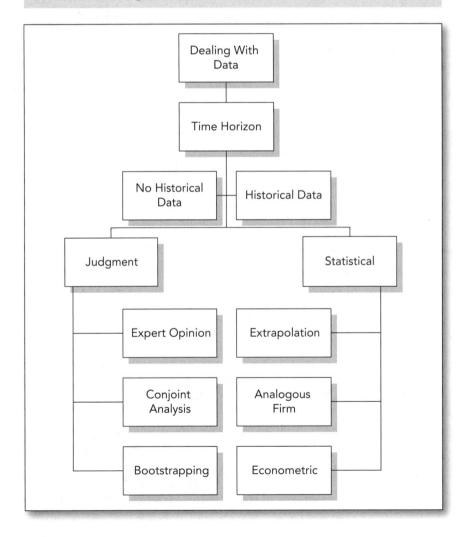

The *time horizon* of a projection and the nature of available data for the projection are key issues that need to be addressed. Generally, time horizons may lengthen given the operating history of the firm and/or the variability of revenues:

1. For startup firms, projections over long time horizons are rarely supported by either historical data or by methodologies that have good predictive power (because of the lack of data and an imprecise understanding of the firm's operating characteristics). There is simply too little history either on the data side or on the operational side to make reliable long-term projections. For the startup firm, 3 to 5 years is a usual time horizon over which to project results, with the last 2 years being very inaccurate.

2. Intermediate-sized firms with substantially more operating history allow projections that range from the 3- to 5-year time horizon to be made. The farther-out years are also not highly reliable but more so than for startup firms; data and methodology can be used to make projections to that time frame.

3. Firms with long operating histories may facilitate projections in the 3- to 7-year time horizon. Projections that range beyond 5 years are rarely accurate and serve negligible purpose.

4. The only exception to this 3- to 7-year limitation is for firms that are utilities or are similar to utilities; firms like this typically have lots of historical or operating data, and the variability of their month-to-month revenue is small. These unique characteristics make longer projections possible. For utilities, 30-year projections are routine.

What data and how much data to consider in a projection are case specific and really depend on the specific circumstances surrounding each projection. As much data should be used as are readily available and coherent. Historical data should be used to the extent that they do not contain discontinuities such as changes in the way the data are acquired or calculated or contain "black swan"–type disruptions. If these types of intervening factors exist in the data, then the flaws need to be recognized and steps taken to adjust for their impact. Depending on the analysis being done, expert opinion or judgment can be applied to the data to improve their relevance to the problem at hand.

The most obvious source of actual data is the firm itself; historical accounting information is the starting point for all projections when it is available. Supplemental data on industry sales come from industry sources, government sources, specialized research reports, and trade associations in the form of census and economic reports. Data on the economy can be found in these same government sources, as well as specialized sources such as the Federal Reserve System and regional economic or industry studies performed by universities, banks, and development agencies. Market sizes are often assessed by reviewing local sales tax records. Sales taxes are reported by category (for example, restaurant sales, clothing sales, and fuel sales). Despite this wide range of data sources, when historical data are limited in their availability, then a number of data sources that have proven to be helpful should be used in the firm's projections.

1. Fee-for-service consultation:
   - AMR Research—supply chain: www.amr-research.com
   - Frost & Sullivan—new technologies and markets: www.frost.com
   - Gartner—IT research: www.gartner.com
   - IDC—broad-based capabilities: www.idc.com
   - DisplaySearch—communications: www.displaysearch.com
   - Jupiter Internet Marketing—Internet: http://jupiterinternetmarketing.com
   - Yankee Group—telecom: www.yankeegroup.com

2. Private company research:
   - Dun & Bradstreet: www.dnb.com
   - Hoover's: www.hoovers.com
   - VentureSource (part of Dow Jones' VentureOne suite of information services): www.venturesource.com
   - VentureExpert (part of Thomson's Venture Economics): http://banker.thomsonib.com/ta/help/webhelp/Thomson_VentureXpert.htm

3. Industry sources:
   - AlwaysOn Network—technology: http://aonetwork.com
   - Charlene Li's Blog—media and marketing: www.charleneli.com/blog
   - Corante—technology, media, and innovation: http://corante.com
   - SEMI—Semiconductor Industry Association—industry research: www.semiconductors.org
   - Datamonitor—public companies and industry analysis: www.datamonitor.com
   - Open Source Technology Group—software: www.openmagazine.net
   - BioWorld—biotechnology (a Thomson publication): www.bioworld.com

- Annual Biotechnology Industry Report, Burrill & Company: www
  .burrillmedia.com/collections/annual-biotechnology-industry-
  reports
- Genetic Engineering News (GEN): www.genengnews.com
- Windhover Information—health care: www.windhover.com
- Clean Edge—clean energy industry research: http://cleanedge.com
- Nanodot—nanotechnology: www.foresight.org/nanodot
- Small Times—nanotechnology: http://electroiq.com/mems

4. Financial information:

- Ibbotson Associates, 2013, *Stocks, Bonds, Bills, and Inflation: Valuation Edition 2013 Yearbook,* Morningstar Inc., Chicago, IL, various pages.
- L. Troy, 2014, *Almanac of Business and Industrial Financial Ratios,* 2013 Edition, CCH, Chicago, IL, various pages.
- BioWorld—biotechnology (a Thomson publication)
- Securities & Exchange Commission—EDGAR: www.sec.gov/edgar .shtml
- Government (federal, state, and local)
- Bank regional econometric forecasts
- Local and state tax authorities
- University research
- U.S. Census: www.census.gov

The availability of historical data is a main driver in the selection of approaches to make the projection. The model and methodology used depend on the data available. If historical data are available, then statistical models and methodologies offer the most logical solutions to making projections. If historical data are not available, then judgment-based models and methodologies will be used.

Statistical methodologies are methodologies that are highly dependent on data to generate results. Included in this class of methodology are the following:

1. Extrapolation, the extension of an existing set of data into the future. Useful methodologies would include flat projection, trended, and regression. The projection considers only the available historical data.

2. Analogous firm analysis, useful for firms where there are limited data or operational history data from an analogous firm, is used to formulate a projection for the subject firm. Franchises are the clearest

example where this type of projection is used. The franchisee is just starting up, and a projection for the new franchise is problematic, but many examples of similar businesses, such as existing franchises, can be used as a template for the startup's projection.

3. Multiple regression and multivariate analysis are techniques that focus entirely on existing data to generate results. The objectives are to search for relations between one or more dependent variables on a number of independent variables. Usually more limited in scope than an econometric methodology, these are more closely designed to describe the day-to-day workings of the firm.

4. Econometric methodology is geared toward looking for relationships between a large number of independent variables of an economic nature and one or more dependent variables. These relationships on their own may or may not seem to be relevant to the firm, its day-to-day business, and the projection of the desired variable.

At every step of the way, *judgment* plays a role in making projections; when historical data are not available, some form of management or expert judgment plays the central role in the construction of the projection when estimates of data are needed. In startup firms, no historical data are available, so the following three sources of data and methodology can be used:

1. Expert opinion is just what it sounds like. An industry expert exercises his or her skill and judgment to make a projection of the key information needed to make a projection of the desired variables. Often the expert is a member of the firm's management, an engaged expert consultant, or a market research firm specializing in market research.

2. Conjoint analysis occurs when a market study is undertaken to identify things like consumer preferences, price sensitivity, market growth rates, and potential size. This type of analysis usually involves focus groups, surveys, and/or beta tests. The results can be assembled into an initial projection of how the product will do over the short to intermediate time frame. This type of analysis is very expensive.

3. When bootstrapping, management makes a forecast based on its judgment of the reasonable expectations of results. Often projections using the bootstrap method focus on the capacity of the firm and a ramp-up from a low initial percentage of capacity to full capacity over time. A variation of this approach is for management to assume a degree of market penetration and then ramp up sales and product to meet that level of sales.

Revenue and Costs Relationships

One question that needs to be answered is, How do you project expenses? The short answer is that you don't project expenses. The cost of some elements of the firm's expenses can of course be projected, but the actual expenses incurred are a function of unit sales, production, and the fixed costs of the firm. If the firm sells 1,000 units of its product priced at $15.00 per unit, the firm's sales revenue is $15,000. The first step of making a revenue projection is projecting unit sales, and the second step is to project a per-unit selling price. The combination of these two projected variables allows for projected revenues to be calculated. It is in this area that the real effort of making projections should be focused—on projecting unit sales and selling price.

When dealing with expenses, costs are not projected in the same manner as revenue. If the cost of raw material is $3.00 per unit, then the raw material expense is a function of the number of units sold, not some other function. This means that the prices of the input elements to the production process should be projected, but the total expense for any given element of production will be a function of the firm's unit sales, except for the cost per unit of material or labor, and not a function of some extraneous relationship. The projection for the firm's expenses should respond to the day-to-day work flow of the firm.

There are two ways to relate the firm's expenses to its unit sales and revenues:

1. The pro-forma method is the simplest. In this system, the relationship between the expense category and the unit sales is held constant. If the relationship between last period's unit sales and the raw material expense was $3.00 on a per-unit basis, then the pro-forma projection will retain that relationship throughout the projection time horizon regardless of any economies of scale that may occur. The pro-forma projection model is easy to implement but does not provide the best day-to-day description of the firm.

2. The input-output method of making projections captures the actual relationships that exist between production levels and component expenses. This type of projection attempts to capture the relationship between raw material and units sold within various production ranges. For example, per unit costs might be $3.00 per unit for the production range of 1 to 999, but the cost might decline to $2.75 per unit when the production range increases to 1,000 to 2,499. The input-output projection model is more complex and gives better results in duplicating the actual workings of the firm on a day-to-day basis. It is somewhat more elaborate and difficult to design and implement.

Both of these projection methodologies need to be used to project cash flow, not just net income or EBITDA. In the valuation section of this book, we discuss how to estimate free cash flow by adjusting net income. Usually, projections of cash flow and cumulative cash flows give the most valuable information for startup firms.

Seasonal Adjustment and Patterns

We have seen that various models and methodologies can exhibit various patterns. Typically, all of the trend-following methodologies produce unique patterns, as do curvilinear regression and econometric projections. These patterns may contribute some information regarding future firm results, but they are artifacts of the computation embedded in the model and method rather than the day-to-day patterns found in the firm. Seasonality is really the gold standard that will relate projections to the day-to-day patterns found in the firm's activities.

Seasonality is a predictable cyclic behavior in the demand for products. Seasonality is distinguished from fluctuations in demand due to noise or casual activities such as price-driven or promotionally driven demand in that it varies independently of these factors (Moore, 2010). Seasonal demand variation is often tied to weather, holidays, or specific events. Seasonality is a phenomenon embedded in almost all business or industrial activity. Some businesses tend to exhibit more seasonality than others. For example, according to the National Retail Federation (2014), the retail industry generates 20% to 40% of its annual sales during the Christmas holiday season. Computing seasonality is important, particularly by using seasonally adjusted numbers when dealing with cash flow forecasts. Being able to combine adjustments for seasonality with other output methodologies is a valuable, useful skill. The process of imposing seasonal patterns on projected outputs is discussed below.

There are two ways to estimate seasonality: (1) Use government data for industry seasonality, or (2) estimate seasonality using historical data. The problem with using government data is that they generate results that are not unique to the case in hand and can vary substantially from the results of the firm. Government numbers come from industry data and do not distinguish between large or small firms or startup firms in their declining years. The problem with determining seasonality using historical data of the firm is that data are needed to do it. Many firms in the early stages of the business have not been around long enough to capture data that will exhibit seasonality. It usually takes at least 2 to 3 years of data to be able to decipher seasonal patterns.

The following example uses the sales data in Table 6.1 to show how to incorporate seasonality into the firm's projections. Table 6.7 indicates the process based on these data using each of the following steps:

1. *Determine the seasonality for each month given the historical data.* Using the historical sales data for 20xx, 20yy, and 20zz, we summed the sales for each month and divided it by the total sales for the 3-year period. For example, total January sales for the 3 years were 39,868 and total sales for the 3 years were 566,897. Therefore, January contributes 39,868/566,897 = 7.03% of yearly sales. As you can see from Chart 6.9, the firm hits a soft patch in sales in month 4 and sees a spike in sales in month 11.

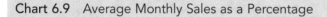

Chart 6.9 Average Monthly Sales as a Percentage

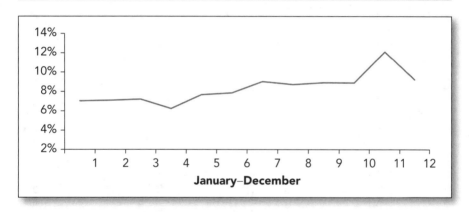

2. *Convert the regression forecast into an untrended forecast.* We previously showed a regression forecast in Table 6.5 and Chart 6.6. To change the regression forecast to an untrended forecast, we simply divide the annual regression-projected sales by 12. In our example, the total of the regression forecast is 301,514, which we divide by 12 to get an average of 25,126 per month.

3. *Calculate the difference due to regression.* By subtracting the untrended forecast from the regression forecast, the amount that is due to the trend can be determined. For January, this would be 21,302 − 25,126 = −3,824.

4. *Seasonally adjust the untrended forecast.* This is done by multiplying the total forecasted sales by the monthly seasonality computed in Step 1. For January, this would be 301,514 × 7.03% = 21,509.

Table 6.7 Seasonality

	January	February	March	April	May	June	July	August	September	October	November	December	Total
Historical unit sales													
20xx	12,505	12,908	13,207	11,906	14,250	14,700	16,780	15,640	15,500	15,780	22,305	17,009	182,490
20yy	13,200	13,027	13,140	10,907	13,798	14,020	16,203	16,240	17,090	16,729	21,910	16,750	183,014
20zz	14,163	14,290	14,517	12,570	15,454	15,825	18,174	17,566	17,957	17,912	24,362	18,601	201,393
Total units	39,868	40,225	40,864	35,383	43,502	44,545	51,157	49,446	50,547	50,421	68,577	52,360	566,897
Seasonal percentage	7.03%	7.10%	7.21%	6.24%	7.67%	7.86%	9.02%	8.72%	8.92%	8.89%	12.10%	9.24%	100.00%
Regression-forecasted sales	21,302	21,997	22,693	23,388	24,083	24,779	25,474	26,169	26,864	27,560	28,255	28,950	301,514
Untrended projection (from regression)	25,126	25,126	25,126	25,126	25,126	25,126	25,126	25,126	25,126	25,126	25,126	25,126	301,514
Difference due to regression	−3,824	−3,129	−2,433	−1,738	−1,043	−348	348	1,043	1,738	2,433	3,129	3,824	0
Seasonal percentage	7.03%	7.10%	7.21%	6.24%	7.67%	7.86%	9.02%	8.72%	8.92%	8.89%	12.10%	9.24%	100.00%

	January	February	March	April	May	June	July	August	September	October	November	December	Total
Seasonally adjusted untrended forecast	21,205	21,394	21,734	18,819	23,138	23,692	27,209	26,299	26,884	26,818	36,474	27,849	301,514
Untrended projection (from regression)	25,126	25,126	25,126	25,126	25,126	25,126	25,126	25,126	25,126	25,126	25,126	25,126	301,514
Difference due to seasonality	-3,921	-3,732	-3,392	-6,307	-1,989	-1,434	2,082	1,172	1,758	1,691	11,348	2,723	0
Untrended regression forecast	25,126	25,126	25,126	25,126	25,126	25,126	25,126	25,126	25,126	25,126	25,126	25,126	301,514
Difference due to regression	-3,824	-3,129	-2,433	-1,738	-1,043	-348	348	1,043	1,738	2,433	3,129	3,824	0
Difference due to seasonality	-3,921	-3,732	-3,392	-6,307	-1,989	-1,434	2,082	1,172	1,758	1,691	11,348	2,723	0
Seasonally adjusted trended forecast	17,381	18,266	19,301	17,081	22,095	23,344	27,556	27,342	28,623	29,251	39,603	31,673	301,514

5. *Calculate the difference due to seasonality.* Subtracting the untrended forecast from the seasonally adjusted forecast determines the amount that is due to seasonality. For January, this would be 21,509 – 25,126 = –3,921.

6. Adjust by untrended forecast by the amount due to the trend and the amount due to seasonality to obtain the seasonally adjusted and trended forecast.

Chart 6.10 presents the seasonally adjusted trended forecast.

Chart 6.10   Regression Projection, Untrended Projection, and Seasonally Adjusted Projection

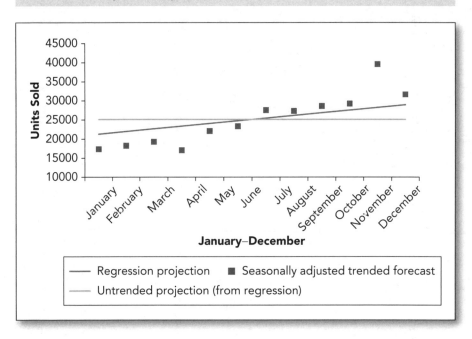

As you can see from the chart, the pattern now looks like the seasonality pattern we saw in Chart 6.9, but the values are magnified due to the trend component.

Summary

As indicated at the beginning of this chapter, making projections is as much an art as a science. When making a projection, the ultimate objective is to minimize the cumulative error between the projected values and actual values over the relevant time horizon. Choices need to be made on the many forms of projection, models, methodologies, and the internal structures describing relationships between unit sales and expenses. These choices offer many routes to a final predictive solution. Key things to remember are the following:

1. Some forms of projection are easier to use and simpler to explain than others. Complexity may not be essential to getting good results. Use the simplest projection that does the job.

2. Data are key to a good projection. Data need to be continuous and calculated in a uniform manner to be helpful. This applies to both historical data and data derived through judgment-oriented processes.

3. Models and methodologies may also range widely in their complexity and difficulty of use. Choose models and methodologies that are adequate.

4. Make projections work the way the firm works. The pro-forma approach to relating expenses to unit sales is quicker, but it does not produce flexible or robust projections. The input-output approach is far superior, but it is harder to execute. It does produce flexible and robust projections.

5. Always project units of sales and prices at which the units will sell. Revenue is a logical computation that flows from these variables. Revenue just in dollars does not give clear, accurate results. Revenue is a function of the two most important variables that a business projection should contain—unit sales and sales price per unit.

Chapter 7

Cost of Capital and Capital Budgeting

Learning Objectives
• To understand the cost of capital
• To understand basic capital budgeting

Case: Mill Pro, Inc.

As a recent graduate of a top 100 business school, Robyn Hunt was the proud possessor of a newly minted MBA. That's not all that had changed; while attending school, she had met the man of her dreams, Tom Dallin. She was now Mrs. Thomas Dallin, MBA. Tom was an engineer by training, and he was running a company his father had started back in the 1940s. The company, Mill Pro, Inc. (Mill Pro), provided custom-made parts to major firms in the aerospace industry. Mill Pro was a successful firm, but like any other firm in its position, it had razor-thin margins in order to compete. Tom was an excellent engineer but lacked business training, and he was happy to have his new bride become both part of his life and the CFO of his business.

Ten years ago, computer numeric control (CNC) machining processes had become the ascendant technology in Mill Pro's competitive landscape. Mill Pro was now using a CNC technology 10 years old, and even though the technology would last another 10 years, it was not now state of the art and was neither as flexible nor as price competitive as the next-generation technology. However, to replace the old technology with new technology was very expensive. While Tom had a general idea that some criteria should be used when making this decision, he did not know what they were. He asked Robyn if she could develop criteria and perform an analysis to decide if it was a smart move for Mill Pro to adopt and purchase the new technology. Robyn remembered that this kind of decision was made up of two parts: (1) the question of the firm's cost of capital and (2) constructing a projection and formatting the analysis. She decided she would review the cost of capital computation and the capital budgeting process.

T he most basic concept of value is that any risky asset is worth the present value of all expected future cash flows discounted back to the present at an appropriate risk-adjusted required rate of return. If we accept this concept, then two problems arise: What are those future cash flows (how certain are they, at what intervals do they occur, and how long do they last), and what is the appropriate risk-adjusted rate of return? In Chapter 6, we indirectly considered the question of what the future cash flows may be by studying the process of making a projection of such future benefits. When entrepreneurial ventures or capital projects are valued, the inherent cash generation capacities of the firm or the capital project are the key elements that should be considered, and projections regarding the relevant future benefits must be made. The second key issue is to determine what the required rate of return should be used as a discount factor when dealing with projected future cash flows.

Chart 7.1 presents a schematic representation of the material covered in this chapter.

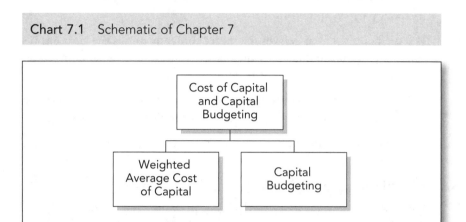

Chart 7.1   Schematic of Chapter 7

Weighted Average Cost of Capital

In calculating the present value of any asset using the **discounted cash flow** (DCF) analysis approach, the expected free cash flows generated by that asset are discounted by a required rate of return, also known as the *weighted average cost of capital* (WACC). The WACC is the average cost of capital representing the expected return on all of a company's outstanding components of capital. Each source of capital, equities, bonds, and other debt is weighted in the calculation according to its prominence in the company's capital structure. A firm's WACC is the overall required return on the firm as a whole. In other words, it is a rate of return offered by investment alternatives with equivalent risk. It is important to note that the WACC embodies both the business and financial risk. The WACC is a weighted average of the cost of equity and cost of debt (including the cost of preferred stock). The *cost of equity* is the rate of return expected by equity holders for taking the risk for investing in a company. The *cost of debt* is the net of taxes cost of debt weighted by type of debt and amount.

The use of WACC is intuitively appealing because of the consistency it affords: The company's cash flows are discounted at a rate reflecting the relative cost of the various components of its long-term capital necessary to generating those cash flows. The formula used to compute WACC is shown as follows:

$$\text{WACC} = \left(\frac{E}{V} * \text{RRR}_{equity}\right) + \left(\frac{D}{V} * \text{RRR}_{debt}(1-T)\right) + \left(\frac{Pfd}{V} * \text{RRR}_{pfd}\right)$$

where

E = the book value of equity of the target company (may be measured by its total market capitalization);

D = the book value of debt of the target company minus the current portion (may be approximated by the market value of any outstanding long-term bonds minus the current portion);

pfd = the book value of preferred stock of the target company (may be approximated by market value of any outstanding preferred stock);

V = the total amount of long-term capital of the target company (i.e., the sum of E + D + pfd);

E/V = the proportion of total firm capital represented by equity;

D/V = the proportion of total firm capital represented by debt;

pfd/V = the proportion of total firm capital represented by preferred stock;

T = the target company's corporate tax rate;

RRR_{equity} = the target company's cost of equity funds, calculated (see below for computational methods);

RRR_{debt} = the target company's cost of debt (see below for computational methods);

RRR_{pfd} = the target company's cost of preferred stock (see below for computational methods).

To calculate WACC at a firm, we need to attach a "cost" to each component of the firm's capital structure. Since there are three generic types of capital components that any firm may have, methodologies must be available to cost each one. These capital components are

1. Equity

2. Debt

3. Preferred stock

The Cost of Equity (RRR_{equity})

Virtually all firms have equity in their capital structure. There are several widely used and accepted methods of estimating the cost of equity. The most common of these are

1. The build-up method

2. The capital asset pricing model

3. The Gordon growth model

The Build-Up Method. The *build-up method* is an additive model in which the expected return on an asset is estimated as the sum of the risk-free rate (RFR) and one or more risk premiums. The RFR is a rate of return that a government bond with a similar maturity to the investment's time horizon earns. The RFR compensates the investor for expected inflation, the premium for forgoing consumption (often estimated to be the long-run growth rate in the economy), and the prevailing relative ease or tightness of credit. When used in its normal context, the build-up method assumes that the two key risk premiums that every risky equity investment should earn are the RFR and the equity risk premium (the required rate of return over the RFR that should be earned on a fully diversified equity portfolio—ERP).

In addition to the RFR and the ERP, two other widely accepted risk premiums can be applied to provide a complete and more specific estimate of the appropriate risk-adjusted rate of return for a single risky asset. These two commonly used risk premiums are industry risk premium (IRP) and company size premium (SP). The IRP reflects the risk that is inherent in the type of industry the company operates in. The SP may also be added in to account for the risk attributed to the company's size. Thus, the build-up method is in essence the sum of all of these historically derived risk premiums. Below is a template for visualizing the method.

The Build-Up Method

The risk-free rate (RFR)	+_____
The equity risk premium (ERP)	+_____
The industry risk premium (IRP)	+_____
Company size premium (SP)	+_____
Estimated cost of equity (RRR_{equity})	_____

Detailed studies are available for the estimation of these various risk premiums. Historical data are used to provide average values, which can be used to approximate the various premiums. One of the better providers of these data is Ibbotson's *SBBI Valuation Yearbook* (e.g., 2012). This data source gives estimates of each of the four premiums that have been discussed. Tables 7.1 to 7.4 are excerpted from the 2013 edition of the Morningstar book.

Table 7.1 Ibbotson Associates' Risk-Free Rate

						U.S. Treasury Bills: Total Returns								
Year	Jan	Feb	Mar	Apr	May	Jun	Jul	Aug	Sep	Oct	Nov	Dec	Year	Jan–Dec[a]
2008	0.0021	0.0013	0.0017	0.0018	0.0018	0.0017	0.0015	0.0013	0.0015	0.0008	0.0003	0.0000	2008	0.0160
2009	0.0000	0.0001	0.0002	0.0001	0.0000	0.0001	0.0001	0.0001	0.0001	0.0000	0.0000	0.0001	2009	0.0010
2010	0.0000	0.0000	0.0001	0.0001	0.0001	0.0001	0.0001	0.0001	0.0001	0.0001	0.0001	0.0001	2010	0.0012
2011	0.0001	0.0001	0.0001	0.0000	0.0000	0.0000	0.0000	0.0001	0.0000	0.0000	0.0000	0.0000	2011	0.0004
2012	0.0000	0.0000	0.0000	0.0000	0.0001	0.00000	0.0000	0.0001	0.0001	0.0001	0.0001	0.0001	2012	0.0006

Source: Ibbotson Associates (2012).

a. Compound annual return.

Table 7.2   Ibbotson Associates' Market Risk Premium

	Value (%)
Long-horizon expected equity risk premium (historical): large company stock total returns minus long-term government bond income returns	6.70
Long-horizon expected equity risk premium (supply side): historical equity risk premium minus price-to-earnings ratio calculated using 3-year average earnings	6.11

Source: Ibbotson Associates (2012).

Table 7.3   Ibbotson Associates' Industry Risk Premium: Industry Premia Estimates Through Year-End 2012

SIC Code	Short Description	Number of Companies	Industry Premia
	Agriculture, Forestry, and Fishing		
01	Agricultural Production Crops	16	−1.24
017	Fruits and Tree Nuts	9	−1.08
02	Agricultural Production—Livestock & Animal Specialties	5	−2.08
07	Agricultural Services	8	−0.47
08	Forestry	6	0.69
	Mining		
10	Metal Mining	55	2.90
104	Gold and Silver Ores	22	−2.91
1041	Gold Ores	20	−3.11

Source: Ibbotson Associates (2012).

While the presentation given here is basic, it does capture the gist of the build-up process. There are various arguments about how to further process historical premium data to make them even more accurate or theoretically "pure." For example, some academics and practitioners argue that SP data

Table 7.4   Ibbotson Associates' Size Premium

Decile	Market Capitalization of Smallest Company (in Millions of U.S. Dollars)	Market Capitalization of Largest Company (in Millions of U.S. Dollars)	Size Premium (Return in Excess of CAPM) (%)
Mid-cap (3–5)	1,912.240	7,686.611	1.12
Low cap (6–8)	514.459	1,909.051	1.85
Micro-cap (9–10)	1.139	514.209	3.81

Source: Ibbotson Associates (2012).

should be adjusted for the asset **Beta;** other arguments are made about the time frame of premium data that should be used, the length of the time frame that should be considered, or even the type of smoothing (if any) that should be applied to the data. There is always the problem of dealing with the problem of using historical data to project future performance. For more information, Ibbotson Associates (2012) provides an in-depth analysis.

Capital Asset Pricing Model (CAPM). The capital asset pricing model (CAPM) is among the most common techniques used to estimate the cost of equity. The central insight of CAPM is that the expected return of a single risky asset is related to the relationship between its unique risk profile and the risk profile of a fully diversified portfolio of risky assets (the market portfolio [MP]). In a traditional CAPM view, there are essentially three different types of risk premiums. As was the case with the build-up method, the starting point is the premium for an appropriate maturity government security (i.e., the RFR), previously explained. Like the build-up method, CAPM is based on the assumption that taking systemic risk (risk associated with economic cycles, environmental events, and political activity) is rewarded by a risk premium that is added to the RFR. Just as with the build-up method, this additional premium is called the market's equity risk premium (ERP).

To deal with the unique risk and return characteristics of a single risky asset, the CAPM makes the assumption that the risk premium of a single risky asset is proportionate to the risk premium of the fully diversified market portfolio. Thus, a coefficient that expresses this proportionality is the best way of explaining the risk premium of the single risky asset. That coefficient

(Beta) when multiplied by the ERP will yield the single asset's risk premium (ARP). (When dealing with equity securities, ERP * Beta is equal to the firm-specific risk premium [FSRP].)

The ARP is proportionate to the degree of co-movement (Beta) of the single asset's returns in excess of the RFR with the returns of a diversified market portfolio return in excess of the RFR. It is important to note that the size effect is not captured by CAPM in its traditional formulation. (However, CAPM can be modified to adjust for a unique size premium [SP]). The following is the CAPM formula:

$$RRR = RFR + (RM - RFR)Beta_{single\ asset}$$

where

RRR = the required risk adjusted rate of return for a single risky equity asset;

RFR = the required rate of return on an appropriate maturity government security;

(RM – RFR) = the equity risk premium (ERP) where the total return of the market is estimated as RM;

$Beta_{single\ asset}$ = Beta or the unique risk coefficient for a single risky asset.

There are two main differences between the build-up method and CAPM. The first difference is that the values for the ERP are viewed in a slightly different manner. The build-up method uses historical data and either an arithmetic average or geometric average to condense that data into usable form. The CAPM method views the ERP similarly but defines the ERP as having a Beta coefficient of 1.0 along a line (it is called the security market line [SML]) defined by the CAPM equation (see above for the equation and Chart 7.2 for the graphical representation). For assets that have Betas other than 1.0, their expected return will plot in the part of the line defined by the CAPM formula. In the CAPM equation, if the Beta is 1.0, then the RRR solution to the equation will be the model's estimate of the current required rate of return for the market portfolio.

The second difference is that the two methods deal differently with computing the RRR of a single asset. The build-up method "builds up" the sum of the RFR and the market's equity risk premium (ERP) to estimate the risky asset's unique risk premium (ARP) by adding in a premium for industry risk (IRP) and a premium for firm size (SP). CAPM relates the "volatility" of a

Chart 7.2 The Security Market Line

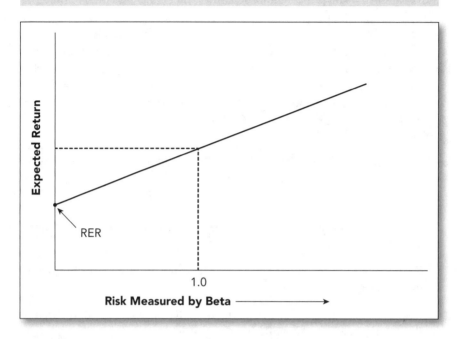

single asset's risk premium to the "volatility" of the market risk premium via a single and unique risk coefficient (Beta). If we plot the per-period change in the risk premium of the market versus the per-period change in the risk premium of a single risky asset and perform regression analysis on the resulting data points, we will get the characteristic line (CL) for that single asset. The slope of the CL is Beta for the single asset. (Remember, Beta is the coefficient that relates the risk premium of the single asset to the risk premium of the market [ERP].) Chart 7.3 demonstrates this concept graphically. Generally, **Alpha** is the average return attributed to the firm-specific risk premium (FSRP) that should be expected when the market's return attributed to the market's risk premium (ERP) is zero.

Gordon Growth Model (aka Dividend Growth Model). In addition to the build-up method and CAPM, the *Gordon growth model* is also used to compute the cost of equity. (This model is also referred to as a continuous growth model.) The model is based on the idea that all firms pay dividends (even if that means that they will pay only a terminating dividend). Furthermore, it assumes that all firms have dividends that will grow at some average rate over the very long term. Finally, the model requires a known or given current price or value for the equity value of the firm being analyzed.

Chart 7.3   The Characteristic Line

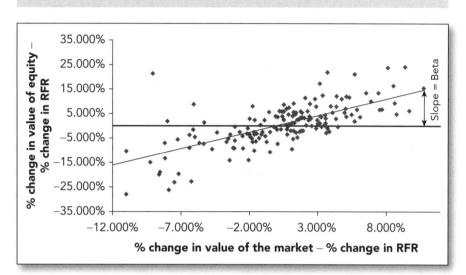

Because the Gordon growth model depends on knowing the current value of the firm's equity before it can be used to compute its RRR on that equity, this model is not quite as useful when trying to determine the RRR equity for firms where the firm's value is unknown and being sought. To use the Gordon growth model in situation compute the cost of equity capital (RRR_{equity}) of a peer group of publicly traded companies and then use an average or weight value made up of these various costs of equity to infer the RRR for the equity for the target firm.

The steps in producing an estimate of an RRR on equity for a specific firm are as follows:

1. Identify some publicly traded firms that serve as a peer group (i.e., dividend paying, same industry, and similar size).

2. For each peer group firm, identify the current dividend.

3. For each peer group firm, estimate the long-run growth rate of the firm's dividends.

4. For each peer group firm, obtain the current market price.

For each peer group firm, plug the variables into the Gordon growth formula (arranged to compute RRR of equity.

$$RRR_{equity} = [D_0 \, (1 + g) \, / \, P_0] + g$$

where

D_0 = the firms' current dividend;

g = the long-term growth rate in the firm's dividends

P_0 = the firm's current market price.

Once the required rate of return for each of the peer group firms has been calculated, the required rate of return values can be averaged together, weighted based on their market capitalization, weighted together in proportion to their Beta coefficients, or otherwise combined to present a proxy for the RRR of equity of the peer group. This resulting RRR can then be used as a proxy for the RRR of the target equity.

There are potential problems with this approach:

1. There may not be a sufficient sample of dividend-paying and publicly traded peer group firms.

2. The sample of peer group firms chosen may have operating leverage, financial leverage, or exposure to foreign exchange rate movements that are uncharacteristic of the industry.

3. The target firm may have operating leverage, financial leverage, foreign exchange exposure, or a technology that is atypical of the industry.

4. It is often difficult to estimate either the dividend or the long-term dividend growth rate.

With respect to all of these methods—the build-up, CAPM, and the Gordon growth model—results are imprecise. The data that all of these methods are based on are historical; the assumptions about what time horizons to use in analyzing the data and whether to use a methodology that adjusts the data by averaging, weighting, or applying statistically based adjustments all affect the ultimate results that are computed. There is virtually no empirical proof that any of these techniques of computing RRR of equity is consistently accurate. The best data need to be used and several methods of analysis applied to generate a range of RRR values that embrace probable RRR of equity.

The Cost of Debt (RRR_{debt})

Most firms have some debt in their capital structure, so calculating the RRR on this debt is a common part of the WACC computation. Unlike equity, the models for assessing the "cost" of debt are few and simple to employ.

The key difference to remember when calculating the RRR on debt is that it must be done on an after-tax basis. The cost of equity capital and the cost of preferred stock are not deductible expenses for tax purposes, but the cost of debt is and, as such, needs to be adjusted for the tax subsidy that the deductibility provides, particularly in the United States.

In its most basic form, the RRR of debt is the interest rate on the debt multiplied by $(1 - T)$, where T is the firm's overall tax rate. However, it is not always the case that interest rate multiplied by $(1 - T)$ is the best estimate for RRR of debt. Over time, the firm's creditworthiness may change, interest rates may change or be variable, lenders may impose commitment fees or upfront lending charges, or the firm may be coming up to a point where its debt is due and it will have to refinance its debt at prevailing higher or lower rates. Some thought should be given to what interest rate will best describe the RRR on debt for the company over the foreseeable future. The basic RRR on debt is as follows:

$$RRR_{debt} = IR \ (1 - T)$$

where

IR = interest rate on debt;

T = the marginal tax rate at the firm.

The value of IR must be adjusted if the interest rate is stepped up or down or pegged to some index, there are upfront loan commitment fees, or there are upfront lending charges. These adjustments are specified in Table 7.5.

A final issue is the consideration of certain mitigating contingencies. The most often encountered contingency is that refinancing is planned or

Table 7.5   Adjustments to Debt Interest Rate for Contingencies

Circumstance	Adjustments	Formula
If the IR is stepped up or down	Use an expected average IR	$IR_{ADJ} = {}^{\wedge}IR_{average}$
If the IR is pegged to an index	Use an expected average IR	$IR_{ADJ} = {}^{\wedge}IR_{average}$
If the lender charges an upfront commitment or loan fee	Adjust IR to account for fee	$IR_{ADJ} = (IR \times Principal$ of Loan$)/($Principal of Loan $-$ Fee$)$

required by the firm's current situation. In this case, the renewal cost of the loan may be substituted for the current cost. Other issues that should be considered are whether the existing or the new loan will involve step-up or step-down interest rates, commitment fees, or variable loan fees. If this is the case, then the adjustments for these features should also be applied to the interest cost of the debt. These adjustments are detailed in Table 7.5.

Once adjustments to the basic interest cost of debt are made per Table 7.5, then computing the RRR on the debt can be done using the following basic equation (except that IR will now be $IR_{adjusted}$):

$$RRR_{debt} = IR_{adjusted} (1 - T)$$

where

$IR_{adjusted}$ = interest rate on debt (IR) adjusted for contingencies;

T = the marginal tax rate at the firm.

If different debt issues are present, then each issue should have its RRR calculated, and the resulting RRRs should be weighted proportionately with respect to their participation in the component. For example, if Debt A has an $RRR_{debt A}$ = 4% and Debt A is 25% of the long-term debt portion of firm capital, and Debt B has an $RRR_{debt B}$ = 8% and Debt B is 75% of the long-term debt portion of firm capital, then Debt A should contribute 1% (.25*4%) to the long-term debt portion of firm capital and Debt B should contribute 6% (.75*8%).

The Cost of Preferred Stock (RRR$_{pfd}$)

Preferred stock is called a hybrid security because it has elements that make it similar to both debt and equity. Sometimes it is referred to as "quasi-debt" and sometimes "quasi-equity." The fact that it comes behind debt in liquidation priority makes it appear to be equity. The fact that it pays a regular dividend that has precedence over the common dividend makes it appear to be a debt. Dividends paid on preferred stock are not tax deductible so, unlike with debt, there is no tax subsidy to account for when computing the required rate of return on preferred stock (RRR_{pfd}).

The most basic model may be used to compute the RRR_{pfd}:

$$RRR_{pfd} = D_{pfd}/Par_{pfd}$$

where

D_{pfd} = the constant dividend in dollars per preferred share;

Par_{pfd} = the par value in dollars of one preferred share.

Two adjustments can be made to this model if circumstances require it:

If the dividend is not constant, then D_{pfd} may be replaced with the average expected dividend (i.e., $D_{average}$). If there is a market price per share or an agreed price per share that is not equal to the par value per share, then that value ($MKTVAL_{pfd}$) may be substituted for the par value per share. If there are different classes of preferred stock outstanding, just as was the case with different debt issues, then each class of preferred stock should have its RRR developed and should be weighted proportionately to all other preferred classes to calculate the RRR for the preferred stock component of capital.

International Issues With Respect to RRR Calculations for Capital Components

A number of issues are currently subject to debate and discussion regarding estimating WACC in an international environment.

The first issue is what the appropriate risk-free rate (RFR) is. Generally, most practitioners and many academics suggest that the choice of the RFR should be governed by two requirements.

1. It should be the rate of return on a government bond that is of a maturity that is consistent with the valuation being performed. This means it should have a maturity that is representative of the time horizon of the data being analyzed. If we are valuing an investment and anticipate liquidating it in 5 years, then the current yield-to-maturity on a 5-year maturity government security should be used as the RFR. If we are valuing the business as a going concern and the time horizon is longer, then the yield-to-maturity of a 10-year or even 20-year government security should be used as a proxy for our RFR.

2. The RFR chosen would ideally be obtained from a government debt that is indigenous to the location where the firm's capital has been raised and the asset being valued resides. If these are different locations, then the place where the capital is being raised is the venue in which to perform the calculation.

Second, a firm's WACC should be derived from data from within the markets where the firm will raise its capital. However, the country that a firm raises its capital in may or may not have information available that would allow for the computation of an equity risk premium (ERP), industry risk premiums (IRP), firm size premium (SP), and/or equity Beta (Beta$_{equity}$). There are a number of possible solutions to this lack of data:

1. The appropriate RFR rate should be readily available since virtually all sovereign governments issue debt.

2. The ERP can be derived from the equity market where the capital has been raised or the asset resides.

3. If data are not available to permit the ERP calculation referenced above, sometimes it's possible to find data that present a unique country-based risk premium that can be added to the U.S.-derived ERP premium to build up to an MRP for the country in question (Ibbotson Associates, 2012).

4. Calculating Beta$_{equity}$ for a security cannot be done without historical prices for the security and the corresponding RFR and ERP. If the ability to calculate Beta$_{equity}$ is not present, then Beta$_{equity}$ can be estimated by computing an average Beta$_{equity}$ of representative U.S. peer group firms, or an average Beta$_{equity}$ for a peer from some other country venue can be computed.

Making the Weighted Average Cost of Capital (WACC) Computation

WACC is a computational methodology designed to identify the appropriate overall risk-adjusted rate or return on a firm's assets that compensates each capital provider on a risk-adjusted basis. That is why RRR is computed for each component of capital individually with models that are specific to the component. After all, the firm's capital comes from a wide range of providers: lenders, preferred stockholders, and equity owners. Providers of capital have different risk and return tolerances with respect to their position in the company's capital structure. WACC is the dollar-weighted combination of each capital provider's risk-adjusted RRR, and it is specific to each capital provider's investment into the various components of the capital structure of the company.

What Is the Firm's Capital Structure?

The capital structure of the firm is the long-term portion of the right-hand side of the balance sheet (i.e., long-term debt, preferred stock, and shareholder equity).

The Firm's Capital Structure

Long-term debt minus current portion	+_____
Preferred stock	+_____
Shareholder equity	+_____
Total long-term capital	_____

All current liabilities are left out of this calculation. For example, the firm's accounts payable, notes payable, or current portion of long-term debt are not considered a part of the firm's long-term capital. These current liabilities are called "spontaneous" liabilities, and they change with day-to-day business activity. Essentially, they are internally financed at most firms with accumulated cash and ongoing accounts receivable collections. It is the providers of the long-term components that we are concerned with when we compute the firm's WACC.

Summary and Special Notes Regarding the WACC Computation

For the WACC formula, the difficulty is not in computing WACC but in how to compute the required rate of return (RRR) for all components of capital that are weighted together to produce WACC. In previous sections of this chapter, some issues have been addressed that complicate the WACC computation. Some of these issues are the following:

1. How is the RRR computed on a particular component of capital?

2. How are adjustments made for special circumstances, such as when market values are available for debt or preferred stock or interest payments or preferred stock dividends are stepped up or down or pegged to a particular index?

3. What security should be used to obtain the RFR when the company is raising its capital in a country other than the United States?

4. What should be used as the $Beta_{equity}$ coefficient in the CAPM model when the company is raising its capital in a country other than the United States?

All of these issues and others complicate the process of determining the appropriate value for WACC is. Our advice is to try to use enough judgment so that the various RRR calculations consider as many of the unique firm circumstances as possible. Also, we suggest that the ranges of value for WACC be calculated. High, low, and expected or average possibilities can be used to produce a range of values when the WACC value is used in the DCF approach to valuing the firm.

There is much discussion about exactly what WACC is and how it should be used. It is important to understand this issue; while WACC is a useful, unique idea, there are some weaknesses embedded in the WACC concept. In addition, the related concept of the marginal cost of capital (MCC) is important to understand. Key ideas relating to WACC and MCC are the following:

1. WACC is the combined required rate of return that earns the appropriate "risk-adjusted" rate of return on each component of firm capital. WACC is constructed in such a way to ensure that all capital providers are adequately compensated for the perceived riskiness of their position within the firm's overall capital structure.

2. When using WACC as the required rate of return in capital budgeting problems, we assume that the capital structure at the firm does not change. This is not likely to be the case, particularly in the long run.

3. When changes in the capital structure of the firm are made, changes in WACC will also change by necessity. This is because (1) the relative weights of capital components will change, and (2) the costs of any or all capital components will change. When the costs of the capital components and the weights of the components within the capital structure are recalculated after such a change, the result is not called WACC but marginal cost of capital (MCC).

4. If changes made to the firm's capital structure have occurred, then the issuance cost of new debt, preferred stock, or equity needs to be considered when calculating their new costs to produce MCC.

Capital Budgeting

A capital budgeting problem can be thought of as a valuation problem; we want to value projects that consume firm capital to ensure that the projects produce positive present values when the firm's WACC or MCC is used as the discount rate. Another way to think of it is to evaluate the internal rate of return on a capital project to determine if it is equal to or higher than the firm's WACC or MCC. The classic capital budgeting example is the sell Machine A and buy Machine B problem. Indeed, this is the problem that Mill Pro is facing in the case at the beginning of this chapter.

One thing to keep in mind is that capital budgeting problems are timeline types of problems. Benefits and costs need to be projected based on both their magnitude and their place in time. Capital budgeting problems should focus on determining the amounts of cash flow for each relevant position on the timeline. The cash flows need to be computed on an after-tax basis.

Example of a Capital Budgeting Problem

Suppose that Mill Pro wants to decide if it should sell a machine (Machine A) that it currently owns and buy a new machine (Machine B), which is a machine that has improved technology and will improve Mill Pro's gross profit margin by $150,000 per year on an after-tax basis (see Table 7.6). A number of steps need to be done to perform the analysis:

1. The first step in the process is to calculate the WACC at the firm (or the MCC if new capital will need to be raised). For the purposes of this example, we have assumed a capital structure and costs of each capital component as shown in Table 7.7. In our example, we specify that the firm does not need to seek additional capital to effect the sale of Machine A and purchase of Machine B, and thus WACC will be the appropriate rate of return we should use in the "sell Machine A and buy Machine B" analysis. (If the firm were to raise new capital, then the appropriate rate of return to use in the problem would be the MCC.) Also in Table 7.7, you will find the calculation of the weight for each component of capital and the product of weight times the after-tax cost for each component (W*K). By adding all of the "W*K" products, we can calculate the WACC for the capital structure found in Table 7.7.

2. The second step that is necessary is to assess the costs that would be incurred at the front end. This would involve estimating the after-tax consequences of the sale of Machine A. Table 7.8 shows the analysis of the sale of Machine A. The result of selling Machine A is that the firm receives $488,000 ($600,000 in sales proceeds—$112,000 in taxes on the sale). The costs associated with the purchase of Machine B are found in Table 7.9.

Table 7.6   Change in After-Tax Operating Cash Flow per Period

After Tax Operating Cash Flow (CF)	
Change in operating profit	$208,333
Tax impact	$58,333
After tax change in CF	$150,000

Table 7.7 WACC Cost of Capital Example

	Cost of Capital				
Component of Capital	Amount (in U.S. Dollars)	Weight (%)	K Component (%)	K * (1 – T) (%)	W * K (%)
Long-term debt–current portion[a]	500,000.00	20	6.00	4.32	0.86
Preferred stock[b]	200,000.00	8	10.00		0.80
Equity					
Capital at par	250,000.00				
Paid in surplus	750,000.00				
Retained earnings	800,000.00				
Total equity	1,800,000.00	72	17		12.24
Total capital	2,500,000.00	100.00			
				WACC =	13.90

a. The interest on debt is tax deductible. Tax rate = 28%.
b. Preferred stock is based on $2.50 annual dividend and $25 price.

Table 7.8 Machine A (at Sale)

Machine A (at Sale)	
Initial price	$400,000.00
Book value	$200,000.00
Sale price	$600,000.00
Tax on $400,000 gain	$(112,000.00)
Life of machine (years)	20
Depreciation per year	$20,000.00

Table 7.9   Initial Net After-Tax Costs

CF at $N = 0$	
Sell Machine A	
Sale Machine A	$600,000.00
± Tax	$(112,000.00)
Total cash inflow	$488,000.00
Buy Machine B	
Price	$(800,000.00)
+ Delivery	$(75,000.00)
+ Installation	$(50,000.00)
+ Testing	$(25,000.00)
Total cash outflow	$(950,000.00)
Total cash flow	$(462,000.00)
Tax rate	28%

3. The third step in the process is to identify the initial net after-tax costs. Table 7.9 shows how these costs are calculated. Note from Table 7.9 that the initial after-tax cash investment required to make the switch between Machine A and Machine B is $462,000.

4. The fourth step is to estimate the amount of the change in periodic cash flows. We already know the after-tax impact on operating revenues. This calculation is shown in Table 7.6. In the day-to-day world, this amount would have been determined by management's review of the impact on sales or costs that would flow from the purchase of Machine B and is case specific. Another factor that affects the periodic cash flow is the change in working capital (WC). An increase in WC represents a cash outflow, while a decrease represents a cash inflow. In this case, the increase in WC is given, but in the day-to-day world, this would also be estimated by management (see Table 7.10). To solve this problem, management would analyze the impact on WC resulting from a change in sales, costs, or both sales and

costs. Finally, any change in depreciation produces either a loss or gain in tax benefits associated with the depreciation. In the case we are dealing with, we see that depreciation goes up, and thus the associated tax benefit also goes up (see Tables 7.11 and 7.12).

5. The final step is to calculate the impacts that occur at the end of Machine B's useful life. Table 7.13 shows this calculation. To estimate the after-tax cash flows that occur at the terminal date of the project, the after-tax cash flow from the sale of Machine B ($450,000 – $126,000 of tax) must be calculated, resulting in the final change in WC ($25,000).

Once all of these numbers have been calculated, the next task is to place the numbers on a timeline so as to locate them at their respective places in the overall project. Table 7.14 indicates where these various sums should be placed on the timeline.

The final task is to calculate the sum of the present value of all the cash flows at a discount rate that is equal to the firm's risk-adjusted rate

Table 7.10   After-Tax Total Cash Flow per Period

Operational CF at $N = 1$ through $N = 10$	
Change in after-tax CF	$150,000.00
Change in WC	$(25,000.00)
Change in depreciation * T	$21,000.00
Total cash flow	$146,000.00

Table 7.11   Machine B (at Sale)

Machine B (at Sale)	
Initial price	$950,000.00
Book value	—
Sale price	$450,000.00
Life of machine (years)	10
Depreciation per year	$95,000.00

Table 7.12 After-Tax Change in Depreciation

After-Tax Change in Depreciation	
Depreciation A	$20,000.00
Depreciation B	$95,000.00
Difference	$75,000.00
Tax rate	28%
Change in depreciation * T	$21,000.00

Table 7.13 Estimate After-Tax Cash Flows That Occur at the Terminal Date of the Project

Terminal CF at $N = 10$	
Sell Machine B	
Gain on Machine B	$450,000.00
±Tax	$(126,000.00)
±Working capital	$25,000.00
Total cash flow	$349,000.00

of return, which is either WACC or MCC depending on whether new capital or changes in the initial capital structure were needed to fund the project. Table 7.15 shows this calculation. As can be seen in the table, the present value of all the respective cash flows is $397,351.74. Since this sum is the combination of the present value of both costs and benefits and the sum is positive, the project should be funded. Management may also calculate the **internal rate of return (IRR)** on the project. IRR is the rate of return that makes the present value of project costs equal to the present value of project benefits. (Computing this number may be arrived at by iteration or by employing the aid of a basic financial calculator with the Excel function.) In this case, the IRR is found in Table 7.15 and is 31.06%. Since this rate of return is higher than the firm's WACC, the project should be funded.

Table 7.14 Timeline

	Years										
	0	1	2	3	4	5	6	7	8	9	10
Terminal CF	—	—	—	—	—	—	—	—	—	—	$349,000.00
Operating CF	—	$146,000.00	$146,000.00	$146,000.00	$146,000.00	$146,000.00	$146,000.00	$146,000.00	$146,000.00	$146,000.00	$146,000.00
Initial CF	$(462,000.00)	—	—	—	—	—	—	—	—	—	—
Total CF	$(462,000.00)	$146,000.00	$146,000.00	$146,000.00	$146,000.00	$146,000.00	$146,000.00	$146,000.00	$146,000.00	$146,000.00	$495,000.00

Table 7.15 Net Present Value and Internal Rate of Return

	Present Value	Years									
		1	2	3	4	5	6	7	8	9	10
Discounted terminal CF	$94,937.04	—	—	—	—	—	—	—	—	—	$94,937.04
Discounted operating CF	$764,414.70	$128,178.11	$112,531.71	$98,795.22	$86,735.51	$76,147.91	$66,852.71	$58,692.15	$51,527.73	$45,237.86	$39,715.78
Discounted initial CF	$(462,000.00)	—	—	—	—	—	—	—	—	—	—
Discounted total CF	$397,351.74	$128,178.11	$112,531.71	$98,795.22	$86,735.51	$76,147.91	$66,852.71	$58,692.15	$51,527.73	$45,237.86	$134,652.82
WACC	13.90%					NPV @ WACC	$397,351.74				
						IRR	31.06%				

If management is faced with a capital budgeting problem where the sale of an old asset is not involved, the methodology outlined above will still work. There will just be no input for the sale of the old asset.

Summary

Cost of capital and capital budgeting are essential subjects to know when assessing the value of a firm, determining the value of an intangible asset, or contemplating making an investment in a capital project. All firms, regardless of size, need to earn the appropriate risk-adjusted rate of return on the assets they deploy. If they do not, then the firms are failing in their duty to pay each provider of capital the appropriate after-tax rate of return. If the firm has internal funds, then it should always view the investment of those funds in new capital projects in light of what the firm's WACC is. If the firm contemplates raising new capital to invest in capital projects, then it should always view the investment of those funds in new capital projects in light of what the firm's MCC is. This is because the alternative to any capital investment is to return funds to capital providers by paying off debt and/or buying back preferred stock or equity. Viewed this way, it is apparent that spending money on capital projects must be justified by earning at least WACC (or if relevant MCC) on those investments.

Chapter 8

Valuation

Learning Objectives

- To know the nuances of the concept of "value"

- To understand the valuation process

- To be able to do a valuation

Case: Franks Brothers LLC

Robert Franks was worried. Since his brother Bill died, Robert's whole life had been turned upside down. He had lost his brother and trusted business partner, and now there were problems with Bill's widow, Marta.

The business had been doing fine, but now Marta was faced with a potentially high and almost impossible-to-pay estate tax assessment. Because of this potential tax bill and her desire to get as much money as possible, Marta was demanding that Robert buy her out of the business. And she was asking a very high price, a much higher price than Robert had money to pay.

Seventeen years ago, Robert and Bill had gone to an attorney to have a "buy-sell" agreement written. The agreement specified that should one of them die or become incapacitated, then the remaining brother would have the option to buy out the interests of the brother who had died or who was incapacitated. If a buyout did not take place within 1 year, then the survivors had the right to sell their share of the business on the open market. There were 6 months left until the option expired.

The root of the present problem was that the price that was to be used in the buyout was to be determined by an appraisal of the business. Marta hired an appraiser who had determined that the price should be higher than anything Robert had felt was reasonable. This high value was also the cause of the high estate tax estimate. Lately, Marta was becoming more strident and vocal about her desire to be bought out, and the situation was beginning to cause general friction in the family as members of the family began to take sides in the matter.

When Robert talked with Marta's appraiser about how the firm's value was determined, Robert was told that the appraiser had looked at analogous public firms with similar growth rates to Franks Brothers and then applied a similar price to equity, price to book, and price to sales ratio to Franks Brothers LLC to determine the firm's value without making any adjustments, such as the fact that Franks Brothers was privately held.

Seventeen years ago, when the buyout agreement was signed, the business had been struggling, but now it was growing rapidly. This rapid growth has been consuming more and more working capital. Since Bill's death, Robert needed to pledge most of his personal assets to securing the working capital loan from the bank to finance this rapid growth. This loan also prevented the company from borrowing additional funds to pay Marta.

To complicate matters more, Bill owned only 45% of the business at the time of his death. Several years prior to his death, Bill had given shares representing 5% of the company to his alma mater. So the share of the business that Marta had to sell was not a controlling interest.

To further complicate the situation, a longtime employee of the company had felt that one of her supervisors had acted improperly toward her; she had quit and was suing the firm for sexual discrimination and harassment. If the company lost the suit, the damages could be substantial.

Robert decided to become more knowledgeable about the process involved in valuing nonpublic businesses. He realized there were many aspects to the Franks Brothers situation that were unique:

1. The company was closely held, and Bill held the controlling interest. Marta was selling shares representing a minority interest.

2. The company did not trade in the public market and had no established market price to determine the firm's value.

3. The company was growing rapidly and was highly leveraged.

4. The employee lawsuit represented a substantial contingent liability.

5. Any appraisal would need to hold up in court, as there could be legal actions with respect to Marta and the employee suit.

Robert now knew that establishing the value of an entrepreneurial venture is complicated and definitely not straightforward. He was resolved to learn about valuing entrepreneurial privately held ventures.

Valuing any risky asset is not always as straightforward as it may seem. If no value can be established in a public market, then the problem of establishing value becomes more difficult. If there is no value that exists in a public market, then what does the concept of value entail? Is the value what two parties agree to? Is it what the accounting records of the firm indicate? Is value what an expert says it is? If valuing were as simple as providing answers to these questions, then parties would rarely disagree on what it is.

The most basic concept of value is that any risky asset is worth the present value of all expected future cash flows discounted back to the present at an appropriate risk-adjusted required rate of return. If we accept this concept, then two problems arise: What are those future cash flows (how certain are they, at what intervals do they occur, and how long do they last), and what is the appropriate risk-adjusted rate of return?

When valuing entrepreneurial privately held ventures, the inherent cash generation of the firm is important, but so are other features of the firm, such as technology, growth, management, industry sector, and strategy. Research into exit strategies for firms financed by private equity sources indicates that 74% of the exits are implemented through those firms being acquired by strategic buyers (i.e., another firm or investor with interest in the industry); about 20% of the exits are implemented through initial public offerings (IPOs) in the public market, and the remaining are through some specialized vehicle like a management buyout, Employee Stock Ownership Plan, trade sale, or a transfer to a family member (Dwivedi et al., 2012).

Since most entrepreneurial ventures are not ultimately sold in public market transactions, the concept of value and the constituents of value become even more key to the entrepreneur's understanding of the potential outcomes—a sale to another firm in the industry, a sale to another businessperson, a sale to a private equity firm, a conveyance to a family member, or a sale through an initial public offering.

Given these outcomes, except for the last one, a range of concepts is needed that describes value under different environments. Each of these concepts exists with the sole purpose of fulfilling a particular role in determining the standards that should be applied to the valuation process under different circumstances. Chart 8.1 presents a schematic representation of the material covered in this chapter.

Chart 8.1   Schematic of Chapter 8

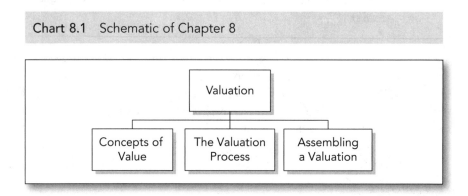

Concepts of Value

Value is generated in many ways; each form may be a composite of one or more sources of value—for example, cash flow, intellectual property, tax impacts, enterprise control, liquidity, or marketability. All or any portion of these sources of value may be relevant at a particular point in time or under a particular circumstance. Depending on the circumstances and context in which the question is being asked, value may take the forms identified below. According to Zukin (1990), the different concepts of value are situational and understood based on the context from which they arise:

> Value cannot be used in isolation. The meaning of value can change, depending upon the context within which the term is used. Lack of clarity concerning these concepts often leads to material disagreements in specific valuations. Therefore, the term should never be used unless defined. (pp. 2–3)

The idea that there can be a number of interpretations of value is a critical first step in understanding valuation in general. Each valuation performed is situational and case specific, and each case drives the person doing the valuation to rely on different types of information, to emphasize different value streams, to consider different timetables over which those benefits occur, and to choose appropriate techniques to employ when considering the stream of benefits. In litigation, arbitration, tax appraisals, and face-to-face negotiations, the relevance of any specific estimate of value is highly dependent on the context and the audience. Ultimately, context drives the choice of valuation technique, type of data relied on, and certainty of conclusion. The American Society of Appraisers (ASA), various courts, government agencies (e.g., Internal Revenue Service [IRS]), and most authors in the field agree that seven types of value are routinely considered. Furthermore, these different valuation scenarios rely on different techniques and emphasize different sources of information and different aspects of value.

1. **Fair Market Value.** This is the most common definition of value. Fair market value is the value at which an asset will change hands when the exchange is between a willing buyer and a willing seller when neither is acting under compulsion and both have a reasonable knowledge of relevant facts. This definition is used by the IRS and the ASA and often referred to simply as *market value*. Market value implies a sale in an impartial market where it is not necessary for the buyer and seller to be face-to-face or to know each other but rather for the transaction to take place in an organized market that has a good supply of buyers and sellers (i.e., marketability) and where the trading action in the market produces regular price movements over time (i.e., liquidity). An example of such a market would be a public stock exchange like the New York Stock Exchange.

2. **Fair Value.** This concept of value often arises in the context of shareholder or owner disputes. This concept is usually related to some

judicial proceedings, for example, a shareholder derivative suit. When developing an opinion of fair value, the standard of practice associated with fair value is to consider all aspects of value that might reasonably affect the asset's value. Such factors would include the market value of comparable assets, cash flows, unique asset values, investment value, and any other factor that may affect the value of the asset subject to the proceeding.

3. **Investment Value.** This is the value that an enterprise has to a specific owner or purchaser. This concept of value is based on the purchaser or owner having special knowledge, expectations, or abilities that permit that purchaser or owner to generate enhanced value through exploitation of a specific niche or through synergy with another entity or firm.

4. **Going-Concern Value.** Two definitions of *going-concern value* are favored by the ASA:

a. The value of an enterprise or an interest in an enterprise as a "going concern"

b. The intangible value of a business enterprise that exists as a result of having a trained workforce, all of the necessary zoning and permits and licenses, having an operational plant with operational procedures, and systems in place.

The value implied under part "a" above is that there is value in being a part of an industry or community of firms within an industry. That value will be enhanced or diminished by other firm-specific characteristics, but first and foremost, there is value in simply being a part of the community of firms. With respect to part "b," the implication is that specific core competencies do, in fact, act as reservoirs of value.

5. **Liquidation Value.** There are two types of liquidation value: orderly liquidation and auction value. Conceptually, these two values differ in the time frame it takes to realize results and in the efficiency with which top values are obtained. The time frame is shortest for the auction, which can happen almost immediately, with an orderly liquidation consuming between 6 and 9 months. An estimate of the proceeds of an orderly liquidation is usually higher than the proceeds of an auction because an orderly liquidation presumes that end user purchasers can be found for the various assets of the firm, while the auction value is usually not as efficient at realizing top-dollar prices because many of the purchasers at an auction are usually not end users.

6. Book Value. The definitions of book value favored by the ASA are as follows:

    a. With respect to specific assets, it is the capitalized cost of the asset less accumulated depreciation or amortization as it appears on the books and records of the enterprise.

    b. With respect to a business enterprise, book value is the difference between total assets (net of depreciation, depletion, and amortization) and total liabilities as they appear on the books and records of the enterprise (it is synonymous with net book value, net worth, or stockholders' equity).

7. Enterprise Value. This is the value of the enterprise calculated as the Market Value of Total Equity (including preferred stock) + Market Value of Total Liabilities minus Cash and Cash Equivalents.

The Valuation Process

To generate value estimates for any firm, you need to consider a number of aspects of the firm value. While it is true that the theoretical value of any risky asset is the present value of all expected future benefits (i.e., free cash flows) discounted back at an appropriate "risk-adjusted rate" of return, the value propositions of a firm are not all locked up in one thing. Future benefits may take the form of free cash flow generated by operations or intangible property (IP), tax impacts or contingent events and premiums, or discounts related to marketability or liquidity. A detailed valuation methodology needs to consider all of these things.

Valuation of a firm can be thought of as a process where various stores and forms of value need to be examined using techniques pertinent to the value therein. One needs to realize that the various categories of value may not initially be manifest in cash flow but may need to be analyzed and considered using appropriate methods to translate the value into cash flow (i.e., future benefits). Valuation should be determined by considering the operating aspects of cash flow generation, IP, tax issues, contingencies, and discounts or premiums for liquidity and marketability.

It is important to note that not all valuation systems and rules of thumb look at every aspect of the firm's value. They may in fact just examine specific aspects of firm value and assume that the measurement of just that part of the firm's value proposition is equal to use as a proxy for the entire enterprise. The best job of estimating firm value involves bringing to bear a certain amount of skill and judgment; this means that the correct valuation techniques to apply to the various parts of the firm need to be used. Each category of value needs to be examined individually using techniques that are relevant to the particular type of asset. In this way, a complete picture of firm value can be obtained.

Chart 8.2 presents a schematic of this broader approach to value. Each of the various types of factors that can affect total firm value appears in its own box. Notice that the firm's operational value is in a box by itself; similarly, the value of the firm's IP, contingencies and taxes, and premiums (or discount) for control, liquidity, and marketability all appear in their own boxes. The firm's total value is the sum of all of these values or the summation of all of these factors.

Chart 8.2   Firm Valuation

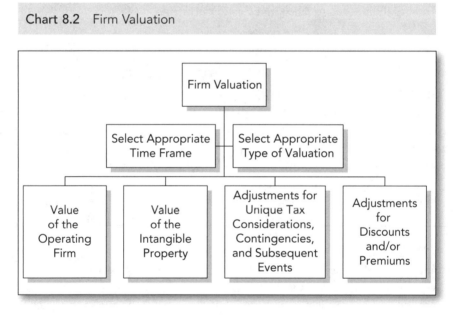

Three Main Valuation Methodologies of an Operating Firm

Generally, three types of methodologies are used to compute the value of an ongoing operation. Virtually all the valuation techniques can be categorized in one of these three methodological classifications. The material in this chapter is aimed at (1) performing a review, with several valuation methodologies available for use in estimating the value of an operational entrepreneurial venture, and (2) discussing the relative merits of these different techniques. Chart 8.3 provides a schematic of these three different valuation methodologies.

Chart 8.3   Value of the Operating Firm

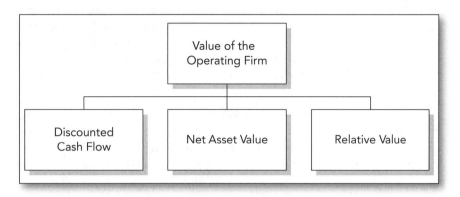

When valuing the operating firm, we focus on the cash flow from operations, not the value of the firm's intangible property (IP), its real estate assets that are held for investment, any tax issues, or the impact of premiums or discounts. We are interested in the cash value the firm produces over time as an operating firm. Therefore, the first step in valuing the firm is to evaluate the cash flow–generating capability of the firm. This means that financial projections must be made, as discussed in Chapter 6. The primary methodology that can be applied to the valuation of operating companies is discounted cash flow analysis (DCFA).

Valuing the Operating Firm Using Discounted Cash Flow Analysis (DCF)

Mike Dinan, president of Dinan & Company (a large "buy-side advisory firm" in the private equity/venture capital space), stated at a lecture at the Thunderbird School of Global Management in April 2012 that discounted cash flow (DCF) "is the *gold standard* [emphasis added] of valuation techniques." In his opinion, the "real value" of a venture is based on an analysis of the present value of the venture's "free cash flow," discussed in Chapter 3.

The DCF method is based on one of corporate finance's most fundamental concepts: The value of an asset (or bundle of assets) today is equal to the present value of the after-tax future cash flows expected to be provided by the asset over its economic life. This DCFA is an income approach to valuation and, when applied to a business venture, suggests that the value of a venture today is the sum of the various future (but uncertain) cash flows to be generated by the operation of the venture, each discounted back to today at some rate of return that reflects the riskiness (and uncertainty) of those cash flows. To employ this method, there are three basic steps: (1) project the future cash flows generated by the each asset being valued, (2) estimate an appropriate discount rate (i.e., weighted average cost of capital), and (3) apply the estimated discount rate to the cash flows and sum up all of the present values.

The DCF process can be illustrated by placing expected after-tax cash flows on a timeline. Positive cash flows are plotted on the top of the line and negative flows on the bottom. Once the appropriate discount rate has been established, that discount rate can be used along with the forecast cash flow projection to compute the present value of all expected cash flows. This present value of expected cash flows is the DCF value of the venture.

Chart 8.4 schematically describes the DCF process, and the formula in Figure 8.1 mathematically describes it.

Chart 8.4   The Discounted Cash Flow Process

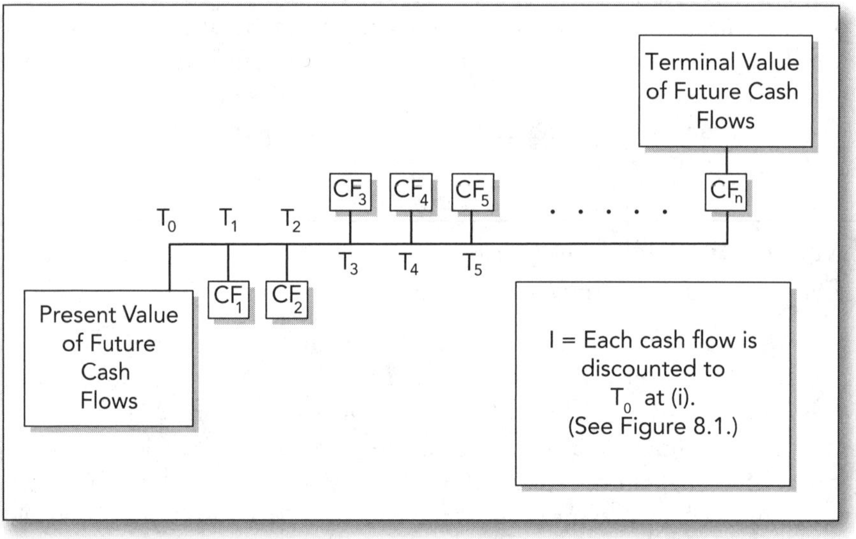

Most firms, even startups, expect to generate cash flows over long time horizons. Even when there is an expectation of long-term cash flows, it is not practical to make very long-term cash flow projections because

1. The accuracy of cash flows projected into the future degrades quickly as you go further out into the future.

2. The value of cash flows declines the further out they are; cash flows that are further away have less and less an impact on the present value of the expected cash flows.

Figure 8.1   The Discounted Cash Flow Formula

$$\text{Firm Value} = \sum_{i=1}^{n} \frac{CF_N}{(1+i)^N} + \frac{\text{Terminal } CF_T}{(1+i)^N}$$

where

CF = the amount of cash flow generated in a particular period
i = (WACC/number of compounding periods)
N = the nominal period that the cash flow occurs
CF_T = the terminal value of any future cash flows beyond CF_N

These two concepts indicate that cash flows should be broken down into two parts. Part 1 consists of the cash flows associated with the forecast period, and Part 2 is the estimated value of cash flows that are expected to be generated beyond this forecast period, as illustrated in Chart 8.4 and Figure 8.1. The first part of the timeline in Chart 8.4 and first part of the equation in Figure 8.1 explain how the present values of forecast cash flows are discounted back to the present; the second part of Chart 8.4 and the second part of the formula shown in Figure 8.1 explain how we provide for separate analysis of cash flows beyond the forecast period. When we are valuing the cash flow generated from the operating firm, the first decision is the time horizon of the analysis period. The second decision is the required rate of return that will be applied to those future cash flows. This concept is covered in Chapter 7. The third decision is the model to use to approximate the cash flows that occur beyond the forecast period chosen.

The Projection Period. For all of the reasons previously discussed, the initial forecast period should be as short as is practical. Three to 5 years should be the maximum forecast period given normal circumstances. If 3 to 5 years does not allow for firm profitability and positive cash flow to be achieved because of the nature of the industry, the forecast period can be extended to a point in time when firm profitability and positive cash flow are established and/or trends in profitability and positive cash flow can be assessed. The entrepreneur must remember that the longer the forecast period, the more error that will occur in the forecast.

Once the time horizon of the forecast is determined, the forecast should be made on a period-by-period basis. Making the forecast is part science and part art. All forecasts have inherent inaccuracies: Care should be taken to minimize these inaccuracies since time alone will inject even more error into the process. A discussion of the techniques that may be used when making a cash flow forecast was a part of Chapter 6.

Computing a Discount Rate. As discussed previously, in the most basic form, the value of any risky asset is the present value of all expected future benefits (i.e., free cash flows) discounted back at an appropriate "risk adjusted rate" of return. The two key questions are the following: (1) What are those "expected future benefits," and (2) What is the "appropriate risk-adjusted rate of return"? While identifying the future cash flow is discussed in Chapter 6, computing the appropriate risk-adjusted rate of return is discussed in Chapter 7.

The required rate of return of risky asset-generating cash flows is referred to as the discount rate, and often this is equated with the firm's weighted average cost of capital (WACC). The importance of WACC in asset valuation was discussed in Chapter 7 along with an outline of some of the widely used methods for estimating WACC, as well as examples of the approaches that may be used to calculate the WACC.

Summary of the DCF Approach. In its most basic form, the DCF approach is nothing more than computing the present value of all expected future benefits (i.e., free cash flows) discounted back at an appropriate "risk-adjusted rate" of return. The real work and struggle in calculating the DCF value of the firm are in making the projection of cash flows and in calculating the necessary WACC. The formula and a graphic representation of the technique are shown in Figure 8.1 and Chart 8.4, respectively.

Valuing the Operating Firm Using Net Asset Value (NAV)

The basic theory of the net asset value method of valuation is that the value of whole is the sum of its parts. In its most basic form, the **net asset value (NAV)** approach is an accounting-based concept. It is most often used to value firms where a holding company parent owns one or more asset-rich subsidiaries. Usually, this methodology is used to value firms where operational activity (like manufacturing or the provision of services) is not the key business of the firm. This model is best applied to situations that are repositories of tangible assets. This method is most appropriate in situations where assets such as real estate, oil and gas mineral rights, mining claims or properties, farmland, timber, or water are held as assets or inventory.

The first type of NAV calculation is based on a purely accounting con-cept. When viewing the problem from an accounting point of view, the procedure is simple; the solution is adding together the equity value of all of the firm's subsidiaries and subtracting the value of the parent company's debt while adding back any cash or securities (see Chart 8.5).

Chart 8.5   First Type of Net Asset Value Calculation

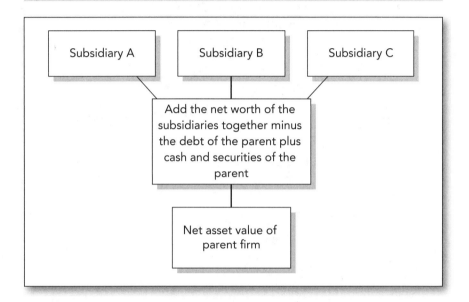

This approach is limited in that it identifies value only from an accounting perspective and is not representative of the actual storehouse of value at the firm. Using this technique means that value at the subsidiary firms is lost or understated because assets are not valued at market value, replacement value, or what appraisers would call their highest and best use.

The second type of NAV calculation is to replace the book values of the long-term assets at the subsidiary company level with market values, replace-ment values, or appraisals. This technique has the impact of expressing the net worth of each subsidiary company in terms of its contemporaneous asset value net of its current level of outstanding debt (see Chart 8.6).

If the subsidiary firms are operating firms, it is even possible to use the DCF method to value them individually and then to use that DCF value as a proxy for firm value by adding the value of the subsidiary firms together.

These two approaches to NAV are basic and are often used when firms are rich in assets.

Chart 8.6   Second Type of Net Asset Value Calculation

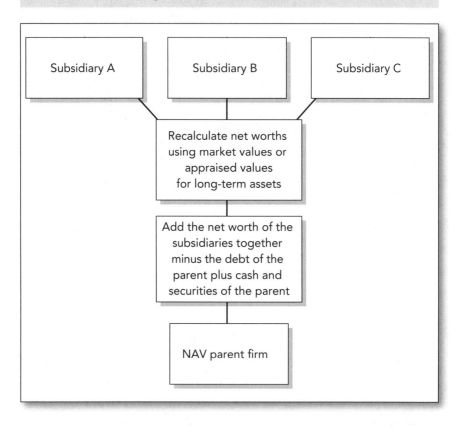

Relative Valuation. The last method that is used to value the operating firm is the **relative value** (RV) method. RV is the least descriptive method when it comes to uniquely considering the details of the firm's operation. However, without a doubt, it is the methodology that is most often employed by investment bankers, private equity principals, and venture capital principals.

Relative value measures are ubiquitous. Basically, they are used as readily available heuristics (i.e., rules of thumb) that are employed in shorthanded ways to estimate value. All of the market ratios discussed in Chapter 4 are forms of relative value and can, on their own, be considered relative valuation techniques. Other ratios not discussed in Chapter 4 also represent various relative value measures. Table 8.1 summarizes the most commonly used relative value measures.

Table 8.1   Various Relative Value Measures

Measure	Computation	Basis of Value
Price to book value (P/BV)	Price of share / book value per share	Expresses what an investor will pay for $1 of book value
Price to earnings (P/E)	Price of share / net earnings per share	Expresses what an investor will pay for $1 of earnings
Multiple of sales	K * sales (annual)	Estimate of firm value expressed as a multiple of annual sales
Multiple of net income	K * net income (annual)	Estimate of firm value expressed as a multiple of annual net income
Multiple of EBIT	K * operating earnings (EBIT)	Estimate of firm value expressed as a multiple of annual EBIT
Multiple of EBITDA	K * operating earning + noncash expenses (EBITDA)	Estimate of firm value expressed as a multiple of annual EBITDA

The various measurements where value is assessed as a multiple of some aspect of sales, cash flow, or profit are the relative value measures most widely used. The interpretation of these measurements is fairly straightforward. Firm value is expressed as a multiple (k) times some other aspect of the firm's financial performance. If the ratio is EBITDA and the multiple (K) is 4, then the firm is worth four times the firm's known EBITDA. The same analysis would hold true if other multiples were used to estimate value, such as (K * sales), (K * net income), (K * EBIT), and (K * EBITDA). In each case, firm value would be expressed as a multiple (K) of some measurement of the firm's income or cash flow statements. Higher multiples imply higher value, at least relative to the price investors are willing to pay for a dollar of EBITDA, EBIT, net profit, or sales.

To know what the appropriate multiple should be is the part of the process that requires the most skill. Investment bankers indicate that they acquire this information through experience. However, it is worth noting that many sources of data accumulate and update this type of information. Firms like Preqin, Pitchbook, Thomson Rueters, Datamonitor, and Standard & Poor's all publish this type of data and can be relied on as a good source of current information.

Summary of Valuing the Operating Firm. Of the three forms of valuing the operating firm, the most time-consuming and involved method is the DCF method. It is most difficult to use because

1. making accurate and robust projections of a firm's sales, profits, and cash flow is very hard to do, and

2. computing the appropriate risk-adjusted rate of return (which we referred to as WACC) is also complicated and involved.

Being successful at both making an accurate projection of profits or cash flow and computing an appropriate WACC is as much art as science. However, the method is the best for valuing the firm because:

1. A good projection will closely duplicate the firm's business processes and will be the best proxy for describing future benefits from operations.

2. The WACC computation generates a rate of return geared at compensating all of the providers of firm capital on a risk-adjusted basis. Although it has some weaknesses, it does represent an appropriate way of associating an appropriate risk-adjusted rate of return to the firm's capital base.

It is best to use several methods to compute RRR_{equity}, covered in Chapter 7, to determine a range of WACC possibilities. This can be accomplished by generating a range of free cash flow (FCF) projections to produce high, low, and expected cash flow projections. By discounting the cash flow projections using the various WACC rates as the discount rate, the analyst will output a range of values that define a range of likely value for the operating portion of the firm. Computing the value of the operating portion of the firm in this manner will generate a combination of outcomes related to the level of WACC and the extent of FCF. This range of outcomes can be arranged in a matrix like the one in Table 8.2.

The value of this approach is that it generates a range of operating firm values that have been derived quantitatively from the firm's cash flow, and this value can serve as the basis for establishing an estimate of the firm's ultimate value after considering IP, taxes, contingencies, subsequent events, and premiums or discounts.

Table 8.2 Range of Discounted Value of the Operating Firm at Different Cash Flow and WACC Levels

	$WACC_{High}$	$WACC_{Average}$	$WACC_{Low}$
CF_{High}			Highest discounted value
$CF_{Expected}$		Average discounted value	
CF_{Low}	Lowest discounted value		

Valuing Intangible Property (Intangibles)

Intangible property is a class of assets that are not included in the process of valuing the operating firm and cannot generally be considered physical objects. These assets can be classified into the following:

1. Intellectual properties, which are assets related to either (1) copyrights, trade names, and trademarks or (2) patents.

2. Customer-related assets such as customer lists, unique customer contracts, or special customer relationships like sole supplier status.

3. Protected processes such as trade secrets, unique fabricating capability, or computer-processing capabilities.

All three of these various categories of assets can be valued, but not as easily as an asset-producing ongoing cash flow stream or an asset consisting of real estate or securities, any of which have more easily obtainable public market prices or comparables. Although sometimes there are publicly disclosed comparables that can be used as reference points for some IP, there is not an organized market in which they trade on a regular basis. There are three primary methods used in valuing intangibles (see Chart 8.7):

1. The market approach

2. The income approach

3. The cost approach

Chart 8.7   Value Intangible Property

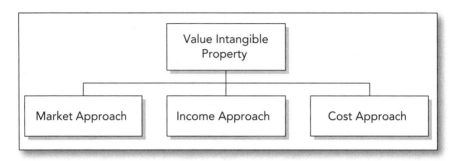

The Market Approach. This method involves finding a similar type of asset that has been traded in a publicly disclosed transaction. There are not secondary markets for intangibles, so information about a comparable transaction is not always available; however, when intangible property is sold, it may generate a press release or report in a trade publication or be noted by the investment banking or business brokerage community. Some general or even a specific record of the sale may be found. These transactions can become the basis for a comparable analysis.

It is not often that intangibles can be valued in a market approach, but some types of intangibles are routinely valued this way. This is usually the case where certain key parts of the firm's profit-generating capability are being bought and sold. The following is a list of assets where the market approach is often applicable:

1. In banking:
   a. Core deposits
   b. Mortgage servicing fees
   c. Loan portfolios
   d. Trust accounts
2. In real estate:
   a. Water rights
   b. Mineral rights and leases
   c. Easements
3. In communications and cable services:
   a. Subscribers
   b. Long-distance customers
   c. Customers involved with data transmission and reception

4. In retail:

    a. Liquor licenses

    b. Franchise agreements (if transferable)

5. Other industries:

    a. Landing rights (in aviation)

    b. Certificates of need

The normal way for these types of intangibles to be valued is using some generally accepted ratio of revenue or cost or, in some cases, a flat amount per unit. For example:

1. Mortgaging servicing is usually valued at 1% to 2% of the principal amount of the mortgage portfolio being serviced. If a financial institution sells a mortgage portfolio with the servicing rights "released," it should add an additional 1% to 2% of value in addition to the present value of the portfolio itself.

2. Water rights are usually valued as a flat amount per acre-foot of water. The exact amount may vary depending on factors like delivery means, type of environment, type of right, and/or end user, but usually there will be a current known price per acre-foot once these factors are accounted for.

Most of the time intangibles are not valued using the market approach, simply because pricing data are not usually available.

The Income Approach. The income approach is very analogous to the DCF approach previously discussed. The same basic model is useful for making the computations. The key questions when using this approach are the same as the key questions that affect DCF valuation. What are the benefits to be valued, and at what rate should they be discounted? In the case of intellectual properties, the benefits we wish to value can be globally organized into two broad categories: (1) the value of new or incremental revenue or (2) the value of avoided or diminished costs. In addition, the appropriate discount rate will be the same in principle but actually different. Some unique considerations need to be taken into account:

1. The time horizon is unique to the specific remaining useful life (RUL) of the intangible property. In other words, the number of future cash flows or benefits to be valued as benefits stemming from the licensing or sale of an intangible is not the same as the number of future cash flows

included in the analysis of the ongoing firm. The time horizons are quite different and need to be analyzed separately.

2. The rate at which the analyst discounts or capitalizes the future benefits is also unique. It is not the WACC of the firm that should be applied to the asset but a required rate of return that is inferred from the potential buyers, users, or industry characteristics to which the intellectual property is relevant. For example, if an unrelated firm intends to license a piece of intellectual property from the firm that owns it, then that third-party firm's WACC or other required rate of return should be used as the required rate of return. This is because the value of the intellectual property is determined by others' use of it. This means that an acquiring firm's WACC, the industry-based required rate of return or a specific firm-based required rate of return, may be used when computing the present value of the intellectual property. Sometimes a "capitalization rate" instead of a required rate of return is used. If a capitalization rate is used, then the annual benefit flow is treated as an amount "in perpetuity," and the capitalization rate is divided into the estimated annual benefit to approximate the value of the perpetual cash flow as discussed below.

3. Sometimes the stream of periodic benefits is not projected over a fixed time frame; instead, this future benefit stream is reduced to an estimate of the amount per year and "capitalized" at an appropriate rate. The capitalization rate is divided into the annual benefit estimate to provide an estimate of the value of the benefit on a perpetual basis. The problem with this method is that it treats the benefit as an amount that will be received in perpetuity when that is not true. Generally, the present value of a projected stream of cash flows or other benefits over a fixed time horizon is the preferred method for computing the value of intellectual property.

Two key issues need to be considered:

1. The capitalization rate or discount rate (or WACC) amount should be consistent with the tax status of the benefit that is being valued. For example, if the net income is being used as the proxy for the benefit of the intangible, then the after-tax rate of return such as WACC should be used as the discount rate in the present value calculation.

2. Care needs to be taken to avoid double counting the benefit of any intangible property. If intangible property contributes to the operating functions of the firm and the intention is to add the value of the intangible property to the value of the operating firm to produce a valuation of the firm,

then the analyst should not count the value of the intangible property that the firm is using when computing the total value of the firm. The value of the intangible property the firm is using is already captured in the form of either higher revenues or lower costs within the valuation of the operating firm. In this situation, the value of the intangible property that can be realized should be determined if it is sold or leased to third parties for their use while the firm continues to use the intangible property for its own purposes.

The Cost Method. The cost of creating an intangible property is another metric of value. Buyers particularly like using this method of valuing the intangible asset. The logic is very simple for the buyer; I can purchase an asset for "x" dollars today that took "y" amount of time and cost "z" amount of money to produce. Building a cost for an intangible is often difficult if only because many businesspeople and even accountants fail to correctly assess all the costs that went into creating the asset. The other issue that can be assessed is the premium for being able to take possession of the asset now.

When computing the cost of an intangible asset, the best guidance is to consider all costs. The actual costs are case specific. In determining the costs of producing an intangible asset, four elements should be considered in the analysis (Pratt & Niculita, 2008):

1. Direct costs (including material, labor, and overhead)

2. Indirect costs (including legal, registration, engineering, administration, etc.)

3. Developer's profit (a fair return on the intangible asset creator's time and effort)

4. Entrepreneurial incentive (the economic benefit required to motivate the asset development process)

Not only is there a physical cost to creating an intangible asset (above), but there is a required commitment of time. An additional feature of the value proposition regarding the intangible asset can be attributed to this time commitment. Not all analysts take this "time premium" into account. Acquiring firms often recognize that this time commitment will be avoided if they purchase rather than develop the intangible asset themselves. The immediacy of the purchase represents an additional form of value. One way to estimate the value of this "time premium" is to analyze the costs developed in Steps 1 to 4 above and then use time value analysis to consider their value.

Such a computation is easy to perform. This process is illustrated by using Firm ABC that is using the cost method to value its intangible assets in preparation for selling them to Firm XYZ:

> Firm ABC performs an analysis of the costs of its intangible assets by building and adding together the cost elements above using historical cost information and, where needed, industry practice. The analysis indicates that the intangible assets are worth $360,000 and that these costs were accrued in roughly equal monthly installments over a 3-year time horizon. Thus, for the purposes of this example, we will say the costs were incurred at the rate of $10,000 per month. These benefits can be plotted on a time line (see Figure 8.2):

Figure 8.2   Benefits Timeline

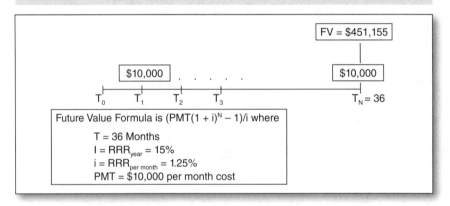

Let's assume the buying firm's (Firm XYZ) required rate of return (RRR) on this type of investment is 15% (the Firm XYZ's WACC can be used if it is determined that it is the appropriate rate), so Firm XYZ's WACC is 15%. If the future value (FV) of this stream of benefits is computed at the end of the 36th month using 15% as the annual required rate of return, the result is $451,155. This means that after considering the required rate of return of Firm XYZ, the $10,000 per month cost spread out over a 36-month time frame would generate a time premium of $91,155 ($451,155 of time-adjusted costs minus $360,000 of identified costs). Thus, the full value of Firm ABC's intangible assets to Firm XYZ is $451,155. This amount represents the cost basis in the assets plus the time premium for the buyer being able to avoid the 36-month development period.

Some use this approach and others do not. This approach is certainly relevant in a selling situation, as it provides a basis for negotiation that covers both the cost and the time premium related to the intangibles.

Summary of the Valuation of Intangible Property. Valuing intangibles is similar to valuing the operating firm. The income method is similar to the discounted cash flow approach except that (1) the time horizon is tied to the remaining useful life (RUL) of the intangible asset and not the time horizon of the firm, and (2) the required rate of return used in the calculation is not tied to the required rate of return of the firm that owns the intangible asset but will originate within industry-standard practice or at the firm that desires to purchase the asset. The market value approach is most similar to valuing real estate where comparable values are heavily relied on. Finally, the cost method is closely associated with the NAV approach.

Unique Tax Considerations, Contingencies, and Subsequent Events

The value of an operating firm and its associated intellectual property represents an important yardstick for assessing the firm's value and its prospects, but it should be recognized as an incomplete measure. Other issues can have impact on what the firm is worth or what its prospects are. Ordinary or unique tax considerations can affect the firm value, as can contingent liabilities and subsequent events. When dealing with firms where ownership is privately held and the ownership does not trade in liquid public markets, liquidity/marketability discounts may apply. Also, at firms where the shares do not trade publicly, then the ownership is either controlling or a minority stake, and invariably a control premium or lack-of-control discount will apply. Chart 8.8 provides a conceptual representation of the elements of assessing these variables.

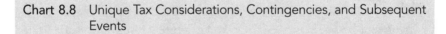

Chart 8.8 Unique Tax Considerations, Contingencies, and Subsequent Events

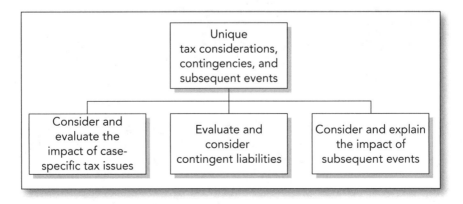

Tax Considerations. The potential for tax implications to affect firm value is normal. Because tax issues are so case specific, it is impossible to prepare a specific methodology aimed at including their impact in a valuation of the firm. As a preface to the following discussion, keep in mind that most valuations of entrepreneurial firms are used when negotiating a sale or the acquisition of another firm or raising capital (although damages for copyright or patent infringement or other disputes are also high on the list). Below are a few examples of some common issues.

1. **Built-in Gain.** This issue comes to the fore when a valuation is being used to set the acquisition price of assets held by a corporation where the assets have been fully depreciated. A sale of the assets by the corporation will trigger capital gains on the assets. The tax will be due at the corporate level. One solution is to have the buyer acquire the corporation that holds the assets instead of the assets themselves, but this approach merely defers the liability and does not solve the problem. Should the new buyer be expected to pay full value for assets within a corporation when the buyer will eventually be required to pay the capital gains tax that was racked up on those assets during the prior owner's ownership? In such a case, how is the present value of the company and its assets affected?

2. **Subchapter S Versus C Corporation Treatment.** Once in a corporation's life the corporation may elect to change its tax status from an LLC to either a Subchapter S or to straight C Corporation status. The type of tax treatment the election will bring the corporation will depend on the original status of the company. There are only two choices. If the one-time election has been made at any time in the past, then the buyer cannot change the tax status of the corporation. The election has been used up. If the buyer does not or cannot function under the current status of the corporation, then there will be tax impacts that the buyer cannot remediate by switching status. Clearly, the value to the buyer is not optimal if he or she can't have the tax treatment he or she wants. Time and expense will have to be dedicated to restructuring the company to work out a solution. This extra effort affects firm value as far as a buyer is concerned.

3. **Existence of Tax Liens or Deferred Tax on the Balance Sheet.** Unpaid taxes will need to be paid, and there may be interest costs or penalties associated with them. These taxes should be deducted from the current valuation of the firm.

4. **Increasing Tax Assessments for Property or Changes in the Tax Code.** Sometimes special tax assessments, tax policy changes, or tax rate changes have not yet been implemented but will be put in place within the near term.

The impact of these changes may not yet have appeared on the firm's income statement, but they may represent an imminent material impact on the corporation's value. The value of the operating firm should be estimated using the most current tax rates that apply, or if changes can be foreseen, then the estimate should use the prospective rates.

Contingent Liabilities or Windfalls. Contingent liabilities are events that have the potential to affect value but have not yet done so, such as the potential sexual discrimination and harassment lawsuit in the Franks Brothers case. The outcome of legal action, the outcome of pending legislation or regulation, and the potential for some other form of environmental change are all examples of contingent liabilities or contingent windfalls. When considering the impact of contingent liabilities and windfalls, the probability-weighted outcome associated with the event needs to be considered. Normally, this means that some type of binomial analysis needs to be constructed to assess the potential impact on firm value. Contingent liabilities or windfalls are always case specific. The biggest problem with assessing the impact that contingent liabilities or windfalls may have on firm value is deciding what the probability is that they actually come to pass. Making the calculation is best described by example.

> Assume that Firm ABC is currently engaged in a product liability dispute that is being settled via an arbitration proceeding. The arbitration is binding and is estimated to be decided in exactly 1 year. If the firm loses the arbitration, the loss will be $1,000,000, which is an amount that includes the plaintiff's legal fees. Another possible outcome of the arbitration is that the firm wins and the plaintiff will have to pay the company $200,000 for its legal fees. There is a third possible outcome—that an arbitration panel will decide that there is no award due but that the company should pay its own legal costs of $200,000.
>
> The situation may be summarized as follows:
>
> A. The company loses the arbitration and *pays* $1,000,000.
> B. The company wins and *receives* $200,000.
> C. There is no damage award but the company is ordered to *pay* $200,000 in legal costs.

The expected value of these outcomes is a function of the combined probability of the three potential outcomes. If the firm's attorneys assess the likelihood of the various outcomes as 30% for Option A, 20% for Option B, and 50% for Option C, then the potential value of the contingency is easily calculated as follows: Value of Contingency = (30% * A) + (20% * B) + (50% * C). This translates into – $360,000 from the computation [(.3 * – $1,000,000) + (.2 * $200,000) + (.5 * – $200,000)]. It is a negative number representing a cost.

Contingent liabilities and windfalls should be evaluated in this way; however, once evaluated, the liability or windfall must be considered in light of its time value, that is, the time until the liability or windfall is realized. In our example, the resolution to the arbitration case is exactly 1 year away; this means that the present value of the arbitration case must be discounted back at the firm's cost of capital (usually expressed as WACC) to understand the impact that the contingency has on firm value in terms of today. Given the terms in our example, the value of the contingency's impact today is the present value of – $360,000 one year away. If we say that the firm's WACC is 15%, then this calculation is FV = –360,000 * (1 / (1 + WACC)), which is equal to – $313,043.

One parting observation—probabilities associated with different contingent outcomes are best supplied by experts in the appropriate field. However, it is usually sufficient to discount contingencies at the firm's WACC.

Subsequent Events. Another type of factor that should be considered when doing a firm valuation is the procedure for considering what is referred to as a *subsequent event*. Basically, a subsequent event is an event or occurrence that has a *material* impact on firm value but has occurred at a time beyond the valuation date and before the completion date of the report. For example, if a valuation of the firm has been prepared using data through December 31 (valuation date) and the valuation is scheduled to be delivered on March 1 (report date), how should an uninsured $1 million casualty loss of the firm on February 1 be dealt with? This loss is what is referred to as a material subsequent event. The loss has not been factored into the estimation of valuation as of December 31, but it is material as it does affect firm value.

When preparing any valuation report, several things must be done regarding subsequent events:

1. Establish a procedure for monitoring company events during the interval period between the valuation date and the delivery date of the report.

2. Should a subsequent event occur, there needs to be a method for determining the "materiality" of the event. A $100,000 one-time write-off of an accounts receivable occurring during the interval between is not material when considering a firm where the estimated value as of the valuation date is $100,000,000, but it is

highly material to a firm whose estimated value is $1.5 million on the valuation date. What constitutes a material event is something that is prone to interpretation. Generally, anything that affects the firm's value by more than 1% is material.

3. As a part of any valuation process, management of the firm need to be asked to disclose and then certify the nature and magnitude of any subsequent events.

Unless there is a legal or regulatory reason for doing otherwise, if subsequent events have occurred and once they have been assessed, subsequent events should be included in the calculation of firm value as of the report delivery date. The basic logic behind this is (1) a determination is made of the firm's value on a particular day (i.e., the valuation date); (2) shortly after the valuation date, a subsequent event occurs that has a material impact on overall firm value; and (3) this material event is considered significant in the value.

Summary of Unique Tax Considerations, Contingencies, and Subsequent Events. All these factors contribute to firm value in some way. They affect value because of the effect on after-tax cash flow or asset value, they represent impacts on value that may or may not come true, or they represent impacts on value that have occurred outside of the period in which the firm is valued. All of these factors need to be considered along with the operating business and intangible property value inherent in the firm to correctly estimate a firm's value or worth.

Adjustments for Discounts or Premiums

If a firm is privately traded, then the firm's value is fundamentally different than if it is traded on an active stock exchange. This difference is attributable to the liquidity and marketability of the firm's shares. If the shares owned represent control, then they are worth more than noncontrolling shares, or if they are not controlling shares, then they are worth less than control shares. Chart 8.9 provides a schematic view of this.

The questions that need to be considered are how and when discounts should be applied to the estimate of firm value. There are three instances when a discount or a premium should be applied:

1. When the firm is not publicly traded

2. If the valuation being prepared is for all or the portion of the firm that represents the controlling interest in the firm

3. If the valuation being prepared is for a minority interest in the firm

Chart 8.9   Adjustments for Discounts or Premiums

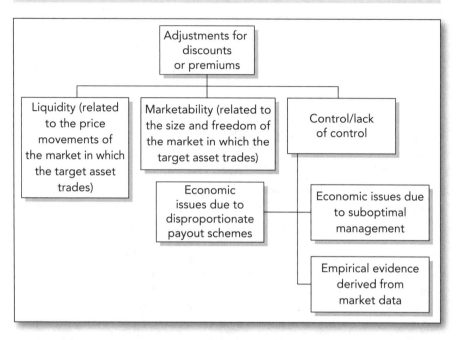

How much of an impact the firm's relative lack of liquidity and market-ability affects the firm's value needs to be considered. The term *marketability* has to do with the ease with which an asset may be sold. The implication is that highly "marketable" assets trade in markets where there are many buyers and sellers and where the time to trade an asset is minimized relative to the asset's category (Downes & Goodman, 1995). The term *liquidity* implies that when the asset is sold, the price trend that is produced by the sale is regular and orderly. Put another way, a highly liquid asset can be sold without experiencing an excessively large change in price (Downes & Goodman, 1995).

It is important to note that there are differing concepts with respect to the terms *liquidity* and *marketability*. Some practitioners like Pratt and Niculita (2008) feel that marketability is the relative ease or promptness with which a security or commodity may be sold when desired, at a representative current price, a large drop in price. Pratt and Niculita, for example, consider liquidity to be a measure of the time it takes to execute a sale. These views are not the same as the view expressed here. But both opinions suggest that liquidity and marketability collectively refer to having a large organized market with many buyers and sellers and being able to sell an asset without suffering too great a loss when executing the trade. Both views suggest that assets that are less liquid and less marketable are not as valuable as assets that are more liquid and more marketable. There is less flexibility in owning these impaired assets; they have the potential to have higher volatility in price, and because they do not trade in markets where instant execution is available, they might not be sold in a timely manner.

A number of studies attempt to capture appropriate discounts for assets having lower liquidity and marketability. These studies can be categorized as (1) studies that are based on prices of restricted stock or (2) studies that are based on analysis of private transactions that take place before initial public offerings in the subject security. The studies are quite elaborate in the way they summarize the results. For example, they can isolate discounts by firm size (measured by net income), total sales, transaction size, net income margin, or days until public trading is initiated. For restricted stock, the discounts themselves range from about 13% to 45% (some even show discount levels in the 80% range, but these kinds of results seem to be outliers).

As to discounts or premiums that should apply to transactions where a controlling share is being valued, there are relatively fewer studies. The studies that are available do demonstrate that, when acquisitions take place in the public market, about 85% of the time they are valued at a premium to market price. This indicates that whenever controlling firm interests are sold, they should be transacted with a premium. Some caution against this flat assumption. They question the idea that a "control" premium may be automatically inferred. They feel that a control premium should be determined relative to the power of the controlling interest itself. The degree of control and the value of that control are the key issues affecting whether a control premium should apply and, if so, how large it should be.

Some factors that should be reviewed are as follows:

1. How much of the company is being transacted?

2. What are the resources that the firm controls?

3. With the control shares that are being transacted, can the new owner reallocate firm resources as he or she sees fit?

4. Do minority shareholders have strong rights and remedies that can interfere with the control owner as he or she exercises his or her power?

The studies of control premiums show premium levels that range from 16% to about 33%. Of course, some of the studies show higher premiums, as high as 44%, but generally speaking, premiums that high are probably outliers. It usually is appropriate that a control premium for 100% of a business entity's ownership (thus giving the buyer complete control over the firm) is at or near 33% if the firm has particularly valuable assets or prospects. The premium might decline as the nature of the firm's value proposition declines and/or as the level of control declines. Individual skill and judgment are needed to scale the premium to the level of control involved and value of the underlying asset being controlled.

Two closing remarks are needed: (1) Pratt and Niculita (2008) provide an excellent technical discussion of control premiums in their book *Valuing a Business*, and (2) the value of minority shares is the inverse of the value of controlling shares when measured in absolute dollars. If we value a firm at $1,000 and if there are 100 shares outstanding and the control premium is 10% for 51% of the firm, then the value of the 51% control position is $561 ((.51*1,000)*1.1) (note: 1.1 represents the premium of 10% added to the identity factor 1) or $11.00 per control share. If the entire firm is worth $1,000 and the 51% control portion is worth $561, then the 49% minority position is worth $439 ($1,000 – $561). This means that each minority share is worth $8.96 per share ($439/49 shares). The lack of control discount for the minority share is –10.41% ((490 – 439)/490). This calculation is explained as follows: ((the value of the minority position given no discounts or premiums – the value of the minority position after giving a premium to the control position) / the value of the minority position given no discounts or premiums).

Assembling a Valuation

The final step in the process of valuing the firm is to combine the analysis that has been done.

The Value of the Firm (or Portion Thereof):

Value of the operating firm	+ $_____
Value of the intangible property	+ $_____
The impact of taxes, contingencies, and subsequent events	± $_____
Total firm value before control premium or discount	$_____
Portion of firm being valued in dollars	$_____
Premium or discount for control or lack of control	± $_____
Value of all or a portion of firm being valued in dollars	$_____

The numeric combination is not the end but should also show a careful summary of the work and the underlying assumptions for each calculation, type of valuation being made, the purpose of the valuation, notes on the disclosures and certifications of management, the dates and time frames for all of the relied-on information (i.e., financial statements and projections), and finally, information on the calculation of the various premiums and discounts that have been applied. This provides true valuation.

Summary

Valuation is an important subject for all entrepreneurs. Most factors in the life cycle of the firm center on the firm's valuation: (1) the day the private (angel) investors commit capital, (2) the day the venture capitalist makes its investment, (3) the day a lender provides the mezzanine line of credit, and (4) the day the firm is sold or goes public. Often, valuations are performed using only the operating company being reviewed or only one method (e.g., the times EBITDA multiple), or no diligence is done on contingencies or no real thought is put into the premiums or discounts that are to be applied. The entrepreneur should know enough about the subject of valuation to defend these haphazard valuation approaches. The future of the firm and those who work there are significantly affected by its valuation.

A thorough valuation giving due consideration to the operating elements of the firm, any intellectual property owned by the firm, subsequent events, contingent liabilities, unique tax issues, and appropriate discounts for lack of control, marketability and liquidity, would provide Robert Franks with a complete perspective regarding the deceased Bill Franks' ownership in Franks Brothers LLC. If Robert Franks had commissioned such a careful and professional evaluation, most of the questions noted in the case would be resolved.

Chapter 9

Raising Capital

Learning Objectives

- To understand the difference between debt and equity funding

- To identify the different financing stages of a venture

- To understand the various sources of capital, including debt and equity financing

- To develop a general understanding of the laws and regulations governing raising private capital

Case: Kickstarter.com

The director, Steve Taylor, was about to give up on his upcoming film, an adaptation of Donald Miller's novel *Blue Like Jazz*, the day before its preproduction as he received the news that two investors backed out of their $500,000 commitment to the project. With no financing, the project seemed doomed. Donald Miller posted the news on his blog, and immediately two fans responded by proposing to start a fundraising campaign to finance the film via Kickstarter.com. While the *Blue Like Jazz* campaign hoped to raise $125,000, it ended up raising $345,992 toward the project (Boudway, 2012; Busch, 2012). The money and awareness of the campaign also lured back the original investors and allowed the film production to go forward. On April 13, 2012, the film was released nationally.

Kickstarter is a website where the general public can contribute financially toward the realization of certain projects ranging from music to complex electronics. In exchange, contributors to the project receive some kind of reward defined in each project. Kickstarter is part of a global trend known as "crowdfunding," where projects are funded through pledges made from people through the Internet. As lending from such typical sources as banks or investors has become more difficult, crowdfunding presents an innovative opportunity for entrepreneurs to obtain the cash they need to start and/or grow their venture.

R aising capital is one of the major challenges facing entrepreneurs worldwide. From "bootstrapping" to venture capital funding, this chapter explores the various sources of funding available to entrepreneurs. Also covered is crowdsourcing and how it can disrupt the traditional sources of financing. Chart 9.1 presents a schematic representation of the material covered in this chapter.

Chart 9.1   Schematic of Chapter 9

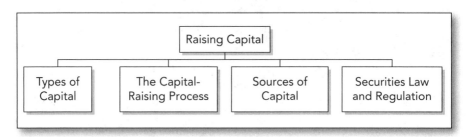

Types of Capital

Capital is basically one of two types: debt or equity.

Debt occurs when an entrepreneur obtains financing in exchange for regular interest payments and paying back the amount borrowed within a certain time frame. Debt can take many forms. It can be structured to be convertible into common stock, to have a floating interest rate, to be accompanied by warrants for the firm's common stock, or to have payments to a sinking fund. Debt may be secured by assets of the firm, guaranteed by the firm's principals, or backed by letters of credit or some other default protection. The permutations are almost endless. Some form of secured or unsecured debt is usually one of the first forms of capital investment raised by the entrepreneurial firm.

The other alternative type of capital is **equity,** which is defined as giving an ownership percentage in the company in return for financing. Like debt, equity may be flexible in its structure. Equity may be structured to have different places in the venture's liquidation preference vis-à-vis other equity owners, be super-voting or have no vote, or have many other permutations.

Each type of capital has its advantages and disadvantages. While debt financing usually only provides cash, equity financing may bring more than just the needed capital. In addition to cash, equity investors may provide mentorship, marketing assistance, or valuable contacts. This is what happened when Facebook received its first angel investment in 2004 from Peter Thiel, co-founder of PayPal. Thiel did not just provide the cash needed for the venture to grow; he also brought his expertise and a network that guided the company in its early stage.

While the press frequently emphasizes the role of venture capital firms in the economy, their investment is in very few companies compared to the total number of ventures financed by private individuals/angel investors. According to the 2011 industry report from PricewaterhouseCoopers, the National Venture Capital Association, and MoneyTree, 3,761 venture capital deals were made in the United States in 2011 compared to 66,230 entrepreneurial ventures financed by angel investors, nearly 18 times more.

The goal of a venture raising capital is to obtain the necessary capital at the best possible terms. Having several offers to consider is obviously the preferred outcome. This chapter will guide entrepreneurs in the capital-raising journey by describing the steps necessary to securing cash to move their ventures to the next level. It is important to remember that entrepreneurs need to be excellent salespersons when raising capital. The ability to sell and come across as a confident entrepreneur will have a dramatic impact on their success in this respect. While we will not cover the art of selling, we advise entrepreneurs to actively study and attend seminars on selling, as it is vital for the success of a venture.

The Capital-Raising Process

The first step is determining how much money the venture needs to raise. A number of issues affect this amount:

1. What is the time frame being considered?

2. What maximum cash flow deficit will occur during that time horizon?

3. What safety margin should be provided?

4. What price in terms of cost and control must be paid?

Based on the venture's financial projections, entrepreneurs can estimate how much capital the venture will need. Often the financial needs of the company occur at milestones, and the funding is contributed at these key points. For example, capital is injected to allow the venture to bring the first version of the product to market. More capital is then invested when sales reach a target level. Progressively larger injections of capital can be made as new milestones are achieved. With respect to establishing milestones, entrepreneurs should underpromise and overdeliver.

Raising the right amount of cash reduces dilution and eases the exit process. If a company raises $2 million on a $6 million premoney valuation for a total $8 million postmoney valuation, investors are typically expecting an exit valued at $32 to $48 million, a four to six multiple of the invested capital. If the company raises $4 million with the same $6 million premoney valuation, the new postmoney valuation is $10 million; the same four to six multiplier would require an exit valuation of $40 to $60 million. While an entrepreneur might be willing to exit at a valuation of $35 million, the investor may not accept anything less than $40 million (or higher). Conflicts between investors and entrepreneurs often arise. While entrepreneurs may consider selling as soon as the opportunity arises, investors, especially venture capitalists (VCs), often want the maximum return possible for their fund. While asking for more money than you need may provide more cushion, it also may lead to pressure from investors.

Financing Stages

Entrepreneurial firms typically have several financing stages ranging from (1) seed or prelaunch, (2) early, to (3) mid and later stage.

Seed stage companies are usually funded through bootstrapping (which will be covered in the next section). Early stage firms have no track record and need capital to create and launch their products/services on the market; this capital usually comes from personal savings, family and friends, or such creative sources as crowdfunding. In very specific cases, angel investors or venture capitalists may be willing to fund seed stage companies. One of the most notable seed funding stories in the history of Silicon Valley is the company Color Labs, Inc. Color Labs raised $41 million prelaunch money in 2011 with no product on the market. The only asset the company had at the time was a very strong founding team composed of renowned personalities such as Bill Nguyen (who sold his company Lala for several million dollars to Apple in 2009), Peter Pham (previously CEO of BillShrink), and D. J. Patil (LinkedIn's chief scientist). However, such cases are rare, even in Silicon Valley.

Early stage companies are already up and running and often have sales. By this stage of their development, the progress is usually material and significant. As a result, firms in this development stage typically request more funding and receive more favorable terms than do seed stage companies. The entrepreneurial team continues to be very important at this stage, however; they must be able to delegate and build an executive team that keeps the company growing.

Mid and later stage companies usually have already achieved significant benchmarks. These benchmarks can range from having significant revenue, having raised previous rounds of investment, having established a market niche, perfecting technology patents or trademarks, and achieving positive cash flow and even profits. At this stage, board pressure, conflict, and voting issues can occur between investors who have provided different levels of funding. All investors require a significant return on their investment, which affects the selling of the firm in terms of timing and amount. If the venture has loyal customers and stable cash flow, bank loans or other forms of conventional debt as well as equity financing may constitute the best forms of financing for the venture.

Sources of Capital

Meeting Capital Formation and Resource Needs

Generally, entrepreneurial firms face more acute problems with respect to raising capital and acquiring resources than do more established performing firms. Entrepreneurial ventures, at least in their early stages, need virtually everything such as capital, office equipment, furniture, computers, legal advice, accounting help, manpower, supply sources, and distribution channels. The entrepreneur needs to arrange for his or her nascent venture to acquire the essential resources needed. There are various ways and methods of accomplishing this task.

Bootstrapping

Bootstrapping is not merely a type of funding but in fact an attitude toward starting a firm. Bootstrapping is defined as the process through which entrepreneurs find creative ways to explore opportunities to launch and get traction for their startup business while having limited resources available (Cornwall, 2009). Bootstrapping is thus a mind-set that the entrepreneur needs to have to obtain the necessary capital and services to advance his or her venture's interests. Included in this mind-set is the willingness to use not only the cash flow and credit of the venture but also the entrepreneur's own resources, the resources of his or her friends and family, barter, and paying performance and stock bonuses for service providers and the founding employees. In short, the "bootstrapping" entrepreneur is creative and will do what is necessary to get the venture through the first critical months or years until more traditional financing is possible.

Bootstrapping is used by more than just entrepreneurs seeking to launch their business when no alternative sources of funding are available. It can be used as a first step to delay external funding and retain equity, minimize risk, increase efficiency within the business, or simply create a company culture where resources are maximized and waste minimized. While aspects of bootstrapping may be viewed negatively under certain circumstances (i.e., delaying payments excessively to employees or suppliers), most entrepreneurs engage in the practice to some degree or other at the start of their entrepreneurial journey. Dissatisfied employees will underperform, and unhappy suppliers will result in shorter terms of payments and a bad reputation that will hurt the company in the long term.

Savings. Most startup companies are funded at the beginning with the entrepreneur's personal savings. Entrepreneurs considering starting their own company often need to be willing to compromise their lifestyle for a period of time to fund their upcoming venture. Depending on the type of business and its cash requirements, the amount of savings necessary for supporting a startup firm will vary. Having savings will allow entrepreneurs to start the venture and finance their own labor when revenue is little or nonexistent. If possible, entrepreneurs should have at least 6 months' worth of expenses saved at the outset of the venture and adapt their standard of living to face a period where they personally will have no income. Entrepreneurs often need to go through a long period of time without a paycheck as the business may take a while to reach a point where they can finally draw a salary.

Some businesses require little capital to get started. That was the case for Chad Mureta. Chad suffered a horrible car accident in 2009 and was heading toward severe financial difficulties as his insurance coverage was limited. With thousands of dollars in debt and his bank account empty, he had little chance of obtaining funding for any entrepreneurial activities. He borrowed $1,800 from his stepfather to create a mobile software application called Fingerprint Security Pro. The software application was distributed through the Apple app store and became an overnight success. The money generated allowed him to build more mobile software applications. Today, Chad is the owner and founder of three companies: Empire Apps, T3 Apps, and Best Apps.

Side Business. Another option that can be used in conjunction with saving is for entrepreneurs to keep their present job. As a result, entrepreneurs are able to have a source of income while they work on building and growing their entrepreneurial venture in their nonwork hours. It is hoped that by the time the entrepreneurial venture requires full-time dedication, it will be generating enough income to provide a salary.

Creative Ways to Bootstrap

There are several creative ways for entrepreneurs to launch and grow their venture. Several ideas that will allow entrepreneurs to bootstrap their way into business are discussed below.

Rent. Apple and Hewlett-Packard are two of the many companies that started in their founder's garage. In fact, more than 50% of the entrepreneurial ventures in the Unites States actually start at home (Kasperkevic, 2013). With the advent of the Internet, having an online presence is easier than ever. Websites such as www.weebly.com or www.wix.com allow entrepreneurs to build an online presence by themselves in hours for less than $10 per month. For certain types of companies, an online presence and a phone number are enough. If large corporations such as Amazon are able to manage their sales from a website, why shouldn't the same be true for startup companies? Meetings can be arranged at local restaurants, hotel lobbies, or, even better, the client's premises.

While an online presence may be enough for certain types of business, others may require a physical space to credibly deal with potential clients. Many free or inexpensive spaces can be used instead of the traditional office. For example, office suite companies now offer workstations or access to a room within a large office suite for rent at a fraction of the price of a traditional office. By using such "corporate identity" programs, entrepreneurs can give a postal address and phone number. In addition, most universities and cities today have incubator centers where young startups can launch and grow their ventures for free or at a lower cost. Some incubators offer rent, utilities, and associated services for free in exchange for equity in the venture. This represents a great way for entrepreneurs to bootstrap their way to success.

There are also more creative ideas, such as occurred in the case of a young Eastern European pianist. She negotiated with a hotel to play 2 nights a week for free in exchange for use of their concert hall during the mornings for both practice and giving private lessons to students. She not only gained credibility for being a great pianist, as she was playing at a renowned hotel, but also used the hotel to advertise her piano classes to people who attended her shows.

Furnishings and Equipment. Furnishings and equipment can represent a large initial cost for a startup venture. Entrepreneurs will have to determine what they really need and if, for example, a new MacBook Air is really necessary at this stage. Always forgo brand-new furnishings and equipment and rent or buy used. Often companies going out of business or upgrading their process or furnishings will sell these at a bargain price. Similarly, good deals can be found online, in local media, and at auctions. The Internet and websites make it easier than ever to find such deals.

In addition, certain types of equipment may be rented instead of purchased. For example, photographers do not need to purchase equipment for specific types of shootings (such as underwater). They can simply rent it for a day or week when needed, thus paying a fraction of the cost of buying it.

Staffing. Some businesses may require manpower beyond the entrepreneurial team to be operational. Employing people is very costly nearly everywhere in the world. It is much more cost-effective to outsource services. If a business needs administrative assistance to take care of paperwork and respond to e-mail, why not outsource it online? Companies such as AskSunday.com provide this type of service at a marginal cost of having to employ someone full-time to do the job. If an entrepreneur requires more technical skills, why not use a website like elance.com where professionals from all over the world offer their services at very competitive rates? Reviews and grading allow entrepreneurs to choose which freelancer they want to hire for the task. An escrow account can be established, and the funds are released when the freelancer delivers a job the employer deems satisfactory.

If a physical presence is required, entrepreneurs may contact placement firms that specialize in recruiting and placing temporary employees (from delivery staff to CEOs). This allows entrepreneurs to bypass full-time employment and the fringe benefits and for a short period of time have the human resources necessary to start their venture.

Another alternative is the recruitment of student interns. Local universities are a great place to find students looking for opportunities to earn school credit and gain professional experience. Interns are usually highly motivated and willing to work for a low salary. Many entrepreneurs value student interns highly given their cost, flexibility, and motivation to perform. Internship programs can be found at university employment or career services offices as well as online through such links as the following:

1. www.internships.com

2. www.InternShipPrograms.com

3. www.aiesec.org

Bootstrapping has the following key characteristics:

1. Has little or no equity give-up

2. Is faster than waiting for banks or investors to make funding decisions

3. Shows commitment to future investors

4. Creates positive pressure to succeed as entrepreneurs' own money is invested

5. Makes the venture more lean because entrepreneurs purchase and finance only what is strictly needed

6. Forces entrepreneurs to focus on revenue early on

7. Offers total control and flexibility, allowing decisions to be made quickly

While "bootstrapping" is a good way to start a venture, a number of sources of capital are important for entrepreneurs. These are discussed below.

Equity Capital

Equity financing is money offered by investors in exchange for an owner-ship share in the business. Such funds may be provided by friends and family members as well as private (angel) investors or venture capital firms. Equity investors want to realize a substantial return on their investment out of future profits of the venture and ultimately exit, usually through a successful sale of the business. Some equity investors, such as angels or venture capital-ists, can also bring more than just cash to the investments, as they usually have a strong network and valuable experience. A discussion of the different types of equity investor follows.

Private (Angel) Investors

Private investors, frequently called **angel investors** (the term used histori-cally to describe the backers of Broadway shows), are high-net-worth indi-viduals who in the United States are certified to be accredited investors under the Securities and Exchange Commission (SEC) rule. In practice, angels are a key resource for entrepreneurs seeking early stage or seed capital. They are known for investing their personal funds (in the form of either debt or equity) in ventures started and managed by other individuals who are neither a friend nor a family member. Normally, angels invest between $25,000 and $500,000. Angels often band together to form angel networks or clubs, which act as clearinghouses for deals and where members of the network can invest together in interesting ventures.

Interestingly enough, the motivation of angels is normally not exclusively financial. While making a return is important, angel investors usually look also for a "qualitative return" that goes beyond money. Typically, angel investors have money, motivation, and time to diversify their investment portfolio with active investments. What this means is that they usually want to be high-worth partners by not only supplying the needed capital but also contributing with their knowledge and network. Angel investors can contribute in several ways. For example, they can leverage their network by opening doors to new clients, distributors, partners, and further sources of financing. They can also have a more involved role by helping entrepreneurs with operational and strategic tasks depending on their experience. Finally, an angel investor's reputation and track record may even result in his or her being a mentor who in times of turbulence brings confidence and calm to the business. They are generally comfortable with 5- to 7-year investments as it usually takes several years for an entrepreneurial venture to show a return. Sometimes, returns can be phe-nomenal, as was the case of Peter Thiel with his investment in Facebook.

In 2004, former Napster employee Sean Parker was looking for a potential investor in the company; he was now president of Facebook. Parker reached out to Reid Hoffman, known Silicon Valley serial entrepreneur and co-founder of PayPal, who at the time held the position of CEO at LinkedIn. Hoffman found potential in the idea but declined the opportunity. He revealed that conflicts could emerge from his actual role at LinkedIn. He recommended Peter Thiel, whom he knew from his time at PayPal. Peter Thiel liked the idea and concept after meeting Sean Parker and the creator, Mark Zuckerberg.

In August 2004, only 5 months after the launch of the venture, Peter Thiel made a $500,000 angel investment in Facebook. In exchange, he was granted a 10.2% equity stake and joined the company's board. This represented the first outside investment in Facebook.

Due to subsequent rounds of funding and movements in Facebook shares under private sales and dilution over the years, Thiel's investment by the time of the initial public offering (IPO) was about 3%. A 3% share of the $100+ billion IPO—Peter Thiel had generated a tremendous return on his investment through angel investing.

Angel investors know that the only way to be part of something big is by investing in the early stage of a venture. When angels begin investing other people's money in deals they believe worth the investment, they become what are known as super angels. They usually make more investments than regular angels and invest not only their own money but also their friends' and other private investors'. When operating in this capacity, they often work as a miniature venture capital firm, and sometimes they are referred to as "micro VCs." Once a super angel raises money, he or she has fiduciary responsibilities similar to those of venture capitalists.

Venture Capital Firms

Venture capital (VC) firms are in the "business of building businesses" and exchange their investment for an equity part of the venture. From a historical perspective, VC investments are far from new. In the 15th century, Christopher Columbus traveled from Portugal to Spain seeking the investment to journey on new ventures that would bring fortune and fame to its sponsors. Venture capital has since evolved into a sophisticated industry, known for its unique structure, which combines risk capital with management and with labor and material to accomplish a common goal—return on investment.

At venture capital firms, the most senior partners in the firm are the managing directors (MDs) or founding partners (if they are the ones who founded the firm). They are the ones responsible for the investment decisions and serve on the board of directors of the companies they invest in—called **portfolio companies.**

The second layer within a VC firm is the principals or directors. While they typically have some influence on a deal, they still require the consent and support from the managing director(s) in the final investment decision.

Associates represent the third layer of a VC firm. They are often composed of recently graduated students who focus on basic research tasks. They generally have no decision-making ability and do not act as principals within the firm.

Some VC firms may also have advisers on a part-time basis who are venture partners, operating partners, or entrepreneurs in residence (EIRs). Such individuals typically have considerable experience in certain fields and bring high added value to the VC firm both during the due diligence process and during the management of the investments. They may also connect the VC firms to interesting deals through their personal networks.

Entrepreneurs should be aware of the structure of the VC firm they are targeting. While they need to work with all members of the firm, entrepreneurs must remember that only managing directors make the final decision. In addition, managing directors are usually with the same firm for many years, while lower-level individuals in a VC firm are often looking for an opportunity for promotion either internally or externally. As a result, entrepreneurs should make sure they have a good relationship not only with the principals but also with the managing directors of the firm.

Differences Between VCs and Angels. A typical venture capital firm usually receives more inquiries for financing than does an angel investor since its contact details are listed publicly in directories. Angel investors usually prefer to remain private and use angel networks as their point of contact where the head of the angel network is the contact for the deals and a screening committee determines the ones to present. Angels themselves receive less deal flow and often take longer to make an investment decision. While VCs expect a percentage of their investments will not be successful, angels like to think all of their investment decisions will generate a positive return, which of course does not happen. Angels do not have any pressure to invest as they are not managing a fund with investor money. VCs have to invest and generate a return to satisfy their fund's investors or **limited partners.**

Angel investors seem to be more concerned with a firm's success in terms of both financials and sustainability, while venture capitalists appear to give more relevance to fast growth and exit strategies. Angel investors are using their own money; venture capitalists are using other people's money as well as their own.

Angel investors usually work part-time on their investments, while VCs are full-time and focused on maximizing their return on investment. A large number of angel investors were in the past entrepreneurs themselves, but that is not as common in the VC industry. While angels focus on a wider variety of enterprises, VCs focus on fewer industries with high growth potential.

Both angel investors and venture capitalists are seeking a high return on their investment. If they do not believe they will make a high return on their capital, they will typically ignore the opportunity no matter how exciting the project is.

Crowdfunding

Crowdfunding is a relatively new way for entrepreneurs to raise financing. While it is just being established and widely used, it allows firms to raise money over the Internet from numerous investors investing small amounts of capital. Typically, an idea for a product or service is posted onto a crowdfunding platform along with a fundraising target. People all over the world can review it and decide if they want to contribute to its development. Donations can be as low as $5 to $10, although some contributions have reached as high as thousands of dollars. In return, "backers" receive a gift such as a copy of the end product.

Globally, crowdfunding platforms raised $1.5 billion in 2011 for one million campaigns, with most of the total raised in North America (Crowdsourcing Org, 2010). Due to its growing popularity and its ability to help firms access capital and increase jobs, crowdfunding received attention from policy makers in the United States. The Jumpstart Our Business Startups Act (JOBS Act) of 2012 opened the door for equity crowdfunding, although the precise details of how this market will develop depend on the SEC. Under the new legislation, a company can raise up to $1 million per year in equity crowdfunding. It is projected that the total market for equity crowdfunding could be $4 billion (Prive, 2012).

What we know is that crowdfunding is premised on large numbers of investors investing small amounts of money. As a result, managing hundreds or even thousands of investors might present a challenge for busy entrepreneurs (Emmanuel, 2013). Furthermore, at a later stage, some sophisticated investors (angels or venture capital firms) may be reluctant to invest in a crowdfunded venture. One way to solve this problem is to have anyone participating in the crowdfunding agree to become one voting block if required for later stage financing.

The Pebble Smartwatch is an example of a firm that used crowdfunding for raising capital. In April 2012, after multiple failed attempts to get funding from venture capital firms, Eric Migicovsky posted his idea of an app-supported Smartwatch that connects to an iPhone or Android smartphone on Kickstarter, one of the most popular crowdfunding platforms. He set his fundraising target at $100,000. Within 24 hours, he had raised $1 million. By the end of the funding period, the project had raised over $10 million from nearly 69,000 backers (Gobble, 2012). Pebble entered mass production in January 2013, with planned production of 15,000 watches per week, with backers who contributed $99 or more getting the first orders filled first (Simonite, 2013).

There are essentially three main types of crowdfunding:

1. **Prize-Based Crowdfunding.** In exchange for their investment, investors receive a tangible item or service (e.g., Kickstrater.com and IndieGogo.com are known for this).

2. **Equity-Based Crowdfunding.** In exchange for their investment, investors receive an ownership position in the company.

3. **Lending-Based Crowdfunding. Investors** lend money, which is repaid over a set period of time.

Prize-Based Crowdfunding. Prize-based crowdfunding allows entrepreneurs to bypass typical investors and pitch their ideas directly to Internet users who may be willing to provide financial support. Using websites such as Kickstarter and IndieGogo, entrepreneurs post online their ideas and products with pictures, text, and videos. Internet users are then offered special rewards such as exclusive merchandise, samples of the product, or even an opportunity to meet the founders of the project in exchange for a monetary donation. In the case of a CD recording, for example, donating $15 will guarantee a copy of the CD, $30 an autographed CD, and $50 an autographed CD and poster. Donations above $500 provide the opportunity to meet the singer and sing part of the album itself.

Gustin Jeans used a prize-based crowdfunding project. The founders of Gustin, a company that provides premium menswear handcrafted in San Francisco, launched a Kickstarter project with the goal of raising $20,000 in exchange for their own products, jeans (Tarnoff, 2013). Within a week, the company had raised $100,000 from more than a thousand different people around the globe. In total, 4,010 people contributed to Gustin Jeans' project, and the crowdfunding campaign raised nearly half a million dollars in less than 35 days!

A significant advantage of prize-based crowdfunding is that entrepreneurs do not give away any ownership or equity stake in their venture, or give up any kind of control. Other sources of cash (i.e., equity-based crowd-funding, venture capital firms, and angel investors) usually require owner-ship or interest repayment of principle in exchange for capital.

Some of the advantages of prize-based crowdfunding include the following:

1. Ideas can be tested and funded easily.

2. No equity is given up.

3. No control is given up.

4. Investors become your word-of-mouth marketing team on social media and among their friends.

5. Entrepreneurs sell their products before they actually exist, providing a good proof of concept.

Lending-Based Crowdfunding. Lending-based crowdfunding occurs when people as a "crowd" lend money expecting that the loan will be repaid with interest. Sites that focus on this approach are SoMoLend.com, LendingClub .com, Microplace.com, Buildingsociety.com, and Prosper.com. This approach is particularly beneficial for companies that do not want to give up equity stakes in the company.

Some advantages of lending-based crowdfunding include the following:

1. No equity is given up.

2. No control is given up.

3. Interest rate charged is usually competitive and allows debt to be available in regions of the world where access to credit is limited.

Equity-Based Crowdfunding. Equity-based crowdfunding allows individu-als to invest in startup companies and small businesses in smaller amounts of money for ownership in the venture. Previously in the United States, only accredited investors were able to invest in privately held companies. Several online platforms focus on this: Fundable.com, WeFunder (United States), CrowdCube.com (United Kingdom), and FundedByMe.com (Sweden, Norway, and Finland).

These three types of crowdfunding provide not only a way to fund entre-preneurial ideas but also "proof of concept" by gauging public interest and having real customers invest their own money in the project. Entrepreneurs in their early stage can benefit from crowdfunding, as it can serve as a cheaper and potentially more reliable alternative to more expensive marketing research studies.

Debt Capital

Debt capital may take many forms. It can be secured or unsecured, bear interest at a variable rate or a fixed rate, be convertible into equity or not, or be structured to have warrants or common stock attached. Debt is a very flexible form of capital.

Today debt is still one of the main sources of capital for entrepreneurs. Debt capital has both advantages and disadvantages. Its advantages include the following:

1. It is usually faster and cheaper than securing equity.

2. The cost of capital is more easily determined.

3. It provides tax benefits.

4. The entrepreneur does not give up ownership in the company.

5. Debt usually is the lowest-cost capital component.

Its disadvantages include the following:

1. Loans can be difficult to obtain.

2. A personal guarantee is often required to secure the loan.

3. Collateral is required on an asset higher than the amount of the loan.

4. The company has to pay back the money borrowed, and the payments must be made in a timely manner.

5. If debt is not paid back, debt can force a company into bankruptcy.

6. Debt appears on the balance sheet as a liability, which makes equity investment less attractive for investors.

The sources of debt capital covered in this section are consumer credit, bank loans, government, and grants.

Consumer Credit. The vast majority of new businesses use consumer credit to provide financing, whether in the form of personal or business credit cards or other short-term borrowing programs. As of the end of 2009, 83% of small businesses reported using credit cards to finance their operations (Board of Governors, 2010). Many small businesses use credit cards as a convenient method of paying for goods and services and of tracking expenses. Some small businesses also use credit cards for borrowing purposes, carrying a balance on the card from month to month.

Small business credit cards differ from consumer cards in that they are issued to firms, rather than individual consumers, and are intended to be used for business purposes. Small business credit cards are also distinct from other types of credit card products designed for businesses, such as corporate cards, procurement cards, and fleet cards, which are usually issued to larger businesses. Small business credit cards are very similar to personal credit cards. Personal and small business credit cards have similar features such as rewards programs, balance transfer programs, and introductory rate promotions. The fees and pricing structures, as well as other terms such as grace periods, can also be similar across the two products.

Examples of business credit cards include American Express Business Platinum Card, Chase Ink, and the CitiBusiness Thank You Card. While all three cards provide financing to small businesses, their fees and rewards vary. The American Express Business Platinum Card, for example, has a $450 annual fee, and the balance needs to be paid in full each month. The card caters more to business travelers, with rewards on major airlines, hotels, and car rentals. The Chase Ink and the CitiBusiness Thank You cards do not charge an annual fee and do allow for balances to roll over month to month. Business owners earn reward points that can be converted to cash or discounts at office supply stores, restaurants, or gas stations, as well as travel benefits.

Bank Loans. Often a bank's primary business is to loan money at an interest rate for profit. Interest rates will vary from bank to bank and the perceived credit risk of the borrower. In general, banks are not receptive to financing startup companies with limited or no revenues and/or assets. When they do, it is often as a personal loan to the entrepreneur disguised as a collateralized business loan. If the business does not have assets or receivables, the bank will usually require the entrepreneur to pledge his or her property as a guarantee for the loan. Entrepreneurs without personal assets to pledge as collateral have little chance of securing a bank loan for their startup.

An alternative to larger commercial or regional banks is the community bank. Community banks are usually friendlier to entrepreneurs than larger, not geographically focused banks. Typically, a community bank is a smaller bank that specializes in more local lending. A complete list of community banks can be found at www.icba.org.

Overall, entrepreneurs seeking any type of bank loan will need to pass a credit analysis in order for the bank to determine their ability to repay both principal and interest. Usually, there will need to be collateral to secure the loan as well as a solid business plan.

The major issue with obtaining a loan from a bank is the required collateral. It is estimated that 90% of first-time business owners pledge their home as collateral for a business loan. While it can be scary for entrepreneurs, this action demonstrates credibility and commitment to the business idea. If the entrepreneur defaults, banks indeed have the right to sell his or her home to recover their loan amount.

Entrepreneurs should be aware that the success of their venture depends mostly on their ability and effort. They should seek the following in any debt obtained:

1. Being able to refinance the terms of the loan at a later stage with no prepayment penalty

2. Being able to improve the terms or extend or add to the amount of the loan if payments are made on time and the firm achieves certain milestones

3. Having a fixed interest rate

4. Having a specified grace period and cure period for noncompliance

Government Guaranteed Loans. Many governments provide some kind of guaranteed or subsidized loans for entrepreneurs. These programs are usually locally focused at increasing or retaining employment in the area. These loans often come with such benefits as a lower interest rate or lower qualification standards than regular banks. The only problem is the bureaucratic process associated with the loan and the reporting system.

In the United States, the Small Business Administration (SBA) has several loan programs for small companies (www.sba.gov). SBA loans have the unique characteristic of being available to entrepreneurs who do not qualify for regular bank loans. To be eligible for an SBA loan, the company must qualify as a small business, have a for-profit goal, and have no internal resources of financing. Further details on which types of companies can and cannot apply to this program can be found at the www.sba .gov site.

While these loans are processed by regular banks, the SBA guarantees up to 85% of the loan principal. The maximum loan under this program is $2 million, of which 75% (1.5 million) is guaranteed by the SBA to the lender. In this case, if the recipient defaults on the loan, the bank lending the money has only a 25% risk because the SBA guarantees 75% of the amount borrowed. While the loan is secured, entrepreneurs should be aware that the amount borrowed is first personally guaranteed and that lenders will request SBA for a refund only after they have assiduously pursued the payment of as much of the loan as possible.

Four of the SBA's main programs are the 7(a) Loan Guaranty, Microloan, 504 (CDC) Loan Programs, and Small Business Investment Company (SBIC), which are discussed below.

The *7(a) Loan Guaranty* program is the most popular of all the programs offered. It provides bank loans where the SBA guarantees 85% of the loans up to $150,000 and 75% for loans between $150,000 and $2 million. Further details can be found at http://www.sba.gov/category/navigation-structure/ loans-grants/small-business-loans/sba-loan-programs/7a-loan-program.

The *Microloan* program is available through nonprofit community-based organizations and offers small and short-term loans (up to 6 years) to small businesses. The maximum loan amount is $50,000 with an average of $13,000 per microloan, and the interest rate charged is usually between 8% and 13%. The purpose of these loans is usually for working capital, purchase of inventory, supplies, furniture, fixtures, machinery, or equipment. Microloans cannot be used to pay down existing debts or purchase real estate. More information can be found at http://www.sba.gov/content/ microloan-program.

The *504 (CDC) Loan* program offers long-term and fixed-rate financing to small businesses to acquire fixed assets such land, buildings, or equipment. This loan cannot be used for working capital, inventory, or to consolidate or repay debt. The loans are delivered through certified development companies (CDC). CDCs are private nonprofit corporations created to promote economic development in their local communities. The 504 loans are usually structured as follows: The SBA provides 40%, a participating lender provides 50% of the total project costs (typically a bank), and the borrower contributes with the remaining 10%. Under specific circumstances, a borrower may be asked to increase its contribution up to 20%. The maximum loan amount in this program is limited to $5 million but may be increased to $5.5 million under specific circumstances. There are more than 260 CDCs in the United States, each covering a specific geographic area. By 2012, the 504 loan program had provided over $50 billion worth of loans. More information about the 504 (CDC) loan program can be found at http://www.sba.gov/content/cdc504-loan-program.

The *Small Business Investment Company (SBIC)* program represents a partnership between the public and private sectors. SBICs are private equity funds that invest in small businesses that meet specific criteria set by the federal government. While licensed and regulated by the U.S. Small Business Administration (SBA), the organization is privately managed. The SBIC program is available only to companies with a net worth below $18 million and after-tax net income for the prior 2 years below $6.0 million. The SBIC program offers both debt and equity capital. Usually, the debt has a 10-year maturity.

Along with the debt capital, the SBIC provides strategic management help. The advantages of this program are that companies get not only cash but also experts willing to assist them. SBIC represents a long-term loan or equity investment but differs from traditional VC funds as SBICs are not allowed to take control of the portfolio companies funded. More information about this program can be found at http://www.sba.gov/content/sbic-program-0.

Community Development Financial Institutions (CDFIs). CDFI programs serve low-income individuals and communities that usually do not qualify for other financing options. The CDFIs' purpose is pursuing a specific goal such as create jobs, promote economic development, or develop affordable housing. CDFI organization makes sense for certain types of businesses where financing from banks and private investors is not an option. Since 1994, the CDFI Fund has provided more than $1 billion worth of financing. For more information, visit the website at http://www.cdfifund.gov.

Foundations and Grants. One source of financing for young companies and entrepreneurs is through grants, which are nonrepayable funds "granted" to businesses by another organization, usually a government department, charitable foundation, or trust. Grants do not require the funds to be paid back. Typically, the grant-giving institution has a mission statement or vision and will provide financing for firms that further the purpose of the organization. While grants do not require the funds to be repaid, many do require a return on their investment in the form of community impact or the fulfillment of a specific social or community benchmark.

An example of a private grant-giving organization is The Kauffman Foundation, based in Kansas City, Missouri. The late entrepreneur and philanthropist Ewing Kauffman established the foundation in the 1960s as a vehicle for providing financing for entrepreneurial companies, advising his associates to "invest in people and be willing to take risks to accelerate entrepreneurship in America" (Kauffman.org). In general, the Kauffman Foundation grants are limited to programs and/or initiatives that have significant potential to demonstrate innovative service delivery in support of education and entrepreneurship. A list of some of the foundation resources is indicated in Table 9.1.

The foundation encourages grant seekers applying for funding to review its founding priorities to see if there is strong congruence between the goals of the foundation and the applicant firm. A letter of inquiry is then submitted detailing a description of the applicant, the purpose for the funds, a proposed time frame, and an estimate of the costs. If approved, the foundation distributes the

Table 9.1   List of Online Resources Regarding Foundations

Cambridge Associates Mission Investing Group	www.cambridgeassociates.com
Confluence Philanthropy	www.confluencephilanthropy.org
Council on Foundations	www.cof.org
Foundation Center	www.fdncenter.org
FSG Social Impact Advisors	www.fsg-impact.org
Global Impact Investing Network	www.thegiin.org
Grantcraft	www.grantcraft.org
Investor's Circle/SJF Institute	www.investorscircle.net
Mission Investors Exchange	www.missioninvestors.org
Monitor Institute	www.monitorinstitute.com
Nonprofit Finance Fund Social Impact Bond Learning Hub	www.nffsib.org
Opportunity Finance Network	www.opportunityfinance.net
Rockefeller Philanthropy Advisors	www.rockpa.org
Social Investment Forum	www.socialinvest.org
The Kauffman Foundation	www.Kauffman.org
Toniic	www.toniic.com

grant money to the organization with the expectation of receiving a "return on their investment" by creating jobs and furthering the organization's specific mission (Kauffman.org). According to its website, the Kauffman Foundation currently has an asset base of approximately $2 billion.

Securities Law and Regulations

In the United States, various state and federal securities laws and regulations must be complied with to raise any kind of capital. Since the interpretation and application of these laws and regulations is very complex, it will not be discussed in detail. In the following section, the U.S. regulatory framework is briefly presented that applies when one raises capital for an entrepreneurial firm. It is incumbent upon the entrepreneur to understand all state and federal regulations that apply to his or her situation. The best way to do this is to engage a competent attorney to deal with these issues.

Basic Securities Laws of the United States

Section 5 of the 1933 Act. Section 5 of the 1933 Securities Act requires securities that are not exempt to be registered with the SEC prior to any sale or distribution. Section 2(a)(3) of the 1933 act defines "sale" as including "every contract of sales or disposition of a security or interest in a security, for value" (Hazen, 2006). It also requires any sale of a security to be accompanied by a prospectus that meets the requirements set forth in the Securities Act. This information enables investors to make informed decisions about whether to purchase a company's securities. The registration documents that a company files with the SEC provide essential facts, including a description of the company's business, a description of the security to be offered for sale, information about the management of the company, disclosure of the risks inherent in the venture, and financial statements certified by independent accountants (SEC.gov).

All securities sold in the United States must be registered or exempt from registration. Certain securities that are issued by certain institutional investors or that have been granted specific exemptions under the Securities Act may not be required to be registered.

Regulation D: The Private Placement of Restricted Securities Offered by Small Firms. Securities issued under the exemption referred to as Regulation D are not required to be registered for sale to the public. Regulation D is the most common exemption from registration that is used by entrepreneurs raising private funds for their ventures.

Regulation D (or Reg D) contains rules providing exemptions from the registration requirements. This exemption from registration allows small issuers to offer and sell their securities without having to register the securities with the SEC. Reg D consists of three separate but interrelated exemptions.

1. Rule 504 provides exemption for certain offerings not exceeding $1 million within a 12-month period.

2. Rule 505 exempts certain offerings not exceeding $5 million within a 12-month period.

3. Rule 506 permits nonpublic offerings to qualified purchasers without any limitation on dollar amount (Hazen, 2006).

A Reg D offering is intended to make access to the capital markets possible for small companies that could not otherwise bear the costs (in both time and money) of a normal SEC registration.

Rules 144 and 144A: The Resale of Restricted or Control Securities. Rule 144 allows public resale of restricted and control securities if a number of conditions are met. Restricted securities are securities acquired in unregistered, private sales from the issuing company or from an affiliate of the issuer. Investors typically receive restricted securities through private placement offerings, Regulation D offerings, or employee stock benefit plans as compensation for professional services or in exchange for providing "seed money" or startup capital to the company (Hazen, 2006). Control securities are those held by an affiliate of the issuing company. An affiliate is a person, such as an executive officer, a director, or a large shareholder, in a relationship of control with the issuer and therefore has the ability to influence, directly or indirectly, management decisions. Five conditions must be met for these securities to be sold:

1. The prescribed holding period must be met.

2. An adequate amount of current information is available to the public regarding the historical performance of the security.

3. The amount to be sold is less than 1% of the shares outstanding and accounts for less than 1% of the average of the previous 4 weeks' trading volume.

4. All of the normal trading conditions that apply to any trade are met.

5. If wishing to sell more than 500 shares or an amount worth more than $10,000, the seller must file a form with the SEC before the sale.

Even if all the conditions of Rule 144 have been met, investors still cannot sell their restricted securities to the public until they have gotten the legend removed from the certificate. Once the sale is approved by the SEC, a transfer agent can remove a restrictive legend, and the sale may proceed.

Rule 144A provides a safe harbor exemption from the registration requirements of the Securities Act of 1933 for resale of restricted securities to qualified institutional buyers (QIBs), as defined in the rule. In general, a qualified institutional buyer is an institutional investor that in the aggregate owns and invests on a discretionary basis at least $100 million in securities of issuers that are not affiliated with the buyer. The SEC's objective in adopting Rule 144A is to achieve "a more liquid and efficient institutional resale market for unregistered securities" (SEC.gov). The rule also permits QIBs to buy and sell securities among themselves. Companies issuing unregistered securities may raise enough capital in the 144A market to remain private. They may also use a 144A offering as an intermediary step toward an initial public offering (IPO).

Selling Securities to the Public Market for the First Time Is Referred to as an Initial Public Offering (IPO). Securities sold in the public market need to go through a more complex issuing process than securities sold through one of the private placement exemptions (Reg. D, Rule 144, and Rule 144A). The procedure is called an *underwriting*. Below is a summary of this underwriting process.

Step 1: Contract with a securities broker/dealer to complete the underwriting process. There are several types of commitments that the broker/dealer may offer.

1. **Strict Underwriting.** The issuer uses an "insuring house," which will advertise and receive subscriptions and applications for shares from the public. The underwriter guarantees to purchase the unsold portion of the allotment.

2. **Firm Commitment.** The underwriter agrees to purchase all the securities from the issuer. The principal underwriter will contact other broker-dealers to become members of the underwriting group (syndicate), who act as wholesalers of the securities to the public.

3. **Best Efforts.** The underwriter does not commit to purchase the entire allotment being offered to the public. Rather than buying the securities from the issuer for resale to the public, the underwriter sells them merely as an agent. This is the most usual type of commitment.

Step 2: Complying with relevant securities law. Section 5 of the Securities Act prohibits all selling efforts by making it unlawful to offer a security for sale unless a registration statement has been filed and has become effective. Section 5 divides the registration process into three time periods: the prefiling, waiting, and posteffective periods.

1. **Prefiling a Registration Statement.** Once the public offering is contemplated, the time prior to the completion of the initial registration statement and filing is known as the prefiling period.

2. **Waiting.** After the registration statement has been filed with the SEC, there is a statutory 20-day waiting period prior to the effective date of registration statement, at which time sales of securities can take place. Although no sales can be made during this period, anyone is free to make an offer to buy or sell the security. The prospectus that meets the requirements of Section 10 of the act can be disseminated during this time.

3. **Posteffective.** Once the registration statement becomes effective, Section 5's prohibitions cease to apply. Market participants are free to buy and sell the registered securities provided they have been given the proper disclosures.

The key to a successful IPO is to engage a reliable, effective underwriting and a competent and reasonably priced law firm. Most IPOs can be done in 3 to 6 months.

Summary

There are many sources of capital available for entrepreneurs, but the competition for this capital is very intense. Identifying potential sources of capital is necessary, difficult, and time-consuming, but being a successful entrepreneur requires being successful at attracting capital.

Most entrepreneurs start by investing their own savings; they then move on to friends and family, angel investors, consumer credit sources, and then banks or venture funds. If they are motivated, capable, and organized, they may be able to do an IPO in the public securities markets.

If the entrepreneur solicits any form of investment capital from third parties, then the process is regulated by federal or local laws, particularly the solicitation process. No matter where the firm is domiciled (whether in the United States or some other country), compliance with securities law and regulation is expensive and requires professional assistance. In addition, the process is almost always very time-consuming. The results of an IPO are never predictable, and occasionally they can be disastrous in that they generate little or disappointing amounts of new funds at a high cost in terms of time and money.

Overall, the process of fundraising is difficult, time-consuming, and definitely not without risk and frustration. Yet it is an essential part of successfully starting and growing a new venture.

Chapter 10

Risks of Doing Business Internationally

Learning Objectives

- To learn about "transaction risk"
- To learn about "translation risk"
- To understand hedging with forwards, futures, and options
- To understand liability swaps
- To understand other methods of controlling risk
- To understand financing trade with letters of credit

Case: Baja'd Out Clothing Company

The Sea of Cortez is located on the west coast of Mexico and lies between mainland Mexico and the Baja California peninsula (which, while Mexican territory, is actually the lower part of California). The peninsula extends southward from the California border 800 miles to where it ends at Cabo San Lucas. Sailing, sport fishing, scuba diving, sun worshipping, and of course cerveza and tequila form the basis of the lifestyle. Having spent enough time on the "sea" to forget everything except these fun things is what is known as being "baja'd out."

The Baja'd Out Clothing Company of Tucson, Arizona, offers apparel that was inspired by the lifestyle and allure of the Sea of Cortez. The 15- to 34-year-old customers of U.S.-based marine stores, scuba diving supply shops, bars, restaurants, and sports shops like the offbeat and radical designs that Baja'd Out was producing. The apparel is good quality, and the designs resonate with the young crowd. Firm sales are growing rapidly as more and more retailers are ordering the line, and the company struggles to make enough product to keep up with demand.

As popular as the clothing line was, however, Baja'd Out was having a problem: Its gross profit margin was shrinking. While the line is primarily sold in the United States, the apparel is manufactured in Mexico; the direct costs are denominated in Mexican pesos, and the sales are denominated in U.S. dollars. The Mexican peso was rising versus the dollar, and that disparity was the heart of the company's shrinking margins. The company had to use more and more dollars to pay for manufacturing its products in pesos. When the firm's costs (incurred and paid in pesos) were "translated" into dollars and then matched with the firm's sales (made in dollars), the rise in the peso versus the dollar was causing the gross profit margin to decline.

A number of things occur when a firm does business internationally. One of the most significant is that it may no longer be paying its accounts payable or collecting its accounts receivable in its normal (country) currency. In addition, its assets or liabilities may no longer be denominated in its normal (country) currency. These currency-related impacts fall into the generic class of risks referred to as foreign exchange (forex)–related risk. Forex is not the only problem that a global environment brings to an international business. Financing the firm's purchase of foreign supplies, goods, or services can also be a problem, as are making sales to foreign customers in general and the tax implications of doing business globally. Chart 10.1 presents a schematic representation of the material covered in this chapter.

Chart 10.1   Schematic of Chapter 10

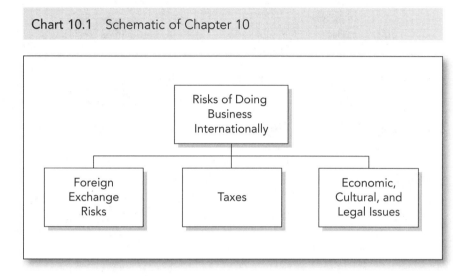

Foreign Exchange (Forex) Risks

One of the most significant problems encountered when doing business internationally is the impact of foreign exchange rates. The world's currencies fluctuate in value every minute of every day. Currency markets are the largest markets in the world, dwarfing all other markets. Any firm that buys a product or service that is denominated in a foreign currency or that sells its products or services in a foreign market has forex exposure. Once understood, forex exposure can be quantified, and once quantified, it can be mitigated. Forex risk manifests itself in several ways, as indicated in Table 10.1.

Quantifying Currency Risk

To control currency risk, a firm must first be able to quantify the risk. The first step is to identify the firm's exposures. Transaction currency exposure is fairly easy to identify because it is specific and directly related to the amount of payables or receivables denominated in the

Table 10.1   Foreign Exchange (Forex) Risk

Main Types of Forex Exposure		
Transaction Exposure	**Translation Exposure**	**Operating Exposure**
Changes in value of outstanding financial obligations or receivables caused by a change in forex rates	Changes in owners' equity due to changes in forex rates	Change in firm value or product demand resulting from change in cash flows due to an unexpected forex change

foreign currency. Similarly, **translation exposure** exists when a company owns a foreign subsidiary or asset.

To quantify **transaction exposure,** a firm should list all exposures for each main currency in which the company has receivables or payables. When listing transaction exposures, a firm should include the currency of the exposure, the amount of the exposure, the time period of the exposure, and the direction of the cash flow (receivable or payable) (Coyle, 2000). The size of its transaction exposure in any currency is the total of its future known receivables and payables in that currency. Exposures can be divided into time frames according to when the receivables and payments will occur. Finally, a cash flow forecast specific to the flows of currencies should be prepared that covers up to 1 year and updated regularly.

Translation exposures are unrelated to cash flow and therefore more difficult to quantify. The total exposure is the parents company's net investment in its foreign subsidiaries. The size of potential losses depends on exchange rate volatility over time.

Natural, Reporting, and Local Currency

Three types of currency relationship are at play when we consider forex risk and particularly forex-caused transaction and translation problems.

1. The "natural" or **functional currency.** This is the currency that the firm is doing business in on a day-to-day basis. In the case of Baja'd Out, the natural currency is U.S. dollars because that is the currency in which the firm makes its sales and in which it reports and pays taxes. The owners are U.S. citizens, and they want their company to earn and grow both profit and net worth in U.S. dollars.

2. The **reporting currency** at Baja'd Out is U.S. dollars. Most of the time, the reporting currency is the same as the "natural" position. However, on rare occasions, it may be different from the "natural" position.

3. When companies have receivables, costs, or assets denominated in a currency other than the "natural" or functional currency, that foreign currency is referred to as the "local" currency.

The interplay between the impacts of various currency rate changes on these three different types of currency exposure is what creates problems of a transaction and/or translation nature.

Transaction Risk

Baja'd Out was incurring transaction risk because it makes its product in Mexico and it pays for the production in pesos; the direct costs at Baja'd Out are denominated in pesos. Obviously, if the peso rises versus the dollar, then direct costs are going up (in dollar terms), and revenue (which is generated in dollars) is not rising proportionally. This results in a decreased profit margin. This income statement impact is called *transaction risk,* and it can occur any time that income statement items are denominated in **local curren-cies** that are not the natural currency or the reporting currency.

Transaction Exposure Example. Baja'd Out, a U.S.-based company, reports its financial statements in U.S. dollars. It purchases MXN $500,000 worth of goods from MexiCANT, its Mexican supplier, on October 1, 2013. Credit terms allow payment in 60 days. Spot exchange rates between the Mexican peso (MXN) and the U.S. dollar (USD) are as follows:

October 1, 2013   USD $1 = MXN $13.50

November 30, 2013   USD $1 = MXN $12.85

At the time of the purchase on October 1, Baja'd Out will record an account payable for USD $37,037.04 (MXN $500,000 * USD $1/MXN $13.50). At the time of settling the account payable, however, the Mexican peso has strengthened (the U.S. dollar buys less Mexican pesos) and Baja'd Out now has to pay USD $38,910.51 (MXN $500,000 * USD $1/MXN $12.85). Therefore, Baja'd Out has incurred a $1,873.47 transaction loss that has to be reported in its income statement.

Conversely, if the U.S. dollar had strengthened against the Mexican peso, Baja'd Out would have needed fewer dollars to pay for the purchase at settlement and therefore would have recorded a transaction gain in the income statement.

Translation Risk

If the company owned the Mexican company where the clothing was made and the Mexican plant used the Mexican peso as its reporting currency, then the currency fluctuation between the Mexican peso and the U.S. dollar would affect the asset balance on the books of the U.S. parent because when the Mexican company's equity is translated into U.S. dollars, there would be an increase in dollar value (because of the rise in the peso). This is called *translation risk*; it affects the parent firm's balance sheet either positively or negatively.

How would this affect Baja'd Out? Baja'd Out decides to establish a wholly owned subsidiary, MexiCAN, in Mexico on January 1, 2014, by investing USD $100,000 when the exchange rate between the U.S. dollar and the Mexican peso is USD $1 = MXN $13.00. In addition, MexiCAN borrows MXN $500,000 from a local bank on January 1, 2014. It uses the capital to purchase inventory and property, plant, and equipment (PP&E) worth MXN $1,400,000. MexiCAN's local balance sheet and U.S. translated balance sheet on January 1, 2014, are indicated in Table 10.2.

During the first quarter of 2014, MexiCAN engages in no transactions; however, the U.S. dollar weakens to USD $1 = MXN $12.25. To prepare a consolidated balance sheet at the end of the first quarter, Baja'd Out must now translate MexiCAN's balance sheet to USD using the current exchange rate. The original investment of USD $100,000 is a historical fact, so the company wants to translate MexiCAN's common stock such that it reflects this amount; therefore, it should use the historical rate of USD $1 = MXN $13.00. All other items are translated at the current exchange rate of USD $1 = MXN $12.25. The balance sheets at the end of the first quarter are indicated in Table 10.3.

As you can see, the USD balance sheet on the right doesn't balance and is off by USD $6,080. This is due to the difference in exchange rate. The subsidiary's assets and liabilities are now worth more in U.S. dollars as the peso has strengthened. A translation adjustment must be made in that amount to keep the balance sheet balanced, as indicated in Table 10.4.

By translating all assets and liabilities at the new (stronger) Mexican peso exchange rate, there will be a positive translation adjustment of $6,080. The positive translation reflects the fact that MexiCAN has a net asset balance sheet exposure (i.e., its translated assets are larger than its translated liabilities). If the peso had weakened in the first quarter, MexiCAN would have recorded a negative translation adjustment.

Table 10.2   MexiCAN's Balance Sheet

	January 1, 2014, in Pesos	Exchange Rate[a]		January 1, 2014, in Dollars
Cash	$400,000.00	$0.0769	Cash	$30,769.23
Inventory	$400,000.00	$0.0769	Inventory	$30,769.23
PPE	$1,000,000.00	$0.0769	PPE	$76,923.08
Total assets	$1,800,000.00		Total assets	$138,461.54
Note payable	$500,000.00	$0.0769	Note payable	$38,461.54
Common stock	$1,300,000.00	$0.0769	Common stock	$100,000.00
Total liabilities + shareholder's equity	$1,800,000.00		Total liabilities + SE	$138,461.54

a. USD $1/MXN $13.00 = .0769.

Table 10.3   MexiCAN's Balance Sheet Showing Translation Problem

	March 31, 2014, in Pesos	Exchange Rate[a]		March 31, 2014, in Dollars
Cash	$400,000.00	$0.0816[a]	Cash	$32,640.00
Inventory	$400,000.00	$0.0816[a]	Inventory	$32,640.00
PPE	$1,000,000.00	$0.0816[a]	PPE	$81,600.00
Total assets	$1,800,000.00		Total assets	$146,880.00
Note payable	$500,000.00	$0.0816[a]	Note payable	$40,800.00
Common stock	$1,300,000.00[b]	$0.0769	Common stock	$100,000.00
Total liabilities + SE	$1,800,000.00		Total liabilities + SE	$140,800.00

a. USD $1/MXN $12.25 = .0816.
b. USD $1/MXN $13.00 = .0769.

Table 10.4   MexiCAN's Balance Sheet Translation Showing Solution

	March 31, 2014, in Pesos	Exchange Rate[a]	March 31, 2014, in Dollars	
Cash	$400,000.00	$0.0816[a]	Cash	$32,640.00
Inventory	$400,000.00	$0.0816[a]	Inventory	$32,640.00
PPE	$1,000,000.00	$0.0816[a]	PPE	$81,600.00
Total assets	$1,800,000.00		Total assets	$146,880.00
Note payable	$500,000.00	$0.0816[a]	Note payable	$40,800.00
Common stock	$1,300,000.00	$0.0769[b]	Common stock	$100,000.00
Total liabilities + SE	$1,800,000.00		Translation adjustment	$6,080.00
			Total liabilities + SE	$146,880.00

a. USD $1/MXN $12.25 = .0816.
b. USD $1/MXN $13.00 = .0769.

Another factor complicating the translation forex problem is that companies having it must choose between the "current method" and the "temporal method" of translating the foreign subsidiary's net worth to the parent's balance sheet. Which of these two methods is used is based on the subsidiary's functional currency versus the parent's functional currency. If the functional currency of the two companies is the same, then the "temporal method" (i.e., the historical currency relationship) is used. If the functional currencies of the subsidiary and the parent are not the same, then the "current method" is used to make the translation. The choice between the two methods determines whether the historical or current exchange rate is used, as well as what line items of the subsidiary company's balance sheet are adjusted and translated to the parent company. The choice between the two methods, as well as its effect on the parent's balance sheet and income statement, is beyond the scope of this chapter and is case dependent. To choose one of these accounting methods to describe a translation forex problem, one should obtain the advice of an accountant. You can read more about translation exposure in the textbook *Multinational Business Finance* (Eitman, Stonehill, & Moffett, 2010).

Hedging Forex Risk

Translation, transaction, and other types of forex risk can be "hedged." This means that the impacts of transaction, translation risk, and the other types of forex risks can be mitigated if the firm has the capital and expertise to effect a counterposition in a security that will negate or substantially eliminate the movements of the foreign currency causing the transaction or translation problem in the first place. Figure 10.1 presents a schematic that assists in visualizing this statement.

Figure 10.1   Hedge Concept

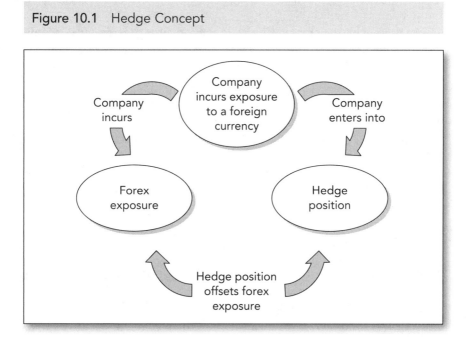

Technically, the term **hedge** means to avoid the possibility of a loss on a natural position by creating a counterposition (i.e., the hedge position). This means that, in the case of a true hedge, the hedging party will necessarily forgo the possibility of gain in excess of the natural position loss and vis-à-vis. As the natural position fluctuates, the up or down movement will be duplicated by an opposite move in the hedge position. When implementing a hedge position, it is critical to understand the hedge vehicle well enough so that a hedge can be constructed in a way that the percentage change in the value of the hedge position will offset the percentage change in the natural position over any period of time.

A number of investment vehicles can be used to create hedged positions, including

1. Forward contracts and swaps

2. Futures contracts

3. Options on futures contracts

Forward contracts are private contracts that bind two parties to complete a specified currency transaction wherein one party must deliver and another must purchase a negotiated nominal amount of a currency at a negotiated future point in time.

The party with the "long position" in the forward contract agrees to buy an agreed amount of a foreign currency at a predetermined price. Alternatively, the party with the "short position" in the contract agrees to sell a certain amount of currency at the predetermined price. Because the price is agreed to up front, each long party knows with certainty the amount of local currency it will need to buy to purchase the foreign currency. Similarly, the party that is the "short side" knows how much and at what exchange rate it will be selling. This certainty eliminates the risk of changes in the spot exchange rates that would otherwise affect both parties. Forward contracts can be customized in terms of size and maturity to suit each party's needs.

A forward contract is not an option. Both the buyer and the seller are obligated to perform under the terms of the contract. However, because forwards are private agreements, they carry of the risk of the opposing party not fulfilling its obligation (counterparty risk).

Below is an example of a forward contract that has worked as intended:

On March 1, Baja'd Out buys from its Mexican supplier goods valued at MXN $500,000 with an agreement to pay in full in 60 days. Suppose exchange rates were as follows:

Spot rate on March 1 for April 30 delivery: USD $1 = MXN $12.40

Because Baja'd Out wants to hedge the currency risk inherent in its account payable, it enters into a forward contract with its bank to buy Mexican pesos at $12.40 with a settlement date of April 30.

Since it has entered into a forward contract, Baja'd Out knows with certainty that it will need USD $40,322.58 (MXN $500,000 * USD $1/MXN $12.40) to buy MXN $500,000 on April 30.

Suppose that as April 30 approaches, the spot rate is USD $1 = MXN $12.00.

Had Baja'd Out not entered into the forward contract and waited to buy the pesos it needed, the pesos would have cost USD $41,666.67 (MXN $500,000 * USD $1/MXN $12.00). This amount represents an increase of USD $1,344.09. Therefore, Baja'd Out has saved money by buying pesos in the forward market.

Note: If the spot rate on April 30 had moved in the opposite direction, Baja'd Out still would have been obligated to buy Mexican pesos at the agreed rate, even though that rate would have been higher than the market rate.

When a forward contract is done directly with another business, with the company having the mirror image of the currency risk of your company, it might be possible to simply swap the two liabilities on the appropriate day. This kind of arrangement is called a *liability swap,* and it works to eliminate forex exposure through a contractual arrangement between two or more companies. Forward contracts are more formal and often involve a number of financial intermediaries, while liability swaps are direct agreements between two companies to "swap" currency-denominated liabilities on a particular day.

Typically, the two companies will negotiate the nominal amount of liability they wish to swap, an interest rate, and the date that they want to make the swap. Essentially, each company is making a loan to the other company in its own functional currency. On the day of the swap, they pay off each other's respective liabilities along with the accrued interest they owe to each other.

In the case of Baja'd Out, the company could find a Mexican-based company that would owe a dollar-denominated liability roughly equivalent to Baja'd Out's April accounts payable. Baja'd Out could agree to pay the Mexican firm's dollar-denominated liability while the Mexican firm would agree to pay Baja'd Out's peso-denominated liability. They would charge each other an appropriate interest rate in the appropriate currency to compensate each other for assuming the other's liability.

The weakness of this approach to "swapping" liabilities is the credit worthiness of the two firms engaged in the swap. Each firm is exposed to the risk that the other firm (counterparty) will fail in its obligation. Trading desks at large investment banking firms are now doing swaps. When a swap is done with one of these institutions, the swap contract is between the firm having the exposure and the investment bank, not the ultimate party. Depending on how the contract is written, this may serve to transfer the counterparty risk to the investment bank and away from the counterparty firm.

Futures contracts can perform the same function as a forward contract (i.e., they allow a party to buy or sell a currency at a predetermined price and date). The difference between a forward contract and a futures contract is that futures contracts are standardized, meaning they can be entered only at preset amounts and for predetermined settlement dates. On the other hand, forward contracts are entirely tailor made. Standardization allows futures contracts to trade on exchanges and allows for the contract to be closed out or sold to a third party. Because they are traded on exchanges, a clearinghouse guarantees payments to parties, eliminating counterparty risk. Futures contracts are marked-to-market daily, which means that daily price changes are settled day by day until the end of the contract. Settlement via a sale in the market for futures contracts can occur at any time up to the contract's expiration date. On expiration, a financial settlement occurs, and physical delivery is not made.

Options contracts are not like forward contracts or futures contracts. If an investor buys an option, he or she does not have the obligation to either buy or sell a currency at a future point in time. Only the seller of an option can be made to buy or sell at some point in the future. Options give the owner of the "option" the right, but not the obligation, to buy or sell a futures contract on a currency at a predetermined price and by a certain date in the future. To enter into an option contract, the owner must pay a premium to the seller (counterparty) to compensate the seller for accepting the obligation to buy or sell an underlying futures contract at a specific price until a specific date.

With respect to options, the predetermined price at which the option may be exercised at is called the *strike price,* and the date that the options matures is called the *expiration date.* Table 10.5 presents a summary of what options entail.

The owner of the option (long position) will ultimately exercise the option only if it is in his or her interest to do so—that is, when the futures contract that underlies the option contract has appreciated beyond the strike price contained in the option. Long positions in options on futures contracts are priced daily but not marked-to-market daily. This means that the value of owning an options contract changes daily in the market, but no daily cash settlement needs to occur with respect to the option holder. Sellers of the option, on the other hand, will be required to meet margin requirements because of the impact of the price fluctuations inherent in the underlying futures contract.

Table 10.5   Options (American Style)

	Call	Put
Buy	You have the option, but not the obligation, to *buy* the currency at a predetermined price (strike price) before a certain date (expiration date).	You have the option, but not the obligation, to *sell* the currency at a predetermined price (strike price) before a certain date (expiration date).
Sell	You give the option buyer the right to buy from you the currency at a predetermined price (strike price) before a certain date (expiration date).	You give the option buyer the right to sell to you the currency at a predetermined price (strike price) before a certain date (expiration date).

Taxes

One of the biggest problems that occur from doing business globally are the consequent tax issues that arise from such activity. Taxes are so case specific that we cannot detail all of the necessary points of analysis that need to be taken into consideration. The solution to this issue is simple: Hire a competent tax accountant. With that said, some general guidelines about tax issues are discussed below.

Profits earned and retained overseas do not get taxed by U.S. authorities until they are repatriated to the United States. This does not mean that profits earned in those foreign jurisdictions are not taxed by local authorities; they are, but usually these local tax rates are lower than current U.S. rates.

Some guidelines regarding overseas subsidiaries include the following:

1. To retain profits, overseas profits must be earned overseas. This means that one or more subsidiaries must be created in the overseas venues to earn the profits in the first place.

2. Transfer pricing associated with the overseas subsidiaries will be key in determining the venue where the profit ends up.

3. Transfer pricing between the U.S. parent and its foreign subsidiaries will affect the ultimate U.S.-denominated value of the parent firm's profits.

4. Overhead and other costs assumed at overseas subsidiaries will also determine subsidiary profitability.

5. Changes in relative currency values will affect the parent's U.S. balance sheet because of translation risk. These changes will not affect the parent's tax situation.

6. Transaction risk at the U.S. parent company will affect the dollar-denominated value of both the firm's profits and the firm's ultimate tax liability.

Once foreign subsidiaries are flush with cash and earnings, the U.S. parent can borrow against those assets to secure domestic lines of credit. Apple, Inc., has recently done this by leaving its profits overseas and borrowing domestically to pay shareholders dividends.

Other Risks Related to Doing Business Internationally

In one way or another, most of the risk of doing business internationally is, at least tangentially, currency related. Other risks, however, need to be dealt with, including the following:

1. Cultural and legal issues

2. Credit, payment, and shipping issues

3. Operating issues

Cultural and legal issues permeate all international relationships and are very case specific. Russia is different culturally as a legal environment from Vietnam, which is different from Peru. In this chapter, it is impossible to cover the gamut of cultural and legal differences that can occur. The nature and enforceability of written contracts, the extent to which trust plays a role in business intercourse, and the ability to arbitrate and settle disputes without court action are important. Companies will often agree to put measures in place to assist them in resolving disputes should they arise. Some of the normal precautions are as follows:

1. The parties may agree to a jurisdiction for potential legal action up front. Often foreign companies are leery of the local courts in locations where they intend to do business. As a result, they negotiate that any disputes will be tried in a nonpartisan location. For example, many foreign companies doing business in Russia have negotiated that any disputes will be tried in Finland. The Finnish commercial

justice system is similar to the Russian commercial justice system, but it is viewed as being less partisan by non-Russian market participants.

2. Another approach is for the foreign company to consider hiring a local agent or enter into a partnership agreement with a local partner. The idea is that a well-known local representative will be able to negotiate the ins and outs of the local business community better than an outsider.

3. Another approach is to negotiate a binding arbitration process between the parties. The objective of such an agreement is aimed at guaranteeing that both parties will be bound by the outcome so that protracted legal wrangling is avoided altogether.

Credit, payment, and shipping issues are always important and can be quite problematic. These aspects of foreign trade are facilitated in any number of ways:

1. Freight-on-board (FOB) invoicing is common. Upon delivery of the product to a shipping point, the invoice becomes due and payable. Title to the product changes at the point when it is released by the manufacturer to its final destination, and there is no continued obligation on the part of the seller to care for or facilitate it on its journey. Payment is made at the same time as final shipment.

2. A partner, agent, or customs broker may be employed to facilitate either or both the payment of invoices and the facilitation of shipping. These arrangements with such firms do add to costs and may not remove the credit risk from the relationship since the agent or partner may not be willing to accept any credit risk.

3. Often the easiest way to facilitate the payment for goods is to use *letters of credit* (L/C). Letters of credit are fairly standardized agreements made by a financial institution to make payment on behalf of its client (an importer) to a beneficiary's (an exporter's) bank under specified conditions. In essence, the importer's bank is substituting its credit for that of the importer. It has guaranteed payment to the exporter, provided that the exporter complies with the terms and conditions of the L/C (Madura, 1992). The bank issuing the L/C is obligated to honor the payment to the exporter regardless of the buyer's ability and willingness to pay, as long as all terms and conditions have been met by the exporter. Letters of credit can be revocable, where the L/C can be

canceled at any time without prior approval from the beneficiary, or irrevocable, in which case it cannot be canceled or amended without the beneficiary's approval. Normally, L/Cs used to finance international trade are irrevocable.

One *operating issue* that affects all companies doing business internationally is the *magnitude and impact that foreign currency movements have on the cross-market demand* for goods and services. Currency movements may serve to make products or services relatively more or less expensive in one market versus another. As currencies move around in terms of price, the nominal cost of goods and services sold by foreign producers changes when measured in the local currency of the country in which they are selling. Essentially, the demand for the company's goods or services changes because the nominal price of the goods or services changes, and the nominal price for the good or service changes because the product or service is paid for in either a relatively more or relatively less expensive foreign currency.

Strictly speaking, this is not a forex problem but a macroeconomic problem. This problem is not amenable to a forex-oriented hedging solution. This problem is related to long-term trends, not day-to-day currency rate fluctuations. Hedging to eliminate such a widespread and persistent event is difficult and costly for several reasons: (1) because it is hard to quantify the risk within a given time horizon, (2) because the cost of the hedge will be expensive, and (3) because of the inability to predict the impact that changes in currency rates will have on product demand as well as the timing of those impacts. Hedges attempted under such conditions will yield very imprecise results.

Companies do a couple of things to mitigate this problem. A foreign company may decide to price its products or services in the local currency of the market in which it is selling. By doing this, it is assuming the long-term forex risk to retain sales and market share. Once a firm has made this decision, it then usually attempts to denominate as much of its costs in that same local currency as is possible. Doing this provides the company with at least a partial natural hedge (by denominating revenues and costs in the same currency). Second, this keeps the firm's products and services available and priced in the local currency and market. Demand should not be adversely affected.

A less used version of the above strategy would be for the firm to price its products or services in a market basket of currencies, thereby assuming a diverse form of forex risk to retain the firm's market share. Such a strategy will diversify the impact of any single currency on product demand. The firm needs to have a great deal of bargaining power to do this, but the strategy can be done.

Occasionally, foreign customers may be required by their government to arrange *countertrade* transactions to offset their contemplated transactions with foreign suppliers. When this requirement is in place, it usually becomes the responsibility of the foreign firm trading partner to make the arrangements. The purpose of countertrade is to provide a quid pro quo for the local economy. For example, if U.S.-based Firm A sells to foreign-based Firm B, then the national government of Firm B can and often does require that U.S.-based Firm C buy a like amount of product from another firm based in its country (Firm D). The result of such a chain of transactions is that the dollar reserves of B and C's countries stay at their original levels.

Countertrade may represent the key to being able to sell one's own product into a foreign venue or an opportunity in its own right. It is a ubiquitous requirement that at some point is likely to become relevant to the business. The Commercial Service Officers (CSOs) of the U.S. Department of Commerce stationed in the foreign country can be helpful in dealing with this. It is also worth knowing that very large companies (like Boeing or McDonnell Douglas) usually have entire countertrade departments tasked with finding U.S. companies to engage in countertrade transactions to help offset their foreign business activities.

Summary

Global business is fraught with unique risks. One of the biggest risks is the risk precipitated by fluctuations between currencies—forex risks. Knowing how to quantify forex exposure, hedge it, and initiate the hedge position is something with which managers may want to get specialized help. Most commercial banks have foreign currency desks through which foreign currencies can be bought or sold. Also, most banks are equipped to issue letters of credit to finance offshore purchases of goods. Larger banks will usually have the ability to do swaps or forward contracts. Brokerage firms are usually better equipped to help with hedges constructed using futures contracts or options on futures contracts.

Even though managers of firms engaged in foreign trade may often choose to obtain specialized help with their currency hedges and trade finance activities, managers of these firms can initiate many day-to-day activities to control both the currency risk and other risks encountered. Managers can adopt policies and procedures such as denominating accounts receivable and accounts payable in the same currency, selecting the proper venue in which to settle disputes, building in binding arbitration processes to settle disputes, taking action to find countertrade opportunities, or hiring a local partner or agent. Finally, managers can manage to minimize tax liability by using optimum structure and transfer pricing to organize the firm for maximum profitability.

Chapter 11

Managing to Maximize Firm Value

Learning Objectives

- To identify the key aspects of maximizing value

- To enact processes that will help create value

- To recognize and minimize risks to value creation

Case: Uni-Net

The year was 1992, and the company, Uni-Net, was just beginning to develop its strategy to grow and prosper in the long-distance communications space. There was substantial competition, with the largest competing firms being MCI, Sprint, and Williams Communications. But management at Uni-Net thought they had a winning strategy. Uni-Net management believed that they should not compete head-to-head with the major players in the industry but would focus on overlooked markets: markets in rural areas and markets where the large players were not active and did not have switching stations to aggregate customer calls and connect to the AT&T long-distance system.

In 1984, the monopoly that AT&T had on the U.S. telephone market was ended via a consent order in the U.S. District Court. AT&T was broken up into Regional Bell Operating Companies, Bell Labs, and a few other subparts. Among other things, the impact of this deregulation was that it opened up the long-distance market to anyone who could aggregate customer traffic by routing it to a local switching station and then, using that switch, to connect to and transmit over the AT&T national landline system to the final destination. This provided the opportunity for many to be a long-distance company and the impetus for many companies to enter the long-distance business.

These new entrant companies could provide long-distance service via their own local switching stations. If a customer wanted to make a long-distance call, then the customer would dial a local access number, be connected to the local switch, and then have the call sent to its ultimate destination via whichever long-distance network was available (usually AT&T). Such long-distance service was cheaper than sending the call directly over the old AT&T system because AT&T was now required, by terms of the consent agreement, to act as a common carrier and accept traffic from all competing service providers.

The value of being a long-distance aggregator was wholly dependent on getting as many customers as possible. The more customers the company had, the more value the company had to a strategic buyer. The largest companies in the industry were focused on the largest urban areas, where the bulk of the national market was. Uni-Net marketed itself in small-town environments, usually where there was a university or college. College students were both target customers and excellent part-time salespersons. It was a conscious strategic choice of management that once the customer base was built, the company would be very attractive to one of the big national resellers like MCI, Sprint, or Williams Communications.

However, during the build-up phase, management wondered what additional considerations they should be giving to both operational and financial issues to maximize firm value.

Whether the entrepreneur's goal is to exit the business, make a potential merger or acquisition, or simply expand the firm through steady growth, a continuous objective should be to maximize the value of the firm. Producing maximum value ensures that the entrepreneur does not leave anything on the table and that he or she is able to get the most for his or her efforts. In this chapter, we look at ways the entrepreneur can implement strategies to increase and maintain value and identify and control the risks that can be detrimental to value creation. Chart 11.1 presents a schematic representation of the material covered in this chapter.

Chart 11.1   Schematic of Chapter 11

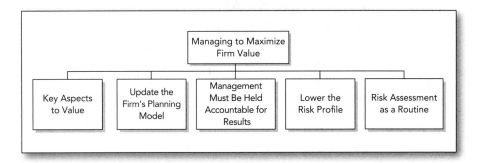

Key Aspects to Value

While there isn't a "one-size-fits-all" approach to maximizing the firm's value, there is consensus in the academic as well as in the business community about measures that entrepreneurs can take to ensure the firm takes advantage of its full potential. The following are some key variables that entrepreneurs should pursue.

Certainty of Cash Flows

The certainty of cash flows takes risk into account. What is risk? In terms of modern finance, risk is the "volatility" of returns over time. By this standard, "risk" can be statistically determined. It is the measured probability that a company will not achieve the results expected. Remember that risk is not uncertainty. Uncertainty is not amenable to statistical determination. There was no way for Tokyo Electric Power to statistically forecast the tsunami of 2011, nor was there a way for Johnson & Johnson to predict the Tylenol murders of 1982. These events represent events that are classed as uncertainties, not risk. Despite the classification, both of these events had lasting impacts on the two firms.

According to financial theory, the value of any risky asset is the present value of its expected future cash flows. To find the present value of those cash flows, they are discounted by the appropriate cost of capital given the risk of the company, as discussed in Chapter 7. Given this concept of value, it follows logically that given a fixed level of cash flow, if we can lower the risk-adjusted required rate of return at the firm, the higher its value will be. To maximize firm value, it is crucial to lower the firm's risk profile.

Inherent in the financial notion of risk is the concept of variability of returns over time. In the case of an entrepreneurial firm, given more variability in expected cash flows, in the eyes of investors, the firm will appear riskier. This higher perceived risk will in turn increase the required rate of return and decrease the value of the firm. An entrepreneur can reduce this risk and maximize firm value by consistently meeting cash flow projections.

A history of meeting cash flow projections will establish that the company has lower volatility than it may first have appeared to have. This technique is effective at enhancing firm value because of the measurable impact that meeting the firm's cash flow projections has on the variability of financial outcomes. Outcomes that are close to expectations are considered less variable if they closely adhere to projected results. While variability may occur, if outcomes are close to projected values, the variability will not be significant compared to management's and investors' expectations.

Grow the Firm

With the advent of social media, growth has taken on a new meaning. Sometimes investors are willing to overlook growth in the top (sales) and bottom line (net income) and focus instead on growth of the firm's user or customer base with the intention of monetizing the client base in the future. This is the case of the mobile messaging service WhatsApp. While sending instant messages within the United States has always been easy and inexpensive, messaging internationally has historically presented challenges. Cell phone providers usually have a presence in just a few countries, and in the past, communicating between platforms has been nearly impossible and expensive.

In 2009, WhatsApp founder Jan Koum created a cross-platform messenger service that allows users to communicate via the app for 99 cents *per year*, bypassing wireless carriers that may charge users 99 cents *or more per message* to use their networks. WhatsApp technology proved especially beneficial in places with a high degree of international communication and fragmented cell phone service like Europe, Asia, and Latin America. As anticipated, the WhatsApp's user base grew exponentially, at times adding 50 million people every 2 months. Its user base reached 200 million in April 2013 and grew to 400 million just 8 months later (Winkler, 2013). Despite its tremendous user base, Mr. Koum sacrificed immediate revenues and earnings and focused instead on building a robust client base. In February 2014, Facebook agreed to buy WhatsApp for $19 billion, a record for any startup. The motivation behind Facebook's acquisition is not WhatsApp's relatively small earnings but the exponential growth of its user base that it expects to monetize in the future.

While revenue and earnings growth are important for the success of an entrepreneurial firm, growing the customer base is critical to maximizing the value of the firm. Virtually all valuation models favor growth. As was the case at Uni-Net and WhatsApp, customer base is extremely important when building and maintaining value. Often startups and early stage firms have not yet had time to build the other accepted measures of firm value, such as customer growth, positive cash flow, and EBITDA (earnings before interest, tax, depreciation, and amortization). Because these other determinants of value are lacking, it should be remembered that growing a customer base is one firm-specific characteristic that is available to all firms, even early stage ones.

Market Position Is Important: Document and Publicize Your Success

Some firms use their market position to command premium valuations. While the firm's revenues might not be impressive, the market's view of the firm's market share, brand, and growth create a positive view of the firm's ability to produce superior profits in the future. Facebook is an example of a firm that used its market position to receive a premium valuation. Facebook started in 2004 as a social media site intended for universities in the Boston area. Facebook gradually increased its presence to universities and high schools throughout the United States. In 2006, the company allowed anyone older than 13 years to open an account. By promising to keep its services free, the company gained a huge market share from other social media sites that charged a fee for its premium services. At the end of 2006, Facebook had 12 million users.

Facebook repeatedly publicized its market share to businesses as a way of attracting them to advertise on the site. In 2007, the company created an ad platform to attract businesses to market on their site. The site's technology allowed for targeting of customers by characteristics like age, gender, and geography. Facebook reached 100 million users in August 2008. By July 2010, the site had reached 500 million users and had surpassed Google as the most popular Internet site. Despite its vast user base, the company's revenue was far behind that of Google. In 2009, Google's revenues were $24 billion, while Facebook's revenue was only $800 million.

The company focused on gaining market share, and by the time the company went public in May 2012, Facebook had gained over 900 million users. Prior to the initial public offering (IPO), the company reported revenues of just over $1 billion while net income was $205 million. The original IPO price was $38 per share, which translated into an extremely high price to earnings (P/E) ratio of 107 (Raice, Das, & Letzing, 2012).

Build Intangible Value and Organization

Key to any organization's value is the worth of its intangible property and the value of its organizational structure and style.

Intangible Property. As indicated in the chapter on valuation, *intangible property* is valued differently and separately from the other parts of the firm. Because the value of intangible property is independently derived, it is worth the firm's effort to document and develop any intangible property it might have. It is also significant that intangible property often has value that can immediately be realized outside the context of the firm's current ongoing activity. Patents, proprietary processes, customer lists, and unique service capabilities may have value to outside firms that will pay to license the capability to use in activities that are noncompetitive to the licensor (i.e., firm that owns the intangible property).

A good example of this kind of secondary use of intangible property involves Strum Ruger & Company. This firm is a well-known sporting firearms company. The company has unique patented processes for performing certain CNC (computer numeric controlled) machining processes. The company has established a separate subsidiary to take advantage of these processes and will license or do CNC work for third-party firms.

Firms that have any form of intangible asset should be looking for ways to document and use the value. Following is a list of procedures that a firm with intangible assets can use to do this:

1. Patent patentable processes.

2. Register copyrights and trademarks.

3. Document all proprietary processes.

4. Keep customer lists in usable and updated form.

5. Have all personnel execute confidentiality agreements.

6. Do periodic searches for third-party misuse of firm intangibles.

A Flat, Flexible Organization With a Productive Workforce Is Valuable

The importance of a flat and flexible organization cannot be overstated. A firm with these attributes is able to recognize trends and adapt quickly to take advantage of them while delivering the highest returns possible. Key to achieving this is having a flexible workforce and cost structure. Not only does this keep material and payroll costs down (and profits up), but it also allows firms to be early market entrants responding to opportunities to take advantage of growth.

A flat organization is one that strips away layers of middle management, removes complex business structures, and gives greater responsibilities to lower-level employees. Firms that limit the unneeded layers of management (and the bureaucracy that comes with them) are more capable of listening to the needs of the customer. A flat organization helps ensure that lower-level employees, who communicate most often with customers and who are in the best position to understand market trends, quickly make customer-related decisions. Importantly, research has shown that employees in flat organizations are more satisfied with their jobs (Willems, 2014). It is important to make a distinction between a manager-less firm and a management-less firm. Although there may be a reduced need for managers under this approach, there will always be a need for some more democratic form of management.

Have a Competent, Productive Workforce. Ideally, entrepreneurial firms will hire only the most essential and capable employees needed to grow the business. The firm cannot afford to have incompetent people handling the most critical decisions at this vital stage of firm development. Nothing is more frustrating to potential investors than looking at the management of the firm and realizing that all key positions are held by family and friends of the owner. Investors are usually looking to have the best qualified persons with expertise in the relevant fields in key roles. Showing nepotism indicates a motivation to serve personal interests and not the interests of the company.

Make Costs Reactive to Sales. One approach to creating an adaptive cost structure is to have more variable costs and fewer fixed costs. Because variable costs are incurred only when there is actual production, a firm is able to limit unnecessary expenses if sales become a problem or decline. Since fixed costs are incurred regardless of sales or production, having more fixed costs impedes the firm from lowering costs in times of declining revenues. While it may seem logical for the firm to use variable costs to the greatest extent possible, fixed costs offer the benefit of operating leverage, which can greatly improve the firm's bottom line. The trade-off between more operating leverage and its risk is explained in detail later in this chapter. However, at least in the early stages of development, keeping operating leverage low is usually a good idea.

Entrepreneurs should be aware of any impact technological advances have on their operations. One of the consequences of rapid technological advancement is the shrinking product life cycle. It is estimated that 50% of annual company revenues across a range of industries are derived from new products launched within the past 3 years (Horn, 2014). This suggests that long-term product "cash cows," which stay in a company's portfolio for many years, are becoming less and less relevant. A firm can no longer afford to invest too heavily in profitable ventures, as these may become obsolete very quickly. By limiting investments to purchasing only enough capacity to meet customer demand and keeping up with technological advances, the firm is able to create a flexible organization with adaptive costs.

On the plus side, advances in technology enable firms to create more adaptive supply chains that rapidly adjust to changing requirements based on real-time demand signals. Automation of any supply chain task is likely to produce a more efficient and less costly process of meeting demand. New technology also allows firms to continually revisit sourcing strategies for new, lower-cost supply sources.

Update the Firm's Planning Model

As previously mentioned, technological advances are reshaping the competitive landscape. This changing environment means that accurate demand planning and forecasting have never been more imperative. Reacting to new information more quickly than competitors allows the firm to quantify the impact and react accordingly. The output of any projection model is only as good as the inputs that go into it. In order for the firm to make better projections on sales, costs, and cash flows, it must continuously adjust the planning model to reflect new information, such as changes in trends or unanticipated costs. In addition, firm projections should "work" the way the firm works. So if a firm's policies or procedures change, so should the firm's model for making projections.

Develop a Useful Historical Database

Developing a planning model that functions like the firm is initially difficult due to the lack of historical data. The entrepreneur is faced with having to make many assumptions that often are guesses, at best. As the firm progresses, it can rely on its own historical performance to update the planning model. Developing a historical database allows the entrepreneur to mine the data for information. This new information can help entrepreneurs identify patterns such as seasonality or preferences among various demographics based on empirical evidence. As more historical data are integrated into the planning model, the entrepreneur can produce a more accurate planning model that has improved power to project results and be the basis for estimating firm value.

Management Must Be Held Accountable for Results

In conjunction with good operating and financial processes, the entrepreneur will need to assemble a capable management team to assist in maximizing firm value. Whether intentionally or not, managers sometimes use the resources of the firm to maximize *their own* self-interests at the expense of the firm. This problem is referred to as **agency risk.** Leaders and boards of directors at entrepreneurial firms need to understand that solving this problem is one of their most important tasks. The problem is best solved by instituting a system of accountability and pay that aligns the interests of the managers with the rest of the stakeholders of the firm. While simple in theory, in practice the task can be arduous.

1. The entrepreneur must assign identifiable and measurable objectives and responsibilities that contribute toward the value of the firm. The board should seek managers' commitment to these goals. It is easier to get commitment when managers understand two things: how the goals benefit them personally and how the goals benefit the firm.

2. Progress needs to be measured periodically and continuously to discover any deviations, whether positive or negative.

3. Feedback needs to be provided on ways to improve performance when it is falling short of management's expectations. It's important to remember that feedback is not only for problem areas; praise for good performance is also a valuable feedback tool. To be effective, feedback should be as close to the measured event as is possible.

4. Linking consequences to results provides external motivation for managers to meet their commitments.

5. Evaluating the effectiveness of the overall system in maximizing firm value usually reveals areas for improvement at the organizational level.

Tailor Pay and Incentives to Results

Linking a manager's compensation to meet the firm's objectives has been a popular strategy for aligning interests; managers will be financially motivated to perform if their results support the long-term interest of the firm. This can be accomplished by setting manager salaries at relatively low levels while giving bonuses based on milestones reached. While salaries should be only a small percent of total potential compensation, bonuses and stock options need to be structured to make up the rest. If certain results are met, such as a certain percent increase in earnings or reaching a threshold in the value of the firm, then managers are entitled to a bonus or additional shares. Zingheim and Schuster (2000) describe this "total rewards system" in their book *Pay People Right!*

Entrepreneurs need to carefully address potential conflicts of interest that pay-for-performance systems can create if the goals are not properly considered. Performance goals that focus on short-term results can lead managers to create unsustainable growth that allows them to reach their goals while not benefiting the firm in the long run. Goals should be set so that the quality of firm performance remains high. This means that results will not come from measuring leverage or manipulating costs but from sound fundamental achievements, like higher margins or better turnover rates. Otherwise, managers may be tempted to manipulate variables to make it seem like results are being met. Some companies now defer payments of bonuses or other incentives by up to 5 years to make sure that the results achieved are sustainable.

Lower the Risk Profile

Maximizing firm value can be divided into three components: maximizing growth, maximizing profits, and minimizing risk. In the first part of this chapter, the focus was on ways of achieving growth and profitability. We now turn our attention to minimizing risk as a source of value creation. While strategies for minimizing risk are not considered as "exciting" as growth strategies, they are nonetheless just as important.

As mentioned previously, risk is commonly defined as the variability of outcomes over time; the greater the variability, the greater the probability that the firm will not achieve results. Risk is a statistical concept. While having a robust planning model can help the firm minimize risk, it is impossible to incorporate all possible outcomes into a projection based on a statistical perspective. This often leads entrepreneurs to underestimate the range of outcomes. An entrepreneur's view of future events tends to be incomplete and slow in adapting new information (Courtney, Kirkland, & Viguerie, 1997). Making sound strategic decisions under conditions of risk argues for analytical rigor with respect to the planning process. Rarely do managers know nothing about their risky environment, even in the most volatile environments. The models of risk assessment described below are powerful tools to incorporate into the firm's planning process.

Liquidity Risk

In Chapter 4 on financial ratio analysis, liquidity was described as the extent to which a company is able to meet its short-term obligations by using its short-term assets (i.e., assets that can be readily transformed into cash). Working capital management refers to the ability of a firm to generate cash when and where it is needed. The goal of effective working capital management is to ensure that a company has adequate access to the funds necessary for the day-to-day operating expenses, while at the same time making sure that the company's assets are invested in the most productive way.

Liquidity contributes to a company's creditworthiness, or the perceived ability of the borrower to pay what is owed in a timely matter. Creditworthiness allows the company to lower borrowing costs and obtain better terms for trade credit. Because debt obligations are paid with cash, the company's cash flows will ultimately determine solvency. Liquidity risk is the risk a company may fail to meet its short-term obligations.

A firm's liquidity risk can be measured by calculating its liquidity ratios. Recall from Chapter 4 that the two most important liquidity ratios are the current ratio and the quick ratio. A firm with low liquidity ratios risks is usually able to cover its working capital needs. The following are some steps that can be taken to minimize liquidity risks:

1. Where possible, appropriate discounts for early payment on accounts receivable invoices should be given.

2. Collect accounts receivable with the highest possible efficiency.

3. Pay collections personnel bonuses based on how well they maintain a low days-sales-outstanding ratio.

4. Where possible, ask suppliers for more moderate terms with respect to making payments on accounts payable.

5. Keep inventory as low as possible.

6. Consider using a just-in-time approach for maintaining inventory.

7. Pay production personnel bonuses on how well they maintain a high inventory turnover ratio (and thus a relatively low inventory turnover ratio).

Operating Leverage

Operating leverage is a type of risk that is attributed to the operating cost structure of the firm. In particular, it is the use of fixed costs as opposed to variable costs in its operations. A firm's total costs are made up of variable costs and fixed costs. **Variable costs,** which are costs that change in proportion to the producing and selling activities of a business, are incurred only if there is production or sales activity. **Fixed costs,** on the other hand, do not vary directly with the production or sales process. Examples of fixed costs include rent or lease payments on machinery or equipment, rent, and salary expenses of supervisors. The greater the fixed operating costs relative to variable operating costs, the greater the operating leverage.

As an organization employs a higher degree of fixed costs in its cost structure, its operating leverage will increase. Operating leverage is greatest in firms where total costs are a function of a relatively large proportion of fixed costs and a relatively low proportion of variable costs. The result of having a high operating leverage ratio is that the firm's break-even point rises. Operating leverage acts as a drag on the firm's ability to generate an increase in net income when sales revenue increases; the greater the proportion of fixed costs versus the firm's variable costs in the firm's cost structure, the greater the impact on profit given a percentage change in sales revenue. With relatively high operating leverage (and thus low variable costs), each unit of sales will provide a higher contribution margin.

A measure of operating leverage is *degree of operating leverage (DOL)*, which may be calculated as follows:

$$DOL = \frac{\% \text{ change in operating income}}{\% \text{ change sales}}$$

The easiest way to calculate this is as follows:

$$\frac{(Price - VC) \times \text{ Units}}{((Price - VC) \times \text{ Units}) - FC}$$

where

Price = price per unit sold;

VC = variable cost per unit sold;

FC = total fixed costs;

Units = units sold.

If the DOL is high, then even a small percentage change in sales can produce a big change in operating income. While a high DOL is beneficial if sales are increasing, it can be detrimental if sales are falling. Managers should remember that high operating leverage creates high volatility of net profit, especially at sales levels near the firm's break-even point.

As mentioned, a firm's operating leverage also affects its break-even point (i.e., the number of units that must be produced and sold so that the company's net income is zero). The break-even point can be thought of as the point at which revenues are equal to total costs. It may be calculated as follows:

$$Quantity\ breakeven = \frac{Total\ fixed\ costs}{Contribution\ margin\ per\ unit}$$

where

Contribution margin = (price per unit – variable costs per unit).

Managing cost structure and operating leverage is a cost-benefit issue. A company with high fixed costs, and therefore high operating leverage, can generate a large percentage increase in net income from a relatively small percentage increase in sales revenue. On the other hand, a firm with high operating leverage has a relatively higher break-even point, or operating risk. The optimal cost structure for an organization involves a trade-off. Management must weigh the benefits of high operating leverage against the risks of large committed fixed costs.

Financial Risk

Financial risk refers to the use of debt to finance a firm's operations. Debt allows equity holders to generate a greater return on their investment by being able to increase income-producing assets with the same level of equity by borrowing additional capital. Remember the accounting equation:

$$\text{Assets} = \text{Liabilities} + \text{Shareholder's equity}$$

While adding debt to the capital structure of the firm has benefits, such as a lower cost of capital and tax deductions on the cost of debt (i.e., tax deduction on interest), adding too much debt poses risks. The more debt the company has, the higher the risk that the firm will not be able to pay its debt obligations. Given the nature of debt, payment of debt has the first claim over the firm's income and assets.

A measure of financial risk is the *degree of financial leverage (DFL)*. DFL explains the impact that a change in operating profit will have on earnings, and EPS is the earnings per share.

$$\text{DFL} = \frac{\% \text{ change in EPS}}{\% \text{ change in operating income}}$$

The easiest way to calculate this is as follows:

$$\text{DFL} = \frac{\text{EBIT}}{\text{EBIT} - \text{Interest}}$$

where

EBIT = earnings before interest and tax (CFA Institute, 2012).

A high DFL indicates that for a given change in operating income, there will be a relatively large change in EPS. The benefits of having high financial leverage when operating income is rising is, to a large extent, offset by the risks of having high leverage when operating income is falling. As with degree of operating leverage, a firm must balance the goal of increasing returns on equity by using debt and the risk of incurring too much debt and thus increasing the risk of lower credit scores or even insolvency.

Worst-Case Scenarios

Although it's difficult to expect the unexpected, the entrepreneur must consider the whims of nature along with the risk and consequences of a catastrophic event. A firm that is unprepared for dealing with worst-case scenarios can see its operations brought to a halt in an instant, sometimes to the point of failure. A firm can lessen the impact of such events by undertaking systematic analysis of its status in the industry and community and attempting to build firm capabilities that are robust enough to withstand unexpected events. Some industries, like investment advising, are required by law to have disaster recovery plans. In general, such recovery plans include the following:

1. Routine backup and offsite storage for business records

2. Proper insurance for the various business assets of the firm (including business continuity insurance)

3. Preidentified alternative locations from which to work or produce

4. Preidentified means of shipping and receiving product

5. Employee training with respect to the implementation and execution of contingency plans

6. Preplanned method of notifying customers, regulators, and suppliers of the firm's status

This type of planning, while important, does not create immediate value, but it does tend to preserve value in the face of external events that would otherwise serve to diminish or destroy firm value.

Risk Assessment as a Routine

Risk assessment provides a mechanism for identifying which risks represent opportunities and which represent potential pitfalls. Done correctly, a risk assessment gives a firm a clear view of variables to which it may be exposed, whether internal or external, retrospective or forward looking. A robust risk assessment process, applied consistently throughout the life of the firm, empowers management to better identify, evaluate, and accept risk in the daily course of business, even while maintaining the appropriate controls to ensure effective and efficient operations and regulatory compliance.

For risk assessments to yield meaningful results, certain key principles must be considered. A risk assessment should begin and end with specific business objectives that are anchored in key value drivers. For example, should the firm enter a new market, should the firm invest in a new production process, or should the firm expand its capacity? These objectives provide the basis for measuring the impact and probability of adverse impacts on the firm. Governance over the assessment process should be clearly established to foster a holistic approach and a portfolio view of the organization's overall risk appetite and tolerance. Finally, assessing leading indicators enhances the ability to anticipate possible pitfalls and opportunities before they materialize. With these basic principles in mind, the risk assessment process needs to be periodically refreshed to deliver the best possible insights.

Models, such as back testing and simulation, estimate both the likelihood and impact of events, whereas nonprobabilistic models like stress testing measure only the impact and require separate measurement of likelihood using other techniques. Nonprobabilistic models are relied on when available data are limited. Both types of models are based on assumptions regarding how potential risks will play out.

Back Testing

Back testing is the processes of using a model or technique developed today that uses historical data to help understand the range of potential outcomes. Back testing uses historical data to evaluate how a projection designed for use now would have explained past results. A key element of back testing that differentiates it from other forms of historical testing is that back testing calculates how a strategy would have performed if it actually had been applied in the past.

Back testing requires building a model with sufficient detail so as to "work" the way the firm works. Back testing, like other modeling, is limited by potential overfitting. That is, it is often possible to find a process that would have worked well in the past but will not work well in the future. Despite these limitations, back testing provides information not available when models and strategies are tested on data that themselves are not historical in nature.

Sensitivity and Scenario Testing

Sensitivity and scenario testing is another tool a firm can use to assess risk. In this type of test, key risk factors such as price, volume, and quality level are "stressed" or given values beyond their normal operating ranges, or they are given values based on an expected future set of conditions. One variable at a time is changed to assess the impact of that single variable on the firm; the technique is called a **sensitivity analysis.** When the analyst varies a number of variables so as to approximate a particular business condition, then the technique is called a **scenario analysis.** The goal is to discover the impact on the firm if the selected risk factors hit abnormal levels. The test may also uncover deficiencies in processes and systems that may cause unexpected problems.

Sensitivity and scenario testing has several strengths. It is easy to set up—one only needs to give extreme or expected values (given a specific scenario) to inputs in the firm's planning model and analyze the results. It exposes hidden problems that can be dealt with early. It reveals the inherent structural limitations of a system that allows operating parameters to be set more realistically or the system to be redesigned. It can also be used by audit and internal controls to evaluate existing controls.

Sensitivity and scenario testing does have limitations. This type of test estimates the impact of an event, not its frequency, and therefore captures only one dimension of risk. It is usually focused on an extreme event or a set "scenario." This technique considers complex effects of combinations and relationships between variables to the extent they are understood. The choice of factors to stress or vary and the linkages between these factors are subjectively but logically assigned. It is critical to the scenario technique that input variables be varied logically in a manner calculated to produce results that are descriptive of an extreme event or sets of circumstances.

Simulation

Simulation is an iterative process that allows testing for many scenarios without requiring the construction of or experimentation with the real system. Simulation is the process of creating a model where each variable varies within a selected range of outcomes and with a specific standard deviation. The purpose of simulation experiments is to understand how a system would react to changes in its variables if the changes in each variable were independent and disconnected to the movements in every other variable; they vary based on the probability of their independent distributions.

Simulation offers several advantages. The simulation model is interesting in that it allows for simultaneous and independent changes to multiple variables to study the results. It can also be used to reproduce large and complex situations that may affect the integrity of the firm. The disadvantage of simulation is that it is not connected directly to any specific real-world event or sequence of events. The simulation requires a specialized computer program and knowledge of the historical distribution levels of various input variables.

Summary

The single most important thing about managing to maximize firm value is to pursue excellence in the creation, production, and delivery of the firm's products and/or services. It is important that the firm view value through all the lenses that it has available. Viewing the various key aspects of value beyond the product creation and sales cycle will provide management with an additional edge when it comes to maximizing the firm's overall value. The act of considering these additional key aspects of value will help prepare the firm and its personnel to weather turbulent future conditions.

Chapter 12

Venture Exits

Learning Objectives

- To determine if and when an entrepreneur should exit the venture

- To understand the different types of exits available

- To indicate both positive and negative exits for investors and entrepreneurs

- To determine an exit value

Case: Camera+ Photo Software Application by Tap Tap Tap

Camera+ is a mobile software application launched by the company Tap Tap Tap in 2010. For $1, users can transform their smartphones into a sophisticated photo camera with a bundle of built-in editing and enhancing filters, effects, granular controls, and even a zoom (Empson, 2012). It allows users to take pictures with their smartphone and instantaneously share them on their favorite social network such as Facebook or Flickr.

After 8 million downloads, the founder, John Casasanta, disclosed he had several offers from large corporations to purchase his company. He revealed offers from companies such as Adobe Systems, Zynga, Google, and even Twitter that few entrepreneurs would ever receive. His response to all the above was very clear: "Not interested!" With Instagram (free photo-sharing software for smartphones) purchased for $1 billion by Facebook, Camera+ could surely have cashed in on the trend and made a generous exit for its founder and team. Instead, John Casasanta preferred to keep its independence and keep doing what he loves, building great mobile software. "We're doing more than fine on our own and we'll continue to do so on our own," he commented on the company's blog (Casasanta, 2012). It seems as if an "exit" is out of the question for the entrepreneur. In fact, with such a lucrative business, generating revenues in the millions and operating with a team of fewer than 20 people, why would John Casasanta even think about selling the company or even raising capital?

The entrepreneurial process is more than just the creation of a new venture. For most entrepreneurs, creating a venture is a means of getting to the ultimate goal: reap the rewards of the time, money, and energy spent to build a successful business. The entrepreneurial process, therefore, does not end with creation but rather with the **entrepreneurial exit** (DeTienne, 2010). Yet many entrepreneurs initiate a business without an exit strategy in mind. Research suggests that fewer than 50% of entrepreneurs consider their exit strategy prior to making an exit decision (DeTienne & Cardon, 2008). Furthermore, according to *Inc.* magazine, only 45% of the 2004 *Inc.* 500 CEOs report that they started their companies with an exit strategy in mind (*Inc.*, 2005). It is perplexing that one of the most important decisions for the entrepreneur and for the business does not attract the attention it deserves.

Perhaps the topic of exiting a business is often avoided by entrepreneurs due to the complexity and emotional effort it entails. The exit usually brings a mix of feelings to entrepreneurs as they are about to let go of the project to which they have dedicated a large part of their life. There is no formula to answer when one should exit as it depends on several factors ranging from the personal interests of the entrepreneur to market conditions. Entrepreneurs must decide if they really want to let go of the business they have started and expanded over the years. Are they still passionate about their business? Does the company still have some major milestones to reach that will increase its value? Is exiting the right choice for the success and growth of the company? Is it too early? What are the risks associated with not selling today? How urgent is the entrepreneur's need for money? Is there another more interesting business idea and opportunity? Those questions haunt the mind of successful entrepreneurs worldwide: Make the cash-out larger by delaying the sale or miss the sale opportunity and end up with a fraction of what could have been.

For entrepreneurs, choosing the time to exit is both a rational and sensitive problem. Yet not considering the exit as part of the entrepreneurial process can stymie a successful venture outcome. In this chapter, we discuss exits as a deliberative and methodical process that need not be an overwhelming experience. Rather, exits consist of choosing the best options to enhance the goals of the entrepreneurs, the firm, and its investors. Chart 12.1 presents a schematic representation of the material covered in this chapter.

Chart 12.1   Schematic of Chapter 12

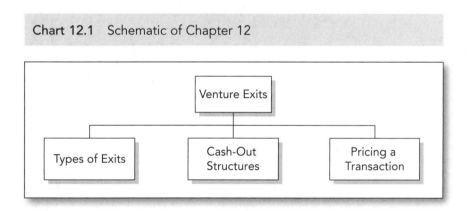

Types of Exits

An "exit" or "cash-out" occurs once a company (or part of it) is acquired or its stock is traded on a public exchange. For investors, this is one of the most important days of their investment journey—payback time. They have invested their own money and their partners' money, as well as obtained bank financing for the venture, and now they expect to realize a lucrative return. While most investment opportunities available on the market have a fair amount of liquidity, investments in privately owned companies are usually illiquid. Investors should always inform entrepreneurs at the beginning of the investment journey that their stock ownership in the company is for sale at any time; it is just a question of price as well as the clauses in the contract. Investors should make clear to entrepreneurs that some day, cash-out opportunities will come and they will exit their investment. In essence, there are seven basic approaches for investors as well as entrepreneurs to exit: (1) initial public offering (IPO), (2) sale to a strategic buyer (trade sale), (3) private exchanges between investors, (4) sale to the owners, (5) selling of shares to corporate partners, (6) reorganization of the company, and (7) liquidation (see Chart 12.2).

Chart 12.2   Types of Exits

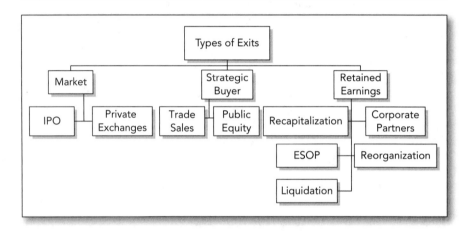

Security Markets

Initial Public Offering (IPO). The most glamorous and almost always the most profitable exit any investor could hope for is through an **initial public offering (IPO)**. In the long run, the public market has the potential to generate higher rewards than any other exit strategy. Entrepreneurs as well as investors have the opportunity to cash out by selling all or a portion of the shares owned.

Despite the fact that the concept of an IPO is very popular and is perceived as the epitome of success for entrepreneurs, it represents only a fraction of the cash-outs made by investors and entrepreneurs. Requirements for IPOs are demanding and very expensive. Companies doing an "IPO" usually need to have a higher than average growth rate and annual revenues in the millions (usually more than $50 million in annual sales). In addition, tightening regulation in recent years has made the process extremely onerous and lengthy. It is estimated that the costs of compliance with the requirements to file an IPO are between $690,000 and $2.87 million (*Study of the Sarbanes-Oxley Act,* 2009). Besides financial costs, the company faces a sudden loss of privacy, pressure from shareholders to exceed expectations, and the obligation to provide time-consuming reports to shareholders and comply with other regulatory obligations. The advantages are obvious, ranging from access to capital, exposure to the market, increased liquidity, and the potential to generate a higher return for investors.

For the founding entrepreneurs, the IPO does not necessarily translate into an immediate exit or a large paycheck. The number of shares registered and sold through the IPO process will be determined by the investment banker (known as the underwriter) the firm chooses. The underwriter will usually require a "lockup" of the owner's shares that are registered. The "lockup" will restrict the amount of shares the original owners can sell over a period of time. Often, no registered shares of the founders can be sold within the first 6 months and sometimes up to a year of the initial public offering.

As a result of securities laws and regulation, if the founders' shares are unregistered, they are subject to many restrictions with respect to selling them to the public. The combination of the underwriter's "lockup" and the restrictions related to securities law and regulation serve to either delay or limit the number of shares an original owner or investor can sell over a given period of time. When a company transitions from being privately held to being publicly traded, there is also a large increase in the amount of regulation and reporting requirements with which the company must comply. IPOs usually bring added challenges for entrepreneurs as they have to devote time and energy to complying with the new rules regarding disclosure of material facts, their personal trading, and the venture's financial information.

The Process of Going Public. Hundreds of brokerage houses can take a company public, but few specialize in public offerings of medium-size and growing companies, with varying criteria as to what kind of companies they are willing to represent. The main criteria center on the company's industrial sector, earnings, expected future cash flows, and the amount of capital to be raised. Since underwriting services come at a premium price, entrepreneurs and investors need to research the market to find an appropriate underwriter willing to take the company public. An underwriter's fee generally ranges from 3% to 10%, with exceptions for companies like Facebook. Given its enormous valuation, Facebook negotiated its fees down to only 1.1% (Saitto, 2012). Besides the underwriter's fee, other costs like legal fees and auditing fees need to be added. Selecting the most competent brokerage house with the most competitive fees is very relevant to the IPO process. In addition, entrepreneurs and investors should choose a well-regarded underwriter. The underwriter's ability to distribute the shares to appropriate investors and support in the secondary market is very important; otherwise, the market for the shares will not maintain itself for any length of time after the initial date of the IPO.

Private Exchanges. The selling of shares of a private company used to be relatively uncommon. The advent of companies such as Facebook, LinkedIn, and Groupon proved that private exchanges are a reality that investors and entrepreneurs need to be aware of. SecondMarket (www.secondmarket .com) and SharesPost (www.sharespost.com) are the leading marketplaces for private company stock trading. These markets allow owners of shares of private companies to cash out before the company either is bought or has gone through an IPO (Hwang, 2010). These *private exchanges* provide liquidity to an asset that under other circumstances is illiquid. SecondMarket and SharesPost offer an auction-style mechanism where they match buyers and sellers of shares of privately owned companies. While the volume of transactions on both websites is still relatively low compared with the level of trade from major public exchanges, private exchanges are becoming popular and represent an opportunity for holders of private shares to exit earlier. The key question regarding these private exchanges is, How will the regulators deal with them? Currently, the issue is unresolved.

Strategic Buyer

Trade Sales. When a publicly traded or private company is looking to acquire another company to grow, the acquiring firm is called a **strategic buyer.** A transaction involving a buyer of this type is called a **trade sale** or "strategic purchase." This type of sale is the most common form of exit for venture-backed companies. It essentially means selling all or part of the company to a strategic buyer that can consolidate the firm with itself and provide both strategic and financial support to take the firm to the next level.

Through acquisitions like these, large corporations are able to strengthen or diversify their core business, as they usually acquire firms that are already profitable with a set of customers and resources. Acquisitions have occasionally been made to capture the talent of the **target company (takeover target).** As a result, being the purchaser in a "trade sale" represents a way for large corporations to grow either vertically or horizontally, obtain technology, improve revenue, capture new customers, or expand to new markets. It can also be used to stymie competition by securing **intellectual property** (IP), market domain, or technology owned by the target organization. This is what happened with Facebook in 2004 when it acquired the company AboutFace for the purpose of acquiring the Internet domain name Facebook.com (Williams, 2007).

Private Equity. Increased attention in private equity as an asset class by institutional investors and high-net-worth individuals has resulted in huge amounts of money committed to private equity firms. It is estimated that between 1998 and 2006, approximately $1.5 trillion flowed into **private equity funds** (Courtois & Jenkinson, 2011). In turn, a large portion of this capital is used to acquire a controlling stake in entrepreneurial firms with the intention of increasing the firm's value and selling it in the future for a handsome profit. According to Courtois and Jenkinson (2011), value creation is attributable to three things:

1. Earnings growth from operational improvements and enhanced corporate governance

2. Optimal financial leverage and repayment of part of the debt with operational cash flows before the exit

3. Multiple expansions depending on preidentified potential exits

According to the Private Equity Growth Council, there are approximately 2,797 private equity funds in the United States (http://www.pegcc.org/educa tion/pe-by-the-numbers/) and perhaps 2,000 firms headquartered in the rest of the world, mostly in Europe. These firms represent a large pool of educated buyers who are interested in buying existing businesses. In addition to the three characteristics mentioned by Courtois and Jenkinson (2011), candidate businesses must

1. Present an interesting investment thesis (unique ability to grow or produce profit or both)

2. Be in the $50-million-in-sales size or larger

3. Have excellent management

4. Have unique proprietary products, market niches, and/or customers

The firms that private equity/venture capital (PE/VC) firms are interested in should be ready for growth and operational improvement. PE-oriented investors like to buy out firm ownership over time and in conjunction with measurable intermediate performance benchmarks. PE/VC investors are not in the business of buying high. Firms in this group will usually be sold on the basis of success payments over time; the owners and specifically the management team are usually asked to stay involved until firm value has increased to the level where the investor has achieved his or her goal.

Retained Earnings

Recapitalization. Recapitalization or "recap" occurs when new capital sources are used to replace old capital sources of the firm. In the event that investors want (or are forced) to exit the venture, the new or remaining owners will seek new capital, usually in the form of debt, to buy out the shares of the exiting investors. It is often done with the purpose of implementing major strategic changes in the firm. A popular form of recap is the **management buyout** (MBO). If the management team believes that they are able to better manage the company, they can take over the firm using a significant amount of leverage to finance the acquisition of the company. MBO managers seek to add value—from improving company operations and growing revenue and ultimately increasing profits and cash flows. The sources of growth include organic revenue growth, cost reduction/restructuring, and acquisition. However, the potential returns in this category are to a large extent due to the use of leverage. This form of recap usually occurs when there are issues between management and shareholders. A recapitalization is often a prelude to a later exit such as an IPO or trade sale.

Selling of Shares to Corporate Partners. It may happen that present investors sell their share of the business to a corporation (known then as corporate partners) interested in owning a part of the business invested in. This situation can be good for the company, as corporate partners may be more useful for the long-term success of the firm than investors. Corporate partners may actually represent a great exit opportunity for entrepreneurs wishing to sell their share of the business.

Employee Stock Ownership Plan (ESOP). The exit strategies previously mentioned often necessitate strong market and business conditions to make the exit worthwhile. Yet one of the most critical mistakes that entrepreneurs make is exiting the venture at the wrong time. Short-term fluctuations in cash flows can have a significant impact on the amount private equity firms are willing to pay (Waldren, 2012). In mature markets or economic down cycles, buyers may not be available or may be unwilling to pay what the owner believes the business is worth (Miller, 2010). Employee stock ownership plans, or ESOPs, represent an alternative exit strategy.

An ESOP is a tax-qualified defined contribution retirement plan designed to invest primarily in the stock of the firm. The investment is made through an ESOP trust. The ESOP owns the stock for the beneficial interest of the employees; the stock is allocated over time based on years of service and compensation. A member needing to exit the firm may sell his or her shares to the trust at fair market value, which is determined through a valuation performed by an independent valuation professional. In a leveraged ESOP transaction, the ESOP borrows money with guarantees of repayment from the company that is used to purchase the shares of the exiting employee. Each year, the company makes tax-deductible employee benefit contributions to the plan that are used to repay the loan (Waldren, 2012). Besides a readily available market, ESOPs offer tax advantages for the firm and seller. Entrepreneurs need to obtain advice and help from a qualified certified public accountant to determine the appropriateness of establishing an ESOP.

Reorganization. Reorganization is a nicer way of saying bankruptcy. This is possibly the worst exit investors can make, as they are at the mercy of bankruptcy courts and creditors. Bankruptcy courts are considered one of the worst possible scenarios for equity investors, as the original amount of money invested is not factored into the bankruptcy plan and is rarely recovered. Large legal fees are usually incurred, and the time to go through the process is usually long. Investors should avoid bankruptcy courts as an investment-saving tool if at all possible.

Liquidation. A last-resort solution for investors can be **liquidation** of their investment. Sometimes a venture can be worth more liquidated than when running. This usually happens in companies with large fixed assets such as land, buildings, or machines that are passing through tough times or were disrupted by new technology. In those cases, the assets, if sold, can be worth more than what the business could ever generate in the future.

Cash-Out Structures

When an entire company or a controlling interest in a company is sold, sellers can be paid for their stock or assets through six different methods:

Cash Sale. As the name suggests, it is an exchange based on cash, where the capital gains are taxed accordingly.

Installment Sale. Instead of exchanging the stock of the company for cash, it can be exchanged for a note that will be paid off over time. Often transactions structured like this generate favorable tax treatment for cash-based shareholders. Sellers should be aware that a note is not cash but a promise of future payments. Sellers should make sure that they know how well secured the note is as well as the creditworthiness of the buyer(s).

Stock Swap. The purchaser may prefer to trade stock instead of cash for an acquisition. Tax advantages to the seller are obvious, as tax will be paid only once the stock received in exchange is sold. Entrepreneurs and sellers should negotiate receiving registered shares that have no restriction on when the stock can be sold and the seller can be cashed out.

Assets for Cash. In the United States, if the entity being sold is a straight C corporation, this approach is generally not recommended, as double taxation occurs (once at the company level and then at the personal level) when the funds are paid to the shareholder. Selling assets for cash may be a good option if the assets are sold below book value.

Asset Sale on an Installment Basis. This occurs when the acquiring company pays for assets through secured notes. Given the complexity of this transaction, an experienced tax lawyer should be used to make sure this makes sense given its associated risks.

Exchanging Assets for Stock. The situation would be similar to an installment sale. By selling assets this way, a gain over book value may be created, which could make sense if the assets are selling below book value. Otherwise, this option is not recommended unless a tax lawyer specifically reviews the deal and advises going forward. The worst-case scenario could end up with having not only double taxation but also an illiquid stock.

Pricing a Transaction

When contemplating or negotiating an exit transaction, one of the relevant questions is always, What should the price be? While of course the price is usually negotiated between the parties, there are a few guiding principles. Below are several key concepts that should be kept in mind when thinking about price as it relates to liquidating transactions. While there are many issues tangent to the various valuation approaches discussed below, details and a more complete analysis are provided in Chapter 8.

Determining firm value generally is a four-part process. Total firm value is the sum of the value determined in each of these four steps.

Part 1: The Value of the Ongoing Firm. For firms with ongoing revenues and expenses, the operating value of the firm should be viewed in light of the revenue stream expected to be generated. Usually the "gold standard" of ongoing firm valuation is to estimate the present value of the firm's "free cash flow" (Dinan, 2012).

Part 2: The Value of the IP and Intangible Portions of the Firm

1. In addition to ongoing firm revenues and cash flow, any intellectual property (IP) that the firm possesses has value. Even with no revenue or cash flow, some firms have substantial worth when their IP is considered. Valuing IP is a very specialized topic. Generally, the value of IP is a matter of how important the IP is to the acquiring firm. Several methodologies can be used to estimate a value of IP; entrepreneurs should take time to learn the basics regarding these techniques. IP is a component of firm value that should never be overlooked, especially with rapidly growing, technologically savvy ventures.

2. "Market share" is another aspect of firm value that should not be overlooked. The same principle holds true for firms that have achieved significant market penetration, as when the firm owns or controls significant IP. Even if the firm does not have revenues, the firm may still have substantial value by virtue of its substantial or unique market penetration.

3. Proprietary processes, exceptional productivity, or unique skills related to sales or production can all create value that is independent of revenues and cash flow.

Formal techniques can be used to develop valuation models for all of the IP and intangible portions of the firm one might wish to consider, as we discussed in Chapter 8. While these various methodologies may be very helpful, it should be remembered that one of the very best estimates of minimum value for the nonoperating characteristics noted above is the cost that the acquiring firm would need to bear to duplicate the acquiring firm. If the acquiring firm would need to expend substantial time and money to achieve the IP, market share, or productivity of the target firm, then the value of these aspects of target firm value should be proportionate to that time and money.

Part 3: Tax Issues and Contingent Liabilities. The third aspect of firm value is rather technical; it has to do with the impact of any tax benefits (or costs) and other contingencies (good or bad). These aspects of value are totally unique to the target firm and need to be considered in a very specific way.

Part 4: The Impact of Liquidity/Marketability and Control. Finally, the impact on firm value attributable to liquidity/marketability and control needs to be considered. Considering these two factors is another specialized topic that is covered in Chapter 8. The main concept to remember is that if control of the venture is being sold, then a control premium should be added to the valuation of the other aspects of the firm.

Venture Capital Method

Due to their stage in the business development cycle and unique financing needs, venture capital firms often do not commit themselves to using the discounted cash flow method to determine the firm's value. VC principals feel that entrepreneur-provided financial projections are simply too imprecise to provide reliable information. There is a simple approach to valuation that is sometimes referred to as the venture capital method, developed by Professor Sahlman at Harvard Business School (Sahlman & Scherlis, 2009). The approach, however, is not necessarily limited to venture capital–backed companies and can be used to value entrepreneurial companies that exhibit startup characteristics (i.e., pre-revenue firms, volatile cash flows, long time horizons, considerable risk).

The *venture capital method* takes the perspective of the investor instead of the firm and is based on the investor's required internal rate of return (IRR) to determine the value of the firm at the time of the investment. Essentially, this method forecasts the terminal value of the firm at the time of exit, usually based on some multiple of earnings, and works backward to calculate the pre- and post-money valuations. The process is as follows:

1. Determine the terminal value (V) of the firm at time of the exit. For example, suppose the firm is projected to have earnings of $4,000,000 in 5 years and price to carnings (P/E) ratio multiples are 6 for comparable companies. The terminal value (V) is

$$V = Multiple * Earnings = 6 * \$4,000,000 = \$24,000,000$$

2. Determine the future value of wealth (W) that investors need to achieve to meet the desired IRR given the investment amount and holding period. Suppose an investor makes an investment for $5,000,000 in the firm and is asking for a 25% IRR in the 5-year holding period. The future value of the firm needs to be

$$W = I * (1 + r)^t = \$5,000,000 * (1 + .25)^5 = \$15,258,789$$

3. Determine the percentage equity stake (E) that the investor needs to hold to achieve the desired IRR. Given V and W, we can calculate the percentage of shares as

$$E = W/V = \$15,258,789/\$24,000,000 = 63.58\%$$

4. Calculate the post-money valuation. In our example, if an investment of $5,000,000 buys 63.58% of the shares, then

Post-money valuation = I/E = $5,000,000/.6358 = $7,864,108

5. Finally, determine the pre-money valuation:

Pre-money valuation = post-money
valuation − I = $7,864,108 − $5,000,000 = $2,864,108

While the concept is simple and requires accurately forecasting terminal value, it is a useful method for developing pre- and post-money valuations for firms with startup features. This method can also be adapted to include multiple rounds of financing if warranted by market conditions.

Summary

Exiting is an essential aspect of entrepreneurial finance. Exit strategies should be thought of at the very beginning of the investment process. When investors commit to an investment decision, they should have in mind a possible exit scenario that is factored into the valuation of the venture. While entrepreneurs tend to consider an IPO as the ultimate exit, it is only one of several possible successful exit possibilities. In this chapter, we covered both positive as well as negative forms of exit.

Choosing one form of exit over another will depend on various factors, such as transaction costs, industry trends, fees, timing, market conditions, size of the firm, revenues generated by the firm, and tax repercussions.

Glossary

accounts payable turnover ratio   A liquidity measure used to quantify the rate at which a company pays off its suppliers during an accounting period.

accounts receivable turnover ratio   A liquidity measure used to quantify the rate at which the receivables portfolio has been collected during an accounting period.

accrual accounting   Accounting method whereby income and expenses are recognized as they are invoiced or incurred, even though cash may not have been paid or received.

agency risk   The risk that the management of a company will use its authority to benefit itself rather than shareholders.

alpha   A coefficient measuring the portion of an investment's return arising from firm-specific attributes as opposed to overall market conditions. It is the abnormal rate of return on a security or portfolio in excess of what would be predicted by an equilibrium model like the capital asset pricing model (CAPM).

angel investors   A single or group of high-net-worth individuals who provide financing to a firm, usually at the startup stage, either in exchange for convertible debt or equity.

assets   Resources owned by the firm having commercial or exchange value that the firm intends to employ to generate revenues.

back testing   The process of using a predictive methodology to test a strategy or idea by using data from prior time periods to get an indication of how the strategy or idea would perform in future scenarios.

balance sheet   A financial report showing the status of a company's assets, liabilities, and owners' equity on a given date.

beta   A coefficient measuring the response of a risky asset's rate of return in relation to return of the market.

bootstrapping   A situation in which an entrepreneur starts a company with little external capital. An individual is said to be bootstrapping when he or she attempts to build a company from personal finances or from the operating revenues of the new company. The term may also apply to building financial projections based on the estimates of management at startup firms. Finally, the term refers to a strategy of repeated sampling to improve overall results in statistical analysis.

business plan   A written document that describes in detail how a new business is going to achieve its goals. A business plan will lay out a written plan from a marketing, financial, and operational viewpoint.

cash accounting   Accounting method that recognizes revenues when cash is received and recognizes expenses when cash is paid out.

cash flow cycle   A measure of the time, usually in days, it takes the company to turn the cash expended on raw material to cash collected from revenues.

cash flow from financing   Cash flow that arises from raising or decreasing cash through the issuance or retirement of equity or debt.

cash flow from investments   Cash flow that arises from investment activities such as the acquisition or disposition of current and fixed assets.

cash flow from operations   Cash flow that arises from normal operations net of taxes.

cost of goods sold   The direct costs attributable to the production of the goods sold by a company. This amount includes the cost of the materials used in creating the good or service along with the direct labor costs used to produce the good or service.

cross-sectional benchmark   Analysis of data for a peer group of companies at a specific point in time.

crowdfunding   The use of small amounts of capital from a large number of individuals to finance a new business venture. Solicitation takes place over the Internet. The regulatory status of this funding strategy is unclear at the time of this writing.

current assets   Assets that are converted into cash, sold, exchanged, or expensed in the normal course of business, usually within 1 year.

current liabilities   Debt or other obligations coming due within 1 year.

current ratio   A measure of a company's ability to pay its current obligations from current assets. It is calculated as the ratio of current assets to current liabilities.

days sales outstanding ratio   A measure of the average number of days that a company takes to collect its accounts receivable.

days of inventory ratio   A measure of how many days' worth of inventory the company has on hand.

debt   An obligation owed by one party, the debtor, to a second party, the creditor. The debtor is obligated to pay the creditor in accordance with an expressed agreement, usually in the form of interest and principal payments. There are many forms of debt, from secured to unsecured to cash flow.

debt to equity ratio   A measure of a company's financial leverage that indicates the proportion of equity and debt the company is using to finance its assets.

debt to total assets ratio   A leverage ratio that defines the total amount of debt relative to total assets.

depreciation   Amortization of fixed assets, such as plant and equipment, so as to allocate the cost over their depreciable life.

discounted cash flow   Value of future expected cash receipts and expenditures at the present date. Cash flows are discounted to their present value using the cost of capital discount rate.

earnings before interest, taxes, depreciation and amortization (EBITDA)   A measure of the firm's production of economic value used to assess the company's worth. EBITDA is net income with interest, tax, depreciation, and amortization added back. This adjustment allows for a more level number when making comparisons among companies and industries since various accounting and financing techniques are not considered.

entrepreneur   A person who is willing to take the risks of starting a new business or taking over an established business for the purposes of increasing its value. In most industries, nations, and markets, entrepreneurs challenge existing assumptions and look to generate value in more innovative and creative ways. Entrepreneurs change the way business is conducted by identifying opportunities and successfully filling them.

entrepreneurial exit   The process by which the entrepreneur exits the venture and relinquishes control of the company that he or she founded. Typically, "exits" involve some form of recapitalization, being bought by another company in the industry or doing an initial public offering.

entrepreneurial finance   The process of making financial decisions for ventures owned or controlled by entrepreneurs. It involves the study of financial statements, cash flow management, raising capital, valuation, and making projections, among other themes.

equity   Ownership interest possessed by a sole proprietor, partners, or shareholders in a corporation. Represents that residual claim to the company's assets after all liabilities have been paid.

executive summary   A section of the business plan that summarizes the longer report in such a way that readers can rapidly become acquainted with a large body of material before reading the detailed presentation of that material. It usually contains a brief statement of the problem or proposal covered in the business plan, background information, concise analysis, and main conclusions. It is considered the most important part of the business plan.

expenses   The economic costs that a business incurs through its operations to earn revenue.

financial leverage ratio   See *debt to equity ratio*

financial projections   Estimate of future performance of the company made by its managers, accountants, or other parties. Making such projections involves estimating future operations regarding the firm, including sales, expenses, net profit EBITDA, and cash outflows and cash inflows. The projection of firm operations is based on an understanding of the day-to-day business processes of the firm and assumptions about future conditions.

financial ratio analysis   The selection, evaluation, and interpretation of financial data to assist in financial decision making. Data are converted into ratios to compare the firm versus its peers (cross-sectional) or to compare its current performance to its own performance in the past (time-series).

financial risk   The risk to shareholders that the firm will be unable to meet its financial obligations, usually debt obligations, due to high leverage.

financial statements   A formal record of the financial activities of the business. They can cover a period of time (income statement, statement of cash flows) or a specific moment in time (balance sheet).

fixed charges coverage ratio   A measure of the firm's ability to generate cash earnings sufficient to cover fixed financing expenses, such as interest and leases.

fixed costs   Costs that are incurred regardless of production or sales volume.

foreign exchange risk   The risk of holding an investment, receivable or payable in a foreign currency that is attributable to changes in currency exchange rates.

forward contract   A contract that allows for the purchase or sale of an asset at a predetermined price and predetermined date to a counterparty who is one of the contracting parties. A forward contract is customizable to the needs of the parties and is not liquid or marketable.

functional currency   The main currency that the firm's day-to-day business is denominated in.

futures contract   A standardized contract that allows for the purchase or sale of an asset at a predetermined price and on a predetermined date and of a standard quality and quantity. Unlike a forward contract, a futures contract is standardized and can be actively traded in the public market, and it has both liquidity and marketability.

gross margin   A measure that represents the percent of total sales that gross profit is.

gross profit   Measure of profit calculated as revenues minus cost of goods sold.

hedge   A strategy used to avoid the possibility of a loss (or gain) on a position (the natural position) by creating a counterposition. The hedging party will forgo the possibility of gain in exchange for the elimination of the possibility of loss.

income statement   A financial report that summarizes all revenues, costs, expenses, gains, and losses the firm incurred during a specific accounting period.

informal risk capital market   Financing for companies, usually small in nature, sourced from nontraditional sources. The sources include family and friend loans and angel investors.

initial public offering (IPO)   A private corporation's first offering of its stock to the public markets.

intangible asset   A nonphysical resource that represents an advantage to the firm's position in the marketplace. Intangible assets have value in their own right.

intellectual property   A work or invention that is the result of creativity to which one has rights and for which one may apply for a patent, copyright, or trademark.

interest coverage ratio   A measure of the firm's leverage indicating its ability to pay the interest on its debt with its operating profit.

internal rate of return (IRR)   A measure used to compare the profitability of various investments. It is also known as the discount cash flow rate of return. Generally, the investment with the highest IRR will be the best.

inventory turnover ratio   A liquidity measure of how many times a firm is able to sell and replace its inventory in an accounting period.

leverage ratio   A financial ratio that provides a measurement of the degree of debt used at an enterprise.

liabilities   Obligations payable by the firm in the short and long term, which includes payables, expenses, taxes, and debt.

limited partner (LP)   Persons or institutions that provide the equity for a PE fund. These persons are the investors who expect to make a return on their investment. In general, they are charged a percentage fee of the invested money by the PE firm. They have some rights in the PE structure but little influence on the mechanics and day-to-day operation of the PE firm's fund.

liquidation   Dismantling of a business, paying off debts in order of priority, and distributing the remaining assets to the owners, usually as a result of bankruptcy or the closing of the business.

liquidity ratios   Measures of the firm's ability to meet short-term (less than 1 year) obligations with current assets.

local currency   The currency of the country that a firm operates in but is not its home country.

long-term liabilities   Obligations, usually in the form of debt, with maturities greater than 1 year.

management buyout   A recapitalization technique that involves the purchase of a controlling interest in a company by the existing management and sometimes new financial partners.

management efficiency ratio (also quality of earnings ratio)   A decomposition of the return on equity (ROE) ratio into pretax net profit margin, total asset turnover ratio, financial leverage, and tax rate. Used to identify the drivers of ROE.

market ratios   For public companies, the value of the firm based on the ratio of a value measure (price, enterprise value) to a fundamental factor (earnings, book value, EBITDA, etc.).

Monte Carlo simulation   A broad class of computational algorithms that rely on repeated random sampling to obtain numerical results; typically one runs simulations many times over to obtain an estimate and distribution of an unknown probabilistic determined result.

net asset value (NAV)   The value of a company or other entity after its liabilities have been subtracted from its assets.

net income   A measure of profitability that accounts for all of the firm's revenues, expenses, gains, and losses. It is the amount profit that is available to the firm's providers of equity capital after all expenses have been paid.

net profit margin   A ratio of net income to revenues that describes the percent of revenues that the firm is able to convert into net income.

noncurrent assets   Assets that are not expected to be converted into cash, sold, or exchanged within the normal operating cycle of the firm, usually 1 year.

operating expenses   Expenses that a business incurs as a result of performing its normal business operations.

operating leverage   A measure of the degree to which a firm incurs a combination of fixed and variable costs. The higher the use of fixed costs in relation to variable costs, the higher the operating leverage is said to be.

operating margin   A ratio of operating profit to revenues that describes the percent of revenues that the firm is able to convert into operating profit.

operating profit   A measure of profitability that accounts only for revenues and expenses that are a result of a firm's normal business operations. Also known as earnings before interest and taxes (EBIT).

options contract   A contract that gives the holder the right, but not the obligation, to buy or sell an asset at a predetermined price and a predetermined date from the counterparty. For this right, the option holder pays the option seller a premium. Options trade on organized exchanges and are securities.

physical assets   Assets that are tangible, i.e., inventory, cash, real estate, etc.

pretax operating income   The primary measurement of the total earnings generated by the firm without regard to taxes or net interest income (expense).

price to book value   A valuation ratio expressing the price of a security compared to its book value per share as reported in the company's balance sheet.

price to earnings   A valuation ratio expressing the price of a security compared to its earnings per share as reported in the company's income statement.

price to sales   A valuation ratio expressing the price of a security compared to its sales per share as reported in the company's income statement.

private equity funds   Partnership interests that are not publicly traded in a market or stock exchange. PE funds receive their capital from limited partners (LPs), and they use the capital to invest in a portfolio of target companies under the direction and management of their general partner (GP). A PE fund has a set of rules governing the rights of both the LPs and the GP (a partnership agreement). It also has a fixed lifetime, usually around 10 years.

private equity management company   A business that raises capital from limited partners through the creation (sponsorship) of private equity funds and then acts as or provides the general partner. The general partners will then invest the capital raised in portfolio firms. The amount of total money raised varies from deal to deal, but it can run into the billions of dollars.

portfolio company   A company that a PE fund invests in. PE funds generally have more than one portfolio company.

profitability ratios   Measures of a firm's ability to generate earnings in relation to sales or balance sheet items (i.e., assets, equity).

quick ratio   A measure of a company's ability to pay its current obligations from its most liquid current assets. Because inventory is not considered a liquid asset, it is usually subtracted from current assets in the calculation.

recapitalization   An alteration of the firm's capital structure where new capital is used to pay off old capital providers.

relative value   Financial ratios that can be used to compare the value of one firm versus another firm or its peer group—price, price to earnings ratio (PE), price to book ratio (PB), and so on. Also, readily available heuristics (i.e., rules of thumb) that are employed in shorthanded ways to estimate firm value. For example, expressing firm value as multiple of EBITDA, EBIT, and free cash flow (FCF).

reorganization   Financial restructuring of the firm due to bankruptcy.

reporting currency   The currency the firm uses to report its financial statements. Usually, it is the same as the functional currency of the business.

return on assets   A measure of profitability that expresses net income of the firm as a percentage of its total assets.

return on equity   A measure of profitability that expresses net income of the firm as a percentage of its common equity.

revenues   The amount of money that a company actually receives during a specific period, including discounts and deductions for returned merchandise.

sales to employee ratio   A measure of management efficiency that captures the amount of sales generated per employee of the firm.

scenario analysis   A process of analyzing future events by considering alternative possible outcomes by logically varying several firm input variables that affect those outcomes and then using a methodology to make a projection of the expected outcome given the assumed values of the variables.

seasonality   A predictable cyclical behavior in the demand for the firm's products or services.

sensitivity analysis   A process of analyzing possible future events by considering alternative possible outcomes by varying a single variable of the model at a time.

shareholders' equity   Represents the amount by which a company is financed through common and preferred shares.

SMEs   Small and medium-sized enterprises. SMEs are smaller enterprises defined by size category that varies by the industry the company is in; it is established by the government of the country.

statement of cash flow   A financial report that provides aggregate data regarding all cash inflows a company receives from its ongoing operations and external investment sources, as well as all cash outflows that pay for business activities and investments during a given accounting period.

strategic buyer   A public or private firm that acquires another firm for strategic purposes, including access to new markets and technologies.

target company (takeover target)   A company that PE funds, venture capital, or other investors are considering making an investment in to gain control.

time horizon   The length of time over which an investment is made or held before it is liquidated.

time-series benchmark   Analysis of data that compare the firm to itself at different points in time.

transaction exposure   Currency exposure that a firm incurs as a result of doing business internationally. It arises from entering into transactions that are denominated in a foreign currency and are subject to foreign exchange risk. Accounts receivable incurred in foreign currency represents a common transaction-related exposure.

translation exposure   Currency exposure that a firm incurs as a result of doing business internationally. It arises when a firm denominates assets, liabilities, and income in a foreign currency and those assets become subject to foreign exchange risk with respect to their value.

total asset turnover ratio   A measure of management efficiency that captures the amount of sales generated per dollar of assets of the firm.

trade sale   A term used to describe a sale of a portfolio company by a PE fund, venture capital, or other investor-owned company. The term gets its name from the fact that the acquiring company usually comes from the same sector or a related sector as the portfolio company.

variable costs   Costs that are incurred depending on the company's production volume.

valuation   The process of determining the current worth of an asset or company. Valuation should consider operating aspects of cash flow generation, intangible property, tax issues, contingencies, and discounts or premiums for liquidity and marketability.

venture capital   Money that is used to purchase equity/partial ownership in companies, usually in early stages. While the size of venture capital funds may be comparable to some PE firms, they generally differ in the type of target companies and the level of ownership they seek.

working capital   A measure of both a company's efficiency and its short-term financial health calculated as current assets minus current liabilities.

References

Abend, L. (2009, April 9). Spain's costumed debt collectors: Final notice? *Time*. Retrieved July 4, 2012, from http://www.time.com/time/magazine/article/0,9171, 1891761,00.html

Abrams, R. (2008, October 17). Strategies: It's a good time to start a business. Really. *USA Today*. Retrieved July 11, 2012, from http://www.usatoday.com/money/ smallbusiness/columnist/abrams/2008-10-17-start-a-business_N.htm

Acs, Z. J., Arenius, P., Hay, M., & Minniti, M. (2005). *Global Entrepreneurship Monitor 2004 executive report*. Babson Park, MA: Babson College and London Business School.

Armstrong, J. S. (Ed.). (2001). *Principles of forecasting: A handbook for researchers and practitioners*. Norwell, MA: Kluwer Academic.

Autio, E. (2007). *GEM 2007 report on high-growth entrepreneurship*. London: Global Entrepreneurship Research Association.

Board of Governors of the Federal Reserve System. (2010). *Report to the Congress on the use of credit cards by small businesses and the credit card market for small businesses*. Retrieved May 27, 2013, from http://www.federalreserve.gov/ BoardDocs/RptCongress/smallbusinesscredit/smallbusinesscredit.pdf

Boudway, I. (2012, May 26). Kickstarter: Financing small movies online. *Businessweek*. Retrieved June 12, 2012, from http://www.businessweek.com/magazine/ content/11_23/b4231052825865.htm

Busch, R. (2012). The new age of patronage: Raising capital and investments from "crowdfunding" websites. *ShortForm*. Retrieved July 4, 2012, from http://www .forbes.com/sites/richardbusch/2012/05/10/the-new-age-of-patronage-raising-capital-and-investments-from-crowdfunding-websites/

Casasanta, J. (2012). Camera+ reaches 6 million sales milestone. Retrieved July 5, 2012, from http://taptaptap.com/blog/cameraplus-reaches-6-million-sales-milestone/

CEON Solutions Pvt. Ltd. website. Retrieved June 27, 2013, from http://ceon.in/ceon/ site/index.php

CFA Institute. (2012). Corporate finance and portfolio management. In *CFA program curriculum 2013* (Level 1, Vol. 4). Hoboken, NJ: John Wiley.

Cornwall, J. (2009). *Bootstrapping*. Upper Saddle River, NJ: Prentice Hall.

Courtney, H. G., Kirkland, J., & Viguerie, S. P. (1997). Strategy under uncertainty, *Harvard Business Review, 75*(6), 67–79.

Courtois, Y., & Jenkinson, J. (2011). Private equity valuation. In *CFA Program Curriculum* (Level II, Vol. 5). Hoboken, NJ: John Wiley.

Coyle, B. (2000). *Introduction to currency risk*. Chicago: Glenlake.

Crowdsourcing Org. (2010). *Crowdsourcing industry report*. Retrieved May 27, 2013, from http://www.crowdsourcing.org/research

Dahl, D. (2010, November 22). How to assess the credit risk of your customers. *Inc.* Retrieved June 21, 2013, from http://www.inc.com/guides/2010/11/how-to-assess-the-credit-risk-of-your-customers.html

DaSilva, C. M., Janezic, M., & Hisrich, R. D. (2012). Five ways to operate and succeed as a venture capitalist in Southeast Europe. *Journal of Private Equity, 15*(2), 84–89.

Dess, G., & Miller A. (1993). *Strategic management*. New York: McGraw-Hill.

DeTienne, D. R. (2010). Entrepreneurial exits as a critical component of the entrepreneurial process: Theoretical development, *Journal of Business Venturing, 25,* 203–215.

DeTienne, D. R., & Cardon, M. S. (2008). Entrepreneurial exit strategies: The impact of human capital. Babson College Entrepreneurship Research Conference (BCERC) 2006 Paper; Frontiers of Entrepreneurship Research 2006. http://papers.ssrn.com/sol3/papers.cfm?abstract_id=1310922

Dinan, M. (2012, April). *Entrepreneurial financing and forecasting*. Lecture conducted at Thunderbird School of Global Management, Glendale, AZ.

Downes, J., & Goodman, J. E. (1995). *Dictionary of finance and investment terms*. Hauppauge, NY: Barron's Educational Series, Inc.

Dwivedi, A., Iliopoulou, M., Jain, P., Kugatkina, O., Lorentzen, C., Neuhoff, J., & Schoenfeld, A. (2012). *Industry, participants, size and prospects* (White paper). Thunderbird School of Global Management.

Eitman, D. K., Stonehill, A. I., & Moffett, M. H. (2010). *Multinational business finance* (12th ed.). Boston, MA: Pearson Prentice Hall.

Emmanuel, G. (2013, February 25). *5 Reasons why equity-based crowdfunding under the JOBS Act won't work. Huffington Post*. Retrieved July 5, 2012, from http://www.huffingtonpost.com/gary-emmanuel/5-reasons-why-equitybased_b_2759580.html

Empson, R. (2012). Camera+ turned down acquisitions from Adobe, Google, Twitter. *TechCrunch*. Retrieved July 5, 2012, from http://techcrunch.com/2012/06/08/camera-plus-turns-2-says-eff-the-vcs/.

Fraser, J. A. (2000). Collection: Days saved, thousands earned. *Inc.com*. Retrieved July 4, 2012, from http://www.inc.com/magazine/19951101/2488.html

Gibney, B., & Howery, K. (2012, January 30). Just how risky is entrepreneurship, really? *Harvard Business Review* Blog Network. Retrieved June 17, 2013, from http://blogs.hbr.org/cs/2012/01/just_how_risky_is_entrepreneur.html

Gobble, M. M. (2012). Everyone is a venture capitalist: The new age of crowdfunding. *Research Technology Management, 55*(4), 4–7.

Gompers, P., Kovner, A., Lerner, J., & Scharfstein, D. (2008). Performance persistence in entrepreneurship (Working paper 09-028). *Harvard Business Review*.

Harman, D. (2010, February 17). Spain uses public shame to collect debts. *Christian Science Monitor*. Retrieved July 4, 2012, from http://www.csmonitor.com/World/Europe/2010/0217/Spain-uses-public-shame-to-collect-debts

Hazen, T. L. (2006). *The law of securities regulation* (Rev. 5th ed.). St. Paul, MN: Thomson West.

Hisrich, R. D. (2013). *International entrepreneurship* (2nd ed.). Los Angeles: Sage.

Hisrich, R. D., Peters, M. P., & Shepherd, D. A. (2013). *Entrepreneurship* (9th ed.). Burr Ridge, IL: McGraw-Hill/Irwin.

Horn, K. (2014). The product lifecycle is in decline. *Sourcing Focus*. Retrieved March 5, 2014, from http://www.sourcingfocus.com/site/opinionscomments/6458/

Humer, C. (2012, March 6). Lehman emerges from 3.5-year bankruptcy. Reuters. Retrieved July 4, 2012, from http://www.reuters.com/article/2012/03/06/us-lehman-idUSTRE8250WY20120306

Hwang, I. (2010). Facebook, Twitter Trading in private spurs questions about financial data. *Bloomberg.com News*. Retrieved July 6, 2012, from http://www.bloomberg.com/news/2010-12-29/private-trades-of-facebook-spur-questions-about-transparency.html

Ibbotson Associates. (2012). *SBBI valuation yearbook 2013: Market results for stocks, bonds, bills, and inflation 1926–2012*. Chicago, IL: Morningstar.

Inc. Magazine Online, 2005. Available at www.inc.com.

Isenberg, D. J. (2008). The global entrepreneur. *Harvard Business Review*, *86*(12), 107–111.

Kasperkevic, J. (2013). Study: Most U.S. entrepreneurs start their business at home. *Inc.* Retrieved June 27, 2013, from http://www.inc.com/jana-kasperkevic/us-entrepreneurs-keep-businesses-close-to-home.html

Kendall, P. (2011, February 7). Angry Birds: The story behind iPhone's gaming phenomenon. *Telegraph.co.uk*. Retrieved July 11, 2012, from http://www.telegraph.co.uk/technology/video-games/8303173/Angry-Birds-the-story-behind-iPhones-gaming-phenomenon.html

Madura, J. (1992). *International financial management* (3rd ed.). St. Paul, MN: West.

Miller, S. D. (2010). The ESOP exit strategy. *Journal of Accountancy*. Retrieved April 9, 2014, from http://www.journalofaccountancy.com/issues/2010/mar/20092046.htm

Mintzberg, H., & Quinn, J. (1991). *The strategy process*. Englewood Cliffs, NJ: Prentice Hall.

Moore, J. (2010). *Seasonality and its effects on lifecycle pricing* (White paper). Revionics, Inc. http://www.financialit.net/white-paper/seasonality-and-its-effects-on-lifecycle-pricing/17158

National Retail Federation. (2014). Retrieved April 4, 2014, from https://www.nrf.com/modules.php?name=Pages&sp_id=1140

Pearce, J., & Robinson, R. (1992). *Strategic management: Formulation, implementation, and control*. Homewood, IL: Irwin.

Pratt, S. P. (2011). *Business valuation: Discounts and premiums*. Hoboken, NJ: John Wiley.

Pratt, S. P., & Niculita, A. V. (2008). *Valuing a business: The analysis and appraisal of closely held companies* (5th ed.). New York, NY: McGraw-Hill.

Prive, T. (2012 November 6). Inside the JOBS Act: Equity crowdfunding. *Forbes*. Retrieved May 28, 2013, from http://www.forbes.com/sites/tanyaprive/2012/11/06/inside-the-jobs-act-equity-crowdfunding-2/

Raice, S., & Ante, S. E. (2012, April 10). Insta-Rich: $1 billion for Instagram. *The Wall Street Journal*. Retrieved July 12, 2012, from http://online.wsj.com/article/SB10001424052702303815404577333840377381670.html

Raice, S., Das, A., & Letzing, J. (2012). Facebook prices IPO at record value. *The Wall Street Journal*. Retrieved August 28, 2013, from http://online.wsj.com/news/articles/SB10001424052702303448404577409923406193162

Robb, A., & Reedy, E. J. (2012). *An overview of the Kauffman firm survey*. Ewing Marion Kauffman Foundation. Retrieved July 12, 2012, from http://www.kauffman.org/uploadedfiles/kfs_2012_report.pdf

Sahlman, W. A., & Scherlis, D. R. (2009). *A method for valuing high-risk, long-term investments: The "venture capital method"* (Harvard Business School Background Note 288-006). Boston, MA: Harvard Business School.

Saitto, S. (2012). Facebook is said to set IPO banker fees at 1.1 percent. *BloombergBusinessweek.* Retrieved July 5, 2012, from http://www.businessweek.com/news/2012-05-17/facebook-is-said-to-set-ipo-banker-fees-at-1-dot-1-percent

Savitz, E. (2011). Raising capital in a choppy market: Cash remains king. *Forbes.* Retrieved July 11, 2012, from http://www.forbes.com/sites/ciocentral/2011/11/23/raising-capital-in-a-choppy-market-cash-remains-king/

Simonite, T. (2013 January 9). A smart watch, created by the crowd, debuts in Vegas. *MIT Technology Review.* Retrieved June 20, 2013, from http://www.technologyreview.com/news/509696/a-smart-watch-created-by-the-crowd-debuts-in-vegas/

Steinberg, S., & DeMaria, R. (2012). *The crowdfunding bible: How to raise money for any startup, video game or project.* Raleigh, NC: Lulu.com.

Study of the Sarbanes-Oxley Act of 2002 Section 404 Internal Control over Financial Reporting Requirements. (2009). Retrieved July 4, 2012, from http://www.sec.gov/news/studies/2009/sox-404_study.pdf

Tarnoff, A. (2013, January 15). Premium denim Kickstarter project continues to grow. *OnMilwaukee.com.* Retrieved June 25, 2013, from http://onmilwaukee.com/market/articles/gustin.html

Thompson, A., & Strickland A. (1992). *Strategic management: Text and cases.* Homewood, IL: Irwin.

Waldren, J. (2012). Is an ESOP your best exit strategy? *Washington Technology.* Retrieved April 9, 2014, from http://washingtontechnology.com/articles/2012/10/29/insights-waldren-esop-benefits.aspx

Waters, R., & Nuttall, C. (2012, April 9). Facebook to buy Instagram for $1bn. *Financial Times.* Retrieved July 11, 2012, from http://www.ft.com/intl/cms/s/0/052cc7c4-8269-11e1-9242-00144feab49a.html#axzz1zgXFwiN5

Willems, M. (2014). Valve's management-light model: New tech trend, or outlier? *SNL Financial Management.* Retrieved Mach 4, 2014, from http://global.factiva.com.ezproxy.t-bird.edu/ha/default.aspx

Williams, C. (2007, October 1). Facebook wins Manx battle for face-book.com. *The Register* (London). Retrieved from http://www.theregister.co.uk/2007/10/01/facebook_domain_dispute

Winkler, R. (2013). WhatsApp hits 400 million users, wants to "stay independent." *The Wall Street Journal.* Retrieved March 4, 2014, from http://blogs.wsj.com/digits/2013/12/19/whatsapp-hits-400-million-users-wants-to-stay-independent

Zingheim, P. K., & Schuster, J. R. (2000). *Pay people right! Breakthrough reward strategies to create great companies.* Hoboken, NJ: John Wiley.

Zukin, J. (1990). *Financial valuation: Businesses and business interests.* New York: Maxwell MacMillan.

Additional Resources

Aernoudt, R. (1999). Business angels: Should they fly on their own wings? *Venture Capital, 1*(2), 187–195.

Benjamin, G. A., & Margulis, J. B. (2005). *Angel capital: How to raise early-stage private equity financing.* Hoboken, NJ: John Wiley.

Benjamin, G. A., Margulis, J. B., & Margulis, J. (2001). *The angel investor's handbook: How to profit from early-stage investing.* Princeton, NJ: Bloomberg Press.

Berkery, D. (2007). *Raising venture capital for the serious entrepreneur.* New York: McGraw-Hill.

Biggs, J. (2013). An interview with Indiegogo CEO Slava Rubin on the wild rise of crowdsourcing. *TechCrunch.* Retrieved March 12, 2013, from http://techcrunch.com/2013/03/11/an-interview-with-indiegogo-ceo-slava-rubin-on-the-wild-rise-of-crowdsourcing/

Bodie, Z., Kane, A., & Marcus, A. J. (2011). *Investments* (9th ed.). New York: McGraw-Hill.

Bragg, S. M., & Burton, E. J. (2006). *Accounting and finance for your small business* (2nd ed.). Hoboken, NJ: John Wiley.

Brealey, R. A., & Myers, S. C. (2002). *Brealey & Myers on corporate finance: Capital investment and valuation.* New York: McGraw-Hill.

Carter, R., & Van Auken, H. (1992). Effect of professional background on venture capital proposal evaluation. *Journal of Small Business Strategy,* *3*(1), 45–55.

Cendrowski, H., Petro, L. W., Martin, J. P., & Wadecki, A. A. (2012). *Private equity: History, governance, and operations* (2nd ed.). Hoboken, NJ: John Wiley.

Community Development Financial Institutions Fund Website. (n.d.). Retrieved June 6, 2013, from http://http://www.cdfifund.gov

Damodaran, A. (2010). *The dark side of valuation: Valuing young, distressed, and complex businesses* (2nd ed.). Upper Saddle River, NJ: Pearson Education.

Davies, J., Finlay, M., McLenaghen, T., & Wilson, D. (2006). Key risk indicators: Their role in operational risk management and measurement. *Risk Business International.* Retrieved May 31, 2013, from http://d.yimg.com/kq/groups/12093474/1290864495/name/McLenaghenTara3.pdf

Dawson, R. (2010). *Secrets of power negotiating, 15th anniversary edition: Inside secrets from a master negotiator* (15th Anniversary ed.). Pompton Plains, NJ: Career Press.

Demaria, C. (2010). *Introduction to private equity.* Hoboken, NJ: John Wiley.

Downes, J., & Goodman, J. E. (1995). *Dictionary of finance and investment terms.* Hauppauge, NY: Barron's Educational Series, Inc.

Eiteman, D. K., Stonehill, A. I., & Moffett, M. H. (1992). *Multinational business finance* (6th ed.). Boston, MA: Addison-Wesley.

Ernst & Young's Guide to Going Public. (2010). Retrieved July 5, 2012, from http://www.ey.com/Publication/vwLUAssets/Guide_to_going_public_2010/$FILE/Guide%20to%20going%20public.pdf

Feld, B., & Mendelson, J. (2011). *Venture deals: Be smarter than your lawyer and venture capitalist.* Hoboken, NJ: John Wiley.

Fields, E. (2002). *The essentials of finance and accounting for nonfinancial managers.* New York: AMACOM.

Fisher, R., Ury, W. L., & Patton, B. (2011). *Getting to yes: Negotiating agreement without giving in* (Rev. ed.). New York: Penguin.

Fried, V. H., & Hisrich, R. D. (1994). Toward a model of venture capital investment decision making. *Financial Management, 23*(3), 28–37. doi:10.2307/3665619.

Gibbons, G., & Stone, H. M. (2011, Winter). PE managers as registered investment advisors. *Journal of Private Equity, 15*(1), 8–15.

Goedhart, M., Koller, T., & Wessels, D. (2010). The five types of successful acquisitions. *McKinsey Quarterly*. Retrieved July 6, 2012, from http://www.mckinseyquarterly.com/The_five_types_of_successful_acquisitions_2635

Harrison, W. T., Horngren, C. T., & Thomas, B. (2009). *Financial accounting* (8th ed.). Upper Saddle River, NJ: Prentice Hall.

Hostess: Twinkies to return to shelves July 15. (2013, June 24). *USA Today*. Retrieved June 25, 2013, from http://www.usatoday.com/story/news/nation/2013/06/23/twinkies-return/2450233/

Ibbotson Associates. (2012). *Ibbotson SBBI valuation yearbook 2013: Market results for stocks, bonds, bills, and inflation 1926–2012*. Chicago, IL: Morningstar, Inc.

Jeng, L. A., & Wells, P. C. (2000). The determinants of venture capital funding: Evidence across countries. *Journal of Corporate Finance, 6*(3), 241–289.

Kaplan, D. A. (2012, August 13). Hostess is bankrupt . . . again. *Fortune, 166*(3), 61–70.

Madura J. (1992). *International financial management* (3rd ed.). St. Paul, MN: West.

Marks, K. H., Slee, R. T., Blees, C. W., & Nall, M. R. (2012). *Middle market M&A: Handbook for investment banking and business consulting*. Hoboken, NJ: John Wiley.

Maxwell, A. L., Jeffrey, S. A., & Lévesque, M. (2011). Business angel early stage decision making. *Journal of Business Venturing, 26*(2), 212–225.

McGinn, J. (2012). *Tail risk killers: How math, indeterminacy, and hubris distort markets*. New York, NY: McGraw-Hill.

O'Donnell, M. J., & Commissaris, A. T. (n.d.). *The venture capital anti-dilution solution*. Palo Alto, CA: Wilson Sonsini Goodrich & Rosati.

Onaitis, S. (2009). *Negotiate like the big guys*. Aberdeen, WA: Silver Lake Publishing.

Osnabrugge, M. V., & Robinson, R. J. (2000). *Angel investing: Matching startup funds with startup companies—The guide for entrepreneurs and individual investors*. San Francisco, CA: Jossey-Bass.

Pedhazur, E. J. (1982). *Multiple regression in behavioral research: Explanation and prediction* (2nd ed.). Fort Worth, TX: Harcourt Brace Jovanovich.

Pratt, S. P. (2007). *Valuing a business: The analysis and appraisal of closely held companies* (5th ed.). New York, NY: McGraw-Hill.

PricewaterhouseCoopers/National Venture Capital Association. (2011). MoneyTree™ report. Retrieved July 4, 2012, from http://www.pwcmoneytree.com/MTPublic/ns/index.jsp

Private Equity Growth Council. Retrieved April 14, 2014, from http://www.pegcc.org/education/pe-by-the-numbers/

Ramsinghani, M. (2011). *The business of venture capital: Insights from leading practitioners on the art of raising a fund, deal structuring, value creation, and exit strategies*. Hoboken, NJ: John Wiley.

Reilly, R. F., & Schweihs, R. P. (2004). *The handbook of business valuation and intellectual property analysis*. New York, NY: McGraw-Hill.

Rogers, S. (2009). *Entrepreneurial finance: Finance and business strategies for the serious entrepreneur* (2nd ed.). New York, NY: McGraw-Hill.

Shane, S. A. (2008). *Fool's gold? The truth behind angel investing in America*. New York: Oxford University Press.

Shane, S. A. (2010). *The illusions of entrepreneurship: The costly myths that entrepreneurs, investors, and policy makers live by*. New Haven, CT: Yale University Press.

Shenkar, O., & Luo, Y. (2007). *International business* (2nd ed.). Thousand Oaks, CA: Sage.

Sherman, A. J. (2010). *Mergers and acquisitions from a to z* (3rd ed.). New York, NY: AMACOM.

Slee, R. T. (2011). *Private capital markets: Valuation, capitalization, and transfer of private business interests* (2nd ed.). Hoboken, NJ: John Wiley.

Smith, J. K., & Smith, R. L. (2004). *Entrepreneurial finance* (2nd ed.). Hoboken, NJ: John Wiley.

Sohl, J. (2012). *The angel investor market in 2011: The recovery continues.* Durham, NH: Center for Venture Research.

Steinberg, S., & DeMaria, R. (2012). *The crowdfunding bible: How to raise money for any startup, video game or project.* Raleigh, NC: Lulu.com.

10 Tips for bootstrapping your marketing. (2010). *Inc.com.* Retrieved July 4, 2012, from http://www.inc.com/guides/2010/06/tips-for-bootstrapping-your-marketing.html

Troy, L. (2012). *Almanac of business and industrial financial ratios.* Chicago: CCH Group.

Whatever happened to IPOs? (2011, March 22). *Wall Street Journal.* Retrieved July 4, 2012, from http://online.wsj.com/article/SB10001424052748704662604576203002012714150.html

Wilmerding, A. (2003). *Term sheets & valuations—An inside look at the intricacies of term sheets & valuations.* Soho, NY: Aspatore Books.

Index

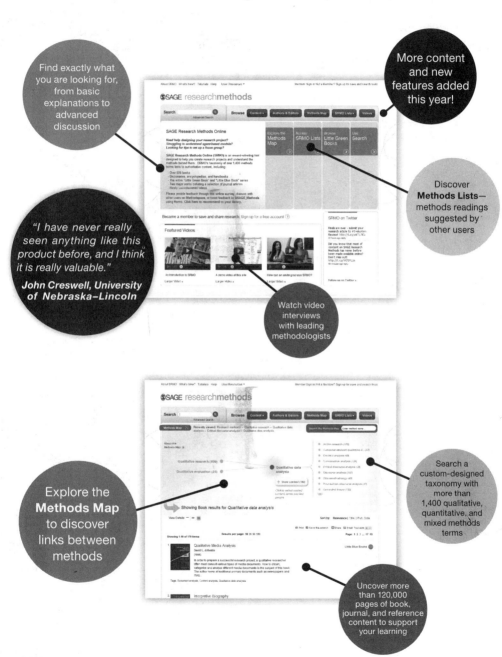